JUSTIFICATION
THE HEART OF
THE CHRISTIAN FAITH

JUSTIFICATION
THE HEART OF
THE CHRISTIAN FAITH

A Theological Study with an Ecumenical Purpose

EBERHARD JÜNGEL

Translated by
JEFFREY F. CAYZER

With an Introduction by
JOHN WEBSTER

T&T CLARK
EDINBURGH & NEW YORK

T&T CLARK LTD

A Continuum imprint

59 George Street
Edinburgh EH2 2LQ
Scotland

www.tandtclark.co.uk

370 Lexington Avenue
New York 10017–6503
USA

www.continuumbooks.com

Authorised English translation of
*Das Evangelium von der Rechtfertigung des Gottlosen
als Zentrum des christlichen Glaubens,* third edition,
copyright © J. C. B. Mohr (Paul Siebeck), Tübingen, 1999

The publishers gratefully acknowledge the support of Inter Nationes, Bonn,
in the preparation of the English translation.

First published 2001

ISBN 0 567 08775 1

British Library Cataloguing-in-Publication Data
A catalogue record for this book is available from the British Library

Typeset by Waverley Typesetters, Galashiels
Printed and bound in Great Britain by
Biddles Ltd, Guildford and King's Lynn

CONTENTS

v

INTRODUCTION

John Webster

Jüngel has always been a (not wholly unwilling) controversialist, and this book, his most sustained piece of theological writing for some time, is no exception. The precipitating occasion for the work was the Lutheran–Roman Catholic *Joint Declaration* on the doctrine of justification, which argued – in line with much recent ecumenical theology and some fashionable Luther scholarship – that the confessional divisions over justification which derive from the period of the European Reformation can and should be re-evaluated, and that in important respects theology and church life may move beyond them. Welcomed by those committed to advancing dialogue between Protestants and Roman Catholics in a certain direction, the *Joint Declaration* – which claimed very little that was not already ecumenical stock in trade – evoked a storm of protest from a large number of significant voices in the German Lutheran theological community. Jüngel's book, which was first published in the midst of the controversy and saw two further editions in rapid succession, is easily the most substantial contribution to that debate from the *non placet* Lutheran side. It is a vintage piece of Jüngel in one of his most characteristic voices: intellectually vigorous, polemical, animated by deep and loving knowledge of Luther's writings, written with an eye not only to fundamental issues in dogmatics but also to pastoral questions of Christian existence and action.

The content and force of Jüngel's argument depends upon his conviction that the doctrine of justification by faith alone is a special-status doctrine which identifies the centre of the

Christian faith. It is, as he puts it, a 'hermeneutical category' for the whole of Christian theology, in that through it the real matter of Christian teaching is concentrated into a dispute about the truth of the gospel concerning the identity of God and of the creatures of God. This explains the (to non-Lutheran readers, perhaps, rather surprising) intensity of Jüngel's commitment to making everything hang on one biblical metaphor for salvation, however central that metaphor may be to the Pauline corpus. It also explains why the book ranges beyond particular soteriological issues into questions of Trinity, ecclesiology and sacramental theology, or ethics.

The shape of the book can be relatively easily described. After an introductory chapter which sketches some of the basic affirmations of the gospel of justification and then fleshes them out by a Christologically focused meditation on the figure of Cain, the argument proper begins with the second chapter on the theological function of the article on justification. Here Jüngel gives a description of justification in its classically Lutheran form as the *articulus stantis et cadentis ecclesiae*. He defends this judgement against, on the one hand, Barth, who – as is well known – disputed the adequacy of any one piece of soteriological doctrine to this task, and, on the other hand, those who followed Fichte in finding the doctrine of justification a regressive attempt to tie the gospel too closely to its Jewish setting. Against Barth, Jüngel argues that giving central place to the doctrine of justification by faith does, in fact, achieve what Barth fears it fails to do: it makes confession of Christ the centre of the church. Against the argument that the idiom of justification is too Judaistic to articulate the catholicity of the gospel, Jüngel argues that the doctrine has virtually unlimited scope: far from being an occasional, polemical doctrine, it identifies the point at which all lines of Christian teaching intersect. Those acquainted with recent New Testament scholarship will look in vain for much interaction with the wide literature on the 'new Paul'; Jüngel's presentation does not substantially advance beyond his early account in *Paulus und Jesus* (1962), which was itself very much in line with Käsemann's understanding of the

Pauline letters. But it would be an uncharitable or theologically tone-deaf reader who did not appreciate the vividness of
Jüngel's presentation or the energy with which he traces the
ramifications of that account of Paul.

From here, the third chapter gives a more analytical presentation of the notion of justification. At its heart is the concept
of well-ordered relations: 'righteousness' is properly a state of
ordered relatedness. Though this sense can be discerned in
Aristotle, the Pauline materials make two distinctive claims. First,
'righteousness' is defined as 'through faith' and 'apart from
law' (the full effect of these qualifications is expounded at
length in chapter five). Second, divine righteousness is not an
incommunicable attribute of God (equivalent to divine eternity
or omniscience, for example) but is rather to be identified with
God's action in declaring and making sinners righteous. Here
Jüngel takes us to the heartlands of classical Lutheran doctrine,
as found in Luther's famous 1545 autobiographical preface to
his Latin works. God is just because God 'practises grace', in
the crucified Christ acting towards us in the crucified Christ in
such a way as to make us just. Here Jüngel envisages the cross as
the supreme act of relation: the relation of God the Father to
God the Son in the Spirit's power, and the relation of the triune
God to sinful humanity. The trinitarian setting of justification
is especially important here (Jüngel's previous expositions of
the doctrine say little about this theme), most of all because he
resists quite firmly the language of human participation in the
life of the triune God which has acquired authority in a good
deal of recent soteriology, including interpretations of Luther's
understandings of salvation.

This emphasis on relation also provides the backcloth for
the presentation of sin in chapter four. As in many other
writings, so here: Jüngel defines sin as breaking away from the
life-giving relation to God and others which form the ordered
ontological structure of human existence, and the replacement
of relation by self-actualization. Sin is thus untruth, the failure
to affirm God's 'affirmation' of us as Creator. As such, sin is
both our action and that which enslaves its perpetrators; hence

an exclusively moralistic presentation of sin is for Jüngel inadequate to describe the human condition. This 'enslaving' character of sin is conceptualized in terms of 'original' sin (as 'primal' rather than 'inherited') – that is, as our pervasive complicity and entanglement in false existence through which we place ourselves under the compulsion to sin. The chapter rounds out the theological phenomenology of sin by discussion of the forms of sin: unbelief, the desire to master the distinction between good and evil, pride, stupidity and guilt. The idiom of the phenomenology is characteristic of the existential Lutheranism which Jüngel imbibed deeply from Bultmann and Ebeling: highly charged, personalist, less concerned with sociological, historical, economic or gender differentiations, but potent in presenting a certain universal ontology of the human situation.

All that has happened so far in the book's argument provides the setting for its centrepiece, the very full doctrinal exposition of justification in its theological and anthropological dimensions presented in chapter five, which makes up almost half of the book. The material is organized around the basic proposal that justification is most properly interpreted out of four exclusives: Christ alone, grace alone, Word alone, faith alone. The force of each *solus* is to reinforce the primacy of the divine initiative; in effect, each reiterates *solus Deus*, God alone. For Jüngel, this means more than anything else the strict exclusion of human work from the economy of salvation, which, as he sees matters, is the chief point of controversy between Protestant and Roman Catholic accounts of the nature of justification.

To affirm that 'Christ alone' is the agent of salvation is to propose a soteriological exclusiveness ('no other saviour') which is at the same time a soteriological inclusiveness (the scope of the saving work of God in Christ is limitless). Jüngel is quite clear that both Protestants and Roman Catholics have normatively upheld the uniqueness of Christ's saving person and act; the disagreement arises over the relation of *solus Christus* to the other exclusive particles. Thus, for example, on

Jüngel's reading of the matter, *solus Christus* is undermined by
Roman Catholic affirmations of 'secondary' soteriological
centres (Mary or the church), and most especially by the metaphysics of grace which he finds in Roman Catholic theology
and which he views as flatly contradictory of proper human
passivity before the creative and saving Word. His discussion of
the Tridentine materials is certainly contestable, and a reader
disposed to be sceptical might feel that Jüngel's rather fierce
repudiation of Trent is driven by a competitive understanding
of the relation of divine and human action, in which acts have
properly to be assigned *either* to God *or* to creatures – an understanding shared of course, by Barth (a decisive influence on
Jüngel's ethical thought), though not necessarily in all respects
by Luther, on some readings of the Reformer. Jüngel's worries
about 'possessing grace' thus may not quite hit the target, shared
as they would be by virtually any Roman Catholic soteriology.

With his discussion of the 'extrinsicism' with which Lutheran
accounts of justification are often charged, however, Jüngel is
on firmer ground. He – rightly – insists that imputed righteousness is not *fictive*. That objection rests on a misconstrual of
the ontology of the human person, failing to see that we are
'outside ourselves'. To be human is not to be the possessors
or realizers of our own being, but to be beyond ourselves
through the creative Word of God. The charge of extrinsicism,
that is, presupposes an unredeemed anthropology in which the
determinative significance of the Christological-soteriological
extra nos has been obscured. In Christ, outside ourselves and
beyond our acts of self-determination, we *are*.

This basic anthropological affirmation is extended by Jüngel
in three directions. It means, first, that the Christian exists *simul
iustus et peccator*, as justified and sinner at one and the same
time – here construed by Jüngel to mean that the justified exist
under two jurisdictions, with primacy accorded to the saving
jurisdiction of God in Christ. Second, as those created by the
Word alone, that is, by the saving divine self-manifestation, the
life of the justified is determined at all points by the same Word.
Life in the Word is not, of course, life without sacraments;

rather, in the sacraments Christ himself is alone at work distributing his grace (a point at which Jüngel records a good deal of *rapprochement* with contemporary Roman Catholic sacramental theology). Third, justification is by faith alone. Faith is neither human decision nor the 'vain confidence' with which Trent charged the Reformers; rather, it is that passive act in which the believer entrusts himself or herself to the saving movement initiated by the Word of God's grace which draws us beyond ourselves to be *nos extra nos*.

Jüngel has often been at pains to defend his account of the Lutheran tradition against the allegation that soteriological passivity entails the elimination of the ethical. For all his tireless insistence on the incompatibility of justification by faith and the self-realizing agent of modern moral and intellectual culture, Jüngel nevertheless draws attention to the imperative dimensions of the indicative of salvation. Justification, in effect, reverses the relation of 'being' and 'doing'. We *are* what God creates, not what we make of ourselves; human acts, therefore, are not self-making but rather the celebration of that which we have been made. This forms the theme of the brief coda to the book in chapter six on 'living out of righteousness' – a topic on which Jüngel has expressed himself many times previously in writing on moral theology.

Such, in brief, is the argument. The book is best read as an essay in positive dogmatics with a certain polemical and practical edge, drawing together and extending much else that Jüngel has written on justification. In his account of Luther, which sees justification as the centre of a massively consistent theological and pastoral programme out of which radiates Luther's teaching on the doctrines of God and humanity, Jüngel acknowledges his debt to Gerhard Ebeling, the *doyen* of existential Luther interpreters, now regarded with some disfavour by interpreters of a more 'catholic' orientation. Like Ebeling, Jüngel expounds justification in relation to the correlative topics of Christ, Word and faith; like Ebeling, he distances Luther both from the theology and spirituality of late mediaeval Catholicism and from modernity; like Ebeling, he finds Luther a particularly rich resource for the construction of a distinctively Christian ontology of the human person as the passive creature of the Word.

Three characteristics of the book make it at first encounter a rather puzzling text for readers from different theological milieux. First, what Jüngel has to say emerges from an exalted view of the place of theology in the life of the church. Theology is, very simply, an exercise of the church's conscience, a point at which it makes its relation to the gospel explicit and stands beneath the gospel's corrective judgement. Exploratory, unattached or ironic modes of theology, familiar in both modern and postmodern forms, are very far from Jüngel's conception of the theologian's task.

Second, the book is a polemical work. Good theological polemic is not intemperate intellectual aggression, but the attempt to draw on a rich store of lovingly apprehended common tradition to dispute and challenge the present directions of church and theology. The hostile reception with which some greeted the work on first publication usually failed to see that point, overlooking how Jüngel's polemic is nearly always undertaken by positive biblical and dogmatic exposition. Nevertheless, many readers will still find strange Jüngel's sense that Christian faith is inherently contentious. He speaks of the dispute between Paul and Peter, 'apostle against apostle, simply for the sake of the truth' as 'after a fashion, the birth of Protestant theology'; on his account, orderly Christian theology 'makes no compromises'. This feature of Jüngel's work cannot simply be explained (away) as a matter of personal intellectual style. Rather, it is generated by an understanding of theology as – at least in some of its genres – a call to intellectual self-examination and repentance. Jüngel's book is neither leisurely nor conversational, and does not think that building consensus means suspension of strong conviction. Rather, its rhetoric and conception of its subject-matter urges its readers to attend to distinctions and make decisions in the face of the critical truth of 'the gospel of the justification of sinners' which 'has caused offence from the beginning'.

Third, this is a genuinely ecumenical work by a genuinely ecumenical theologian who has been involved in work for the reconciliation of separated Christian traditions from his early days in the former East Germany and has co-published and enjoyed cordial relations with leading Roman Catholic theologians such as Rahner and Kasper. But it is a book which is critical of what have become some ecumenical conventions, both methodological and substantive. On the methodological side, Jüngel refuses to accede to the notions that ecumenical advance involves the relativization of confessional traditions, or that confessional divisions can be overcome by offering historical and contextual (rather than dogmatic) explanations of the disputes of the past. Over matters of doctrinal substance, Jüngel works with a very different constellation of doctrines from those which have emerged as normative in much ecumenical theology: he has a sharp sense of the distinction between divine and human action; he does not favour making ecclesiology into the centre of gravity of an account of the Christian gospel; he is firmly opposed to the kinds of affirmations about the continuity between God's saving work and the life of the church which come to expression in the notion of the church as a sacramental 'realization' of Christ; more than anything else he has a powerfully operative theology of the Word which governs his approach to all issues. In short, for Jüngel, contending about the truth is itself a contribution to ecumenism, since it is the truth of the gospel which is the only ground of the church's peace.

Jüngel's book invites and expects counter-argument. Not all will be sympathetic to his reading of the Roman Catholic tradition as a singular and consistent whole; not all will share his interpretation of Luther; not all will agree with the identification of *evangelische Theologie* with the theology of Wittenberg (Geneva? Strasbourg? Cambridge?). Furthermore, one of the major areas of debate – already raised in Barth's critique of Ernst Wolf's presentation of the centrality of justification – will be whether Jüngel's proposal narrows the scope of soteriology by making justification the centre of the whole. There are

undoubtedly exegetical questions to be raised here; and it could
be that the focus on justification (rather than, for example,
sacrifice) may press Jüngel to overemphasize human passivity.
On the other hand, it is equally true that the book does not so
much exclude other soteriological motifs but rather makes
justification into the centre around which other theological
material on salvation can be ranged. Again, some critics may be
concerned about the trinitarian shape of the soteriology which
Jüngel presents. In particular, the clear separation of the work
of Christ and the work of the Christian may indicate to some a
pneumatological deficiency. Anxieties about synergism may be
relieved if the bond between Christology and anthropology is a
function of the Spirit's action, rather than (as Jüngel fears) of
an overdeveloped moralism or sacramentalism. Jüngel's reply
would be that his concern is not with the separation of the
divine and the churchly but with their right ordering, with
identifying a distinction which affirms both the primacy of grace
and the genuine humanity of the church which is compromised
if it becomes a medium or bearer of divine reality.

It is precisely such issues which Jüngel challenges theology
and church to engage. Like all his work, it is both an a exercise
of and a call to theological responsibility, answerability to the
gospel. Only a theology or a church which has grown sleepy
and careless, or ceased to believe in the regenerative power of
theological ideas, will fail to profit from the careful and critical
study which this book undoubtedly deserves.

TRANSLATOR'S PREFACE

It may be of help to the reader to make some comments on the decisions which had to be made in the process of translation. Jüngel's style shows a seriousness and weightiness appropriate to his subject, and he makes frequent use of italics to emphasize a word or phrase. On the other hand, there are many playful elements, as he experiments with neologisms to convey an idea, or uses one root to form three different words, showing their interrelatedness, yet emphasizing a contrast between them. Endeavouring to capture something of this variety has been a very enjoyable exercise. Of course, there are places where it has been impossible to find an English equivalent which would capture something of the wordplay in the German.

There are, however, some elements which make heavy going in English. Jüngel will frequently repeat several times in a few lines a long phrase such as 'the article concerning the justification of the ungodly'. Where this seemed to me to produce an unwanted effect in English, I have avoided such repetition. For similar reasons, I have broken up some sentences and paragraphs into more manageable bites. There follow a few comments on some of the most important issues involved in translating particular words and ideas. I have tried to keep translator's notes to a bare minimum.

Some German terms have been rendered in different ways for the sake of clarity and variety. The word *Gerechtigkeit* (and its related forms) yields two word groups, *justice* and *righteousness*, in English. In each case I have tried to choose terms from one group or the other to bring out the most appropriate meaning.

However, here, perhaps above all, and this in one of the most important discussions in the book, there is a subjective element in the translation.

The German term *das Ereignis*, which is usually translated as *event*, can lead to very heavy, and indeed incomprehensible English phrases. The third major section heading in chapter three is an example of this. To translate *Das Ereignis der Gerechtigkeit Gottes in der Person Jesu Christi* as *The Event of the Righteousness of God in the Person of Jesus Christ* would be sheer obfuscation. Consequently, I have opted for an explanatory paraphrase: *The Righteousness of God is Shown in the Person of Jesus Christ*. However, the concept of an event is sometimes crucial for understanding the author's meaning, and I have used *event* or a synonym on occasions where this did not seem to make the whole phrase too clumsy.

I have variously employed *we*, *I* and *you* to avoid the overuse of the German singular *der Sünder*, and of *der Mensch*, which I have sometimes also translated as *human beings*. *Man* in English suffers from being a coalescence of two concepts into one linguistic form. It had the sense of *human being* on the one hand, and of *male adult* (cf. German: *Mensch / Mann*; Latin: *homo / vir*; Greek: ἄνθρωπος / ἀνήρ) on the other. It has unfortunately become difficult to separate the two meanings. This has meant recourse to a great deal of ingenuity and occasionally lengthy paraphrase by translators and others wishing to make their meaning clear. The present work is thus at times more wordy than Jüngel's original.

Two comments on minor points of style are in order. German favours the full title *Jesus Christus*, where English will often choose *Jesus* or *Christ*. I have followed this practice. The German word *wer*, introducing a clause, makes very clumsy 'translation English' when rendered as *whoever*. I have almost always chosen an alternative phrase.

Once or twice, I have quoted more of the published English translation than was given by Jüngel, in order to make his meaning clear. On occasion, I have altered the published translation for the same reason, or because it did not reflect the original

German or Latin accurately enough for our purposes. However, I have generally quoted the established translations of German works, which sometimes use archaic English. This reflects Jüngel's own use of archaic German in his quotes from German writers of earlier generations.

In this translation, the New Revised Standard Version of the Bible (NRSV) has been used, unless otherwise noted. A fairly full list of abbreviations has been supplied to reduce the already cumbersome bulk of footnotes. I have shortened only those footnotes in which Jüngel gives a range of instances from an author such as Luther, where one or two readily available examples in English translation would suffice to demonstrate his point. The Latin text of quotes has been included in the form in which Jüngel gives it, with an English translation. The footnotes themselves correspond in their numbering exactly to those in the German edition. Since these notes appear on almost every page, this numbering should act as a guide to the reader wishing to compare the two texts.

In order to make the English edition easier to use, to the General Index I have added indexes of authors mentioned, of Biblical references and of Latin and Greek terms used theologically. German terms referred to, principally in the Translator's Notes, have been included in the General Index. In the half dozen cases where this is relevant, I have translated the title of a sermon by Luther in the footnotes. It will be readily apparent by the following reference to *WA* instead of *LW* that the work itself is in German. The German titles appear in the Index of Authors under Luther.

It has been a stimulating project to work at bringing this latest and very relevant work by Eberhard Jüngel to readers of English.

JEFFREY F. CAYZER
Sydney, March 2001

ABBREVIATIONS

AÖR	*Archiv für öffentliches Recht*
ApolCA	*Apology of the Augsburg Confession*
APrTh	*Arbeiten zur praktischen Theologie*
BC	*The Book of Concord. The Confessions of the Evangelical Lutheran Church*, ed. T. G. Tappert, Philadelphia: Fortress Press, 1959
BGB	*Encyclopaedia Britannica: Great Books of the Western World*
BEvTh	*Beiträge zur evangelischen Theologie*
BK	*Biblischer Kommentar*
BSLK	*die Bekenntnisschriften der evangelisch-lutherischen Kirche*
CC	*Creeds of the Churches*, ed. J. H. Leith, Atlanta: John Knox Press, 3rd edn, 1982
CChr. SL	*Corpus Christianorum: Series Latina*
CD	*Church Dogmatics*
CwH	*Calwer Hefte* . . .
DH	*Denzinger-Hünermann* (H. Denzinger, *Enchiridion symbolorum definitionum et declarationum de rebus fidei et morum*, ed. P. Hünermann, 1991)
EK	*Evangelische Kommentare*
EKK	*Evangelisch-Katholischer Kommentar*
EvTh	*Evangelische Theologie*
FC.SD	*Formula of Concord: Solid Declaration*

GE	*Joint Declaration on the Doctrine of Justification* [*Gemeinsame Erklärung*]
GGA	*Göttingische gelehrte Anzeigen*
HUTh	*Hermeneutische Untersuchungen zur Theologie*
JTS	*Journal of Theological Studies*
KD	*Kirchliche Dogmatik*
KEK	*Kritisch-Exegetischer Kommentar*
KJ	*Kirchliches Jahrbuch (für die Evangelische Kirche in Deutschland)*
KuD	*Kerygma und Dogma*
LThK.E	*LThK² = Lexikon für Theologie und Kirche* (2nd edn). *Das Zweite Vatikanische Konzil. Dokumente und Kommentare*, ed. H. S. Brechter *et al.*, 3 vols, Freiburg-im-Breisgau: Herder, 1966–8.
LW	*Luther's Works*
MdKI	*Materialdienst des Konfessionskundlichen Instituts*
ND	*The Christian Faith in the Doctrinal Documents of the Catholic Church*, ed. J. Neuner and J. Dupuis, London: Collins, 1983 (revised edn)
NF	*Neue Folge* (*New Series*)
NIV	*New International Version of the Bible*
NZSTh	*Neue Zeitschrift für systematische Theologie*
NZZ	*Neue Zürcher Zeitung*
ÖTh	*Ökumenische Theologie*
P	The Priestly source, one of the four editorial sources responsible for the shape of the Pentateuch, according to the Graf-Wellhausen hypothesis
PG	*Patrologiae Graecae* (ed. J.-P. Migne)
PL	*Patrologiae Latinae* (ed. J.-P. Migne)
RGG	*die Religion in Geschichte und Gegenwart*

StZ	*Stimmen der Zeit*
TCC	*The Teaching of the Catholic Church*, compiled by J. Neuner and H. Roos, ed. K. Rahner, trans. G. Stevens, Cork: The Mercier Press, 1967
TCT	*The Church Teaches: Documents of the Church in English Translation*, St Louis: B. Herder, 1955
TE 1	*Eberhard Jüngel, Theological Essays*
TE 2	*Eberhard Jüngel, Theological Essays 2*
ThStKr	*Theologische Studien und Kritiken*
ThZ	*Theologische Zeitschrift*
Tr	*Translator*
TRE	*Theologische Realenzyklopädie*
WA	*Weimarer Ausgabe*
WMANT	*Wissenschaftliche Monographien zum Alten und Neuen Testament*
WSAMA.T	*Walberberger Studien der Albertus-Magnus-Akademie – Theologische Reihe*
WUNT	*Wissenschaftliche Untersuchungen zum Neuen Testament*
ZdZ	*Zeichen der Zeit*
ZThK	*Zeitschrift für Theologie und Kirche*

PREFACE TO THE THIRD EDITION

It is not only academic vanity that causes the author to be delighted at the printing of a third edition less than a year after the book's first appearance. My pleasure is far greater because pastors, teachers of religion, and many other Protestant and Catholic folk who are seriously desirous of being Christians and are thus looking for some basic direction, have obviously perceived this slim volume as offering an improved Christian self-understanding. This was precisely the underlying intention, to help Christians and the church towards a self-understanding in keeping with the gospel. The fact that the realization of this intention was accepted, not as a piece of confessional posturing, but really as a study written totally without compromise with a view to ecumenical understanding, makes me certain that this little book – despite a few disputed points – may play its role in the aim 'that all may be one' (John 17:21).

That is why it seems to me appropriate in this new edition to make at least some brief reference to the discussion which in recent months has defined the attempts at ecumenical agreement about the doctrine of justification. I should mention by way of reminder that the *Joint Declaration on Justification* worked out by the Vatican and the Lutheran World Federation was criticized fairly clearly by myself, and, as far as I can see, at the beginning by myself only. My aim in this was, of course, not to impede ecumenical agreement. As a result of my critique there was a wave of protest from more than 160 professors of Protestant theology, which served to strengthen the criticism. Yet I could not identify with the letter of protest from my colleagues, even though I agreed with it in many respects and a significant portion of the phraseology had been suggested by me. This was because some of the statements appeared to me to be expressions of confessional sterility. Nor was the mere possibility of the Vatican reacting with similar confessional sterility – if not with 'great might', then at least with 'deep guile'* – for me anything like a sufficient reason to strike up a chorus of 'Luther, Luther über alles'. Martin Luther is, of course, a doctor of the church without peer. Nor has probably any theologian since the apostle Paul thought through so thoroughly and emphasized so clearly the gospel of justification of the ungodly as did Luther. Yet not the least of the reasons why he is such an incomparable doctor of the church is that he expressly forbade his own transformation into an infallible theological authority: 'What is Luther? After all, the teaching is not mine . . . Neither was I crucified for anyone . . . How then should I – poor stinking maggot-fodder that I am – come to have men call the children of Christ by my wretched name? Not so, my dear friends . . .' (*LW* 45, 70).

Additionally, it should be said that those who listen to this doctor of the church and are ready to learn from him will be richly rewarded. I have tried to do so. That is precisely the reason that I am quite perplexed by the latest protest action by certain professors and the critical votes which accompany them, coming as they do from colleagues whose theological views are otherwise rather close to my own. The more recent protest is directed against the *Common Statement*, issued early in 1999, which completes the *Joint Declaration*, together with its Appendix. These Supplements to the *Joint Declaration* offer in my opinion – to use Schleiermacher's words – those 'conciliatory formulae' which allow the mutual condemnations of the sixteenth century to be declared obsolete. The objection is that the jointly pronounced Reformist claims – that human beings are justified by faith alone (*sola fide*) and that those thus

* The reference is to a line in the first stanza of Luther's hymn 'A Mighty Fortress is Our God' (Tr).

justified are simultaneously righteous and sinners (*simul iusti et peccatores*) – have been expounded here contrary to their Reformation meaning and in the sense of the Tridentine decree on justification, so that it is alleged we are basically dealing with a hyper-Roman text. I am totally unconvinced by this objection. And a strange misunderstanding of Paul's doctrine of justification is shown in the claim that the Prefect of the Congregation for the Faith, in an interview in an Italian newspaper, interpreted this text as anti-Reformation, even anti-Pauline, and with his assertion 'those who are not righteous are not justified either' was even expressing the idea that 'the Roman Catholic Church rejects the gospel of justification of the ungodly (Rom. 4:5)' (*epd-Dokumentation* No. 36/99: 'Streit um die Texte zur Recht-fertigungslehre' [18], 30 August 1999, 1). Cardinal Ratzinger for his part was said to be able to quote Luther concerning the most contentious statements of the interview. It is even more annoying that the interview contains a string of highly regrettable remarks. Among these is the audacious comment that one 'always [!] receives very inadequate responses' from Lutherans today when one asks 'what they understand by the term justification' (art. cit., 6). What Lutherans is the Cardinal mixing with?

This Preface to the new edition is not the place to expound more fully and justify my position regarding the Supplements to the *Joint Declaration* and the objections which were voiced by some Protestant lecturers. Instead, I refer the reader to two of my own publications. My first response to these additional texts appeared in No. 23 of the *Deutsches Allgemeines Sonntagsblatt* on 4 June 1999, entitled 'Ein wichtiger Schritt'. More information is to be had in the November issue of *Stimmen der Zeit* (No. 11/99) under the title 'Kardinale Probleme'. You may also find there the challenge to not only translate the gospel of justification of the ungodly into the *language* of our time, but also to emphasize it in church practice as the truth which guides such practice.

To this challenge is linked an unavoidable question: How is it possible to reconcile an ecumenical 'consensus about fundamental truths of the doctrine of justification' with the Pope's announcement of a Jubilee indulgence for the year 2000? An even more pressing issue is how to square that consensus with the spiritual outrage that, from the Roman Catholic point of view, there can still be no fellowship at the Eucharist between Protestant and Catholic Christians. Can we really, as the authors of the *Joint Declaration* expressly do at the end (No. 44) 'give thanks (εὐχαριστεῖν) to the Lord for this decisive step forward on the way to overcoming the division of the church', when we are not authorized to celebrate the *Eucharist* together?

I am grateful to my colleague in Bonn, Wolfgang Schrage, for those few textual amendments that occur in this edition. I hope in the foreseeable future, in a book on the subject of eternal life, to grant his desire to see a more exhaustive treatment of the relationship between justification and the judgement according to works.

EBERHARD JÜNGEL
Tübingen, October 1999

PREFACE TO THE SECOND EDITION

The author wishes to record his delight at the welcome, given almost without exception, to the first edition, which was quickly sold out. I have gladly incorporated several suggestions in the second edition. Certain phrases that could have been taken as attacking other points of view were moderated. Several misprints and occasional errors were corrected. Special note should be taken of my essay 'Amica Exegesis einer römischen Note', which appeared in *ZThK, Beiheft [Supplement] 10: Zur Rechtfertigungslehre*, 1998, 252–79, and of the exchange with my Catholic colleague in Tübingen, Bernd Jochen Hilberath, in *Herder Korrespondenz* 53 (1999), 22–6 and 154–7. It is to be hoped that agreement with those of my own Confession will be equally promising. If the book received such a positive welcome by, let's say, Finnish Lutherans as it has hitherto from Catholic theologians, I would be content.

But why go so far abroad? The *Materialdienst des Konfessionskundlichen Instituts* of Bernheim says that the book is 'extremely useful . . . for all those who wish to be convinced of the potential of the justification paradigm for hermeneutics, for shedding light on our existence and for practical living' (*MdKI* 50 [1999], 1, 19f.). Nevertheless, a book which attracted such high praise has also been strongly criticized for being 'a very German book', which limits itself to referring to such exegetical 'sources' as Bultmann, Bornkamm and Käsemann. Principally, however, it was said to be a disappointment for anyone 'looking for ongoing consideration of the question of an ecumenical hermeneutic'. Well, what can we say to all that? I have to agree in large measure with the reviewer, though not in the sense that he meant. To even suppose that there is such a thing as a special 'ecumenical hermeneutic' is, I believe, pernicious. Granted, ecumenical theology suffers from certain problems of comprehension. However, the hermeneutic necessary for solving these problems can be none other than that competent teaching which is essential for the understanding of all opinions about life, be they in written or in oral form. I share the view that 'theological thinking . . . cannot be released from its obligation to reflect on what is required of thinking'. It appears to have escaped the notice of the reviewer that the whole first part of my book is an attempt to do that very sort of reflecting, not least by arguing with my teacher Karl Barth, but also in my engage-ment with Fichte. Obviously, we have different understand-ings of such a requirement. The reviewer, taken as typical of many 'ecumenists', demands reflection 'on what is required of thinking' a thought, so as to smooth out its claims to truth. Evidently, the truth claim is being relegated to the level of proclamation. It is claimed that there is a 'difference between proclamation that makes *assertiones* (Luther) and theological thought'. This is a slap in the face to what Luther meant by *assertiones.* As if an assertion didn't have to be thought out, and we could thus dispense with reflecting on what is required of thinking! A thorough reading of the beginning of Luther's essay *On Free Will* would quickly make it clear that it is not acceptable in Reformation theology to emphasize any such distinction between 'proclamation' and 'theological thought'. To attribute a desire for 'meta-reflection' to the *Joint Declaration* – a desire which the reviewer regrets is lacking in my book – is obviously to presuppose an idea of *reflection* which is, in fact, inconsistent with my understanding of *thinking.*

Now a word on the other complaint made by this reviewer, that my biblical exegesis does not go beyond what was done in the 1970s, because I only mention Bultmann, Bornkamm and Käsemann as sources. The reviewer evidently assumes that the one he is criticizing has no exegetical judgement of his own. In fact, in this book I deliberately decided not to go into the current exegetical controversies on the issue. I did not wish to continue the discussion on the matter which can be read in my dissertation *Paulus und Jesus,* not only – as I said in the Preface to the first edition – because, in deference to readers who are not professional theologians, I 'almost entirely abstained from referring to the scholarly literature'. I also did not wish to go into the latest exegetical ideas because only too often they are merely variations on those earlier positions 'though with other motives and completely opposite purposes' (K. Kertelge, 'Rechtfertigung II. Neues Testament', in *TRE* 28, 1997, 286–307, 300, 4f.).

The situation is different in the case of the opinion held by some – for example, my Catholic colleague Michael Theobald (both in agreement with and over against that of English-speaking exegetes). They say that there is a pre-Pauline 'Sitz im Leben' for the passages in Galatians 2:16 and Romans 3:28 which are used to support the message of justification. This pre-Pauline setting is the primitive Christian mission where the idea was to make the admission of Gentiles (who were Christians) to the eschatological people of God not depend on their obedience to the Torah. The message of justification would then have originally had an ecclesiological orientation. According to this position, the anthropological relevance of the preaching of justification does emerge in Paul, but it only became the dominant view when the question of incorporating the Gentiles into the eschatological people of God no longer posed a problem (cf. Eph. 2:5, 8f.). This seems plausible, although it must be stressed that even that original ecclesiological intention has anthropological, and even, in the strict sense of the word, theological implications. After all, only God decides on who belongs to his eschatological people.

There is a position on this matter which one encounters among English-speaking exegetes. According to this view, the message of justification was limited to setting aside the Jewish 'identity markers' (e.g. circumcision, Sabbath observance, etc.) for Gentile Christians, but it had no relevance to Jewish Christians. This view, I believe, founders on the fact that Paul speaks of the justification of the ungodly in the same context as he speaks of the justification of Abraham (Rom. 4:5). Furthermore, it would be difficult to grasp why, in Galatians and Romans, Paul, with his systematic interpretation of the gospel as a message about the cross that justifies sinners, had undoubtedly devoted so much attention to such a subject. I draw the reader's attention to the article by E. Lohse ('Theologie der Rechtfertigung im kritischen Disput – zu einigen neuen Perspektiven in der Interpretation der Theologie des Apostels Paulus', *GGA*, 249 [1997], 66–81), who has interacted with the works of E. P. Sanders (*Paul and Palestinian Judaism*, Oxford, 1977), and J. D. G. Dunn ('The New Perspective on Paul', in idem, *Jesus, Paul and the Law: Studies in Mark and Galatians*, 1990, 183–214; idem, 'The Justice of God: A Renewed Perspective on Justification by Faith', *JTS*, New Series 43 [1992], 1–22).

PREFACE TO THE FIRST EDITION

What does Protestant mean? Who are the Protestants and why are they Protestants? Why do they still exist? To my surprise, such questions have been expressed more and more vocally in recent times. The question is posed in the so-called public arena, but also within the Protestant church. And there are times when you have the impression that this is where the question is least understood – in the Protestant church.

It is quite proper to ask the questions listed above at any time. But the fact that at present the question 'What does it mean to be called Protestant?' is being asked more than ever is due to a struggle currently being waged with some intensity among Protestant Christians in Germany. The quarrel is about what earlier ages used to call the 'cornerstone of Protestant belief', that is the article of faith that concerns the justification of the ungodly by faith alone. The quarrel arose when a *Joint Declaration on Justification*, negotiated by representatives of the Lutheran World Alliance and the Vatican, was publicized. This document makes the claim to have formulated a 'consensus on basic truths of the doctrine of justification', and so thanks God at its conclusion 'for this decisive step forward on the way to overcoming the division of the church'.

I was delighted at this good news, as part and parcel of my theological life from the very beginning has been a passionate interest in coming to an understanding with Catholic Christianity. In the German Democratic Republic, in which I had studied and commenced my teaching, such an understanding was self-evident for those of us who were at that time young theologians faced with the challenge of atheism. So I was also one of the co-founders of the first ecumenical working group of Catholic and Protestant church lecturers in the GDR.

Then, later, meeting with Karl Rahner and his 'pupils' contributed greatly to my discovery of genuine evangelical substance in Catholic theology. This experience was intensified on the one hand by a congenial proximity to Walter Kasper in Tübingen, and on the other hand by a quite special neighbourly friendship with Hans Küng. But in addition, the ecumenism practised by the Protestant and Catholic seminaries in Tübingen was of great importance. The trip to Rome with the former head of the Catholic seminary, Kilian Nuss, remains memorable, as do the encounters and discussions in the Roman Germanicum,* which were preceded by the no less lively encounters and discussions at the theological faculty of the University of Innsbruck. All this and much more led to the fact that for me it was an indispensable duty to look for solid theological bases for a promising path towards the visible unity of the churches.

I mention all of this to make clear the sense of disappointment that took hold of me when I studied more closely that *Joint Declaration* which had promised so much. In my judgement at least, there were no sound theological foundations laid here 'on the way to overcoming the division of the church'. For here decisive insights of the Reformation were either obscured or surrendered. Certainly there is much in this text that the Protestant churches and the Roman Catholic Church can say in common. But these are pronouncements which almost without exception move in the area and on the level of the *Decree Concerning Justification* which the Roman Catholic Church had adopted at the Council of Trent in 1547 on the basis of, and more particularly *against*, the Reformers' doctrine of justification.

---

* One of the three foundations set up in Rome for priests from the German-speaking lands (Tr).

That was precisely why I was unable to discover in the *Joint Declaration* the breakthrough it believes itself to be. It is far too brief for that. And the understanding that allegedly has been reached rests on ground which proves at places quite slippery. When the apologists who wrote the *Joint Declaration* chimed in with their arguments, which, instead of restoring clarity, only created confusion (there is no doubt at all that there will be a thesis written about what the representatives have achieved in this regard, particularly on the Lutheran side), I knew that I was obliged for ecumenism's sake to sound the alarm. I demanded 'For God's sake – Clarity!' ('Um Gottes Willen – Klarheit', *ZThK* 94 [1997], 394–406).

It came to verbal blows, and this affected the public. The squabble was reported in the secular press far more carefully and objectively than in its religious equivalent. (The fact that religious leaders accused the *Frankfurter Allgemeine Zeitung* of bias, when it had rendered an exceptional service by informing its readers about this matter better than almost any other German-language newspaper, can only be noted as a curiosity considering the reporting in the church papers. And the attempt to denigrate a reputable journalist by character assassination is such an embarrassing occurrence that it too will no doubt become the object of an 'academic study'.) It is precisely this squabble, so carefully followed in the media, that has led people in Germany to ask again: Who or what then really deserves to be called *Protestant*?

Nothing is better able to answer this question than the 'basic Protestant article of belief' of the justification of the ungodly by faith alone. That is the purpose of this book. It is not a book that takes pleasure in compromise. An ordered theology makes no compromises. This is what differentiates theology from church leadership, which necessarily has to make compromises, but which, in order not to make uneasy ones, needs to be accompanied by a theology which quite simply makes none.

Nevertheless, this book is written with ecumenical intent. For ecumenism only flourishes when we on both sides become more Protestant in the best sense of the word. Then we on both sides also become more Catholic in the best sense of the word. I dare to claim that agreement about this can also be reached with the Roman Congregation of the Faith.

The book only occasionally goes into the *Joint Declaration*. What needed to be said about this text has been adequately set forth elsewhere. E. Maurer, *Rechtfertigung. Konfessionstrennend oder konfessionsverbindend?* (Ökumenische Studienhefte 8, 1998) gives brief, but excellent information about the 'ecumenical dialogue'. What I am concerned about is to discuss the factual problems in view of our present experiences and questionings. For this the Pauline letters are, of course, of fundamental importance. It is likewise self-evident that the insights of the Reformers are quoted with particular frequency in a Protestant theory of justification. But reflecting on the Reformers' discoveries is no goal in itself. For the discoveries of our fathers only have a legitimate function when they help us turn the articles on justification to good account in the framework of our own present-day awareness of problems. In the early 1970s the *Lehrgespräche der Evangelischen Kirche der Union und der Vereinigten Evangelisch-lutherischen Kirche in der DDR* (the German text may be consulted in *KJ* 98 [1971], 295–322; 99 [1972], 301–9; 100 [1973], 227–39) undertook this in exemplary fashion under the particular conditions of socialist reality. In such expositions of the article on justification it again became clear how much of what to our present day appears at first sight completely unproblematical was at that time a problem. For truth, which is what the gospel of the justification of the ungodly is about, shatters not a few of what were to us till now self-evident beliefs. But it does this only to generate new self-evident beliefs: ones which can stand before God. This is how Luther says it in his Christmas carol: 'The light of heaven to us descends; Sunshine new to earth it lends.'*

---

* 'Das ewig Licht geht da herein, gibt der Welt ein' neuen Schein.' These are the first two lines of verse 4 of 'Gelobet seist du, Jesu Christ, Daß du Mensch geboren bist'. The English translation of 1851, by Arthur Tozer Russell, quoted here, captures Luther's meaning reasonably well, but of course misses the other, key meaning of 'Schein' (Tr).

This book is by no means written for so-called professional theologians – in fact, for them least of all. As I wrote it I was thinking above all of the many ministers and teachers of religion who have to expound and announce the gospel, and who love doing this and want to do it with, theologically speaking, a good conscience. I also thought of all those Christians who are not afraid of a little intellectual work-out in order to be able to give an account of the truth of the faith. Those are the ones I wanted to help. For that reason I have almost entirely abstained from referring to the scholarly literature. I wanted the case to speak for itself. And to put a case means to put it in its present-day form.

In order to make the case more accessible, the book has been organized in such a way that foreign-language quotations are given at the same time in translation. In addition, the Reformation German was carefully modernized. For this I used the Luther texts of Karin Bornkamm and Gerhard Ebeling (Martin Luther, *Ausgewählte Schriften*, 1982). It will be obvious to a well-informed reader how much I owe to Gerhard Ebeling in factual matters. In the matter at hand it became necessary to engage with Karl Barth. Our well-informed reader will certainly also notice that I have tried to take up and turn to fruitful purpose for my own argument as ecumenical knowledge – in the best sense of the phrase – Barth's pivotal pronouncements on this matter.

Among the co-workers who have given me valuable help in producing this manuscript, I may mention as a representative of the whole group my assistant, Mrs Christiane Steiding. Many thanks! I also wish to thank Mr Georg Siebeck for his readiness to bring the manuscript into print at such short notice. It is good to know that theology can still depend on the Mohr Siebeck publishing house. I am also thankful for the contributions from the churches towards printing costs, which have enabled the book to be available at an affordable price: the Evangelische Kirche der Union and the Evangelische Landeskirche in Württemberg have assisted generously.

This book is dedicated to the colleague and friend whose unerring sense of truth is as agreeable as his distinctive Berlin style of *humanitas*.

The church does not satisfy expectations; it celebrates mysteries.
(CARLO MARIA CARDINAL MARTINI)

The greatest of all mysteries is the Mysterium Paschale
which justifies the ungodly.

1

INTRODUCTION

I. The difficulty of understanding something easy

The gospel tells the story of Jesus Christ, the source of a great joy for all people (Luke 2:10). It is – in its most incisive form – news that is at the same time both simple and revolutionary: it is *the message about the cross* (1 Cor. 1:18), which promises life to all people on the basis of the death of a single person. This message gets to the heart of what is narrated in the Gospels. The message about the cross announces the death of Jesus Christ as the decisive event for the life and death of human beings and the world in which they live. In this message there is to be found a focusing of the proclamation so that it is hard to imagine it being more focused or a more notable proclamation: *God for the ungodly! Life for those threatened by death, for those enslaved by death! The hope of salvation for a humanity which is hopelessly lost in a slough of despond of its own making! Liberating truth for people who suppress the truth (Rom. 1:18) and who, in the way they handle truth, entangle themselves and their fellow human beings in a deadly sham existence.*

The apostle Paul's favourite description of this concentrated proclamation, which Friedrich Nietzsche said implied a 're-valuation of all antique values',[1] is *justification of the ungodly*. At the same time Paul gave to this gospel of the justification of the ungodly a form which was the result of theological reflection: the so-called Pauline doctrine of justification. The expression *doctrine* is appropriate because, in the relevant passages of his

---

[1] F. Nietzsche, *Beyond Good and Evil*, trans. R. J. Hollingdale, Harmondsworth: Penguin, 1990, 75. On this, also see below, pp. 38f.

letters, Paul not only tells and announces, but at the same time explains and argues, that is to say he engages in theological reflection.

Of course, no historical account, no proclamation properly so called, can manage without implicit theological reflection. But in the doctrine of justification the theological reflection becomes explicit. It becomes a tool of persuasion. Indeed, as an apologia for the truth of the gospel it becomes downright polemical. The apostle Paul even felt compelled to withstand, in public and face to face, another apostle who had brought the truth of the gospel into question by his behaviour. This was, of course, the one who was later called the Prince of Apostles and the supposed representative of Christ on earth. The apostle Paul countered the behaviour of the apostle Peter, when Peter was threatening by his practice to reduce the truth of the gospel *ad absurdum*, with . . . *arguments* (Gal. 2:11–21). Apostle against apostle, simply for the sake of truth; it was, after a fashion, the birth of Protestant theology.

The fact that the gospel of the justification of the ungodly *was able* to take on such a markedly deliberated form is connected with its potential for truth. Paul stresses the fact that the gospel raises a truth which must win acceptance if the gospel itself is to hold its own. Obviously the gospel of the justification of the ungodly not only *was able to* take on a theologically intentional form, but it *had to*. This fact is not ultimately based on the revaluing of all the values of antiquity which Nietzsche noted as the meaning of the gospel's claim to truth and which he helped us to comprehend. It is not only the values of antiquity, but all human values that are called into question when the claim to truth of the gospel of the justification of the ungodly starts to be heard.

The message about the cross puts the person *in the right* who is *in the wrong*, not (only) in the wrong in the eyes of the world, but before God. That person therefore deserves to be accused and condemned. Nevertheless, for everything to be above board, this demands an explanation, and that is why a reasoned argument is required. The doctrine of justification is an attempt at a reasoned argument which is appropriate to the truth claim of the gospel.

Now this claim to truth is anything but obvious to so-called common sense. First of all, it is to common sense, as it was to the Greeks in the apostle's time, pure foolishness, if not a blasphemous scandal, as it was to the Jews of that day (1 Cor. 1:23). Some effort is necessary to understand that this foolishness conceals a profound, life-saving wisdom and so that it is in fact a beneficial scandal. If the intentional nature of the doctrine of justification demands from those who wish to get to the heart of it something of a straining of the term, then the unfathomability of the matter increases even further the difficulties of understanding. But for those who demand of themselves the effort of thinking, the gospel of the justification of the ungodly becomes what it essentially is, quite simple.

II. The heart of the matter

It is advisable firstly to paint with broad strokes what we are talking about when we say that the gospel of the justification of the ungodly makes its truth claim:

1. We are talking, to put it quite simply, about life and death, or more exactly, about the either/or of life and death. And since life, in the judgement of theology, always means life together, it is more specifically about whether I have the right now and forever to live together with God, or on the other hand am unable to live together with anyone and so belong to the realm of Death. For, in death, life itself disintegrates along with shared life.

2. We are talking about my personhood, that is about me, about the personhood of the Ego. Who or what makes me into the person whose value is so unassailable? Do I myself do it? Does society? Or does God?

3. We are talking about God and the question of what really is divine. And it is about what sort of humanity corresponds to the divinity of God in human beings who see themselves as being in the image of God. So: Who or what is a really divine God? Who or what is a really human human being?

4. What we are talking about is more crucial than all these other questions: The relationship of God to human beings and the relationship of human beings to God. We are talking about the story where this mutual relationship takes place. Even more specifically, we are talking about the central event within this story: the death of Jesus Christ on the cross. Does this death have anything to say? It if it does have something to say, if it has something to say to us – what exactly is that something? At whose behest, by whose authority and by what power does such a message about the cross speak? By the authority of a story which ends in this death and perhaps is completed in this death – that is, with the authority and power of the past? 'Once upon a time . . . ?' Or with the power of a future just beginning, a future that has the strength to return creatively to the past of a life lived and ending in death, so that the truth and meaning of this life and this death is brought to light? Is the message about the cross a funeral oration, or is it a word that releases life, new life, a life that conquers death? To put it briefly: We are talking about the raising of Jesus Christ from the dead and about our participation in his life and resurrection.

5. So we are talking about participation, about being given a part, taking part and having a part in the story of Jesus Christ. How is all this accomplished: our being given a part, our taking part and having a part? If Jesus Christ is the one who gives us a part in his story, how and in what sense are we then those who take part and those who have a part? And how, in what way, is Jesus the one who gives us a part?

Is it through the message about the cross and therefore the gospel alone that Jesus gives us a part in his story? Or does the law, with its claims on us, have a role to play? And if so, how? And if it is through the message about the cross alone that Jesus gives us a share in his story, what role do the so-called sacraments have to play? Do they confirm the theory that Jesus gives us a part in his story through the message about the cross alone? Or are the sacraments in competition with the cross?

And what about our own taking part? Is it by faith and faith alone that we have a share in the story of Jesus? Or do we participate on the basis of our successful living, on the basis of our good works, that is, through what we ourselves do and achieve? Is that it?

And beyond our current taking part in the event of faith do we also have a continuing part in this story? And if so, in what form? In the form of the church? But what is the church? Is it something other than or even more than the community of justified sinners?

6. But above all, and all in all, we are talking about righteousness: about God's righteousness and our righteousness. How does God in his righteousness deal with our unrighteousness? And running parallel, or perhaps combined with that, we are talking about God's grace and our guilt. What relationship does God's grace have to his righteousness and what relationship does his grace have to our guilt?

7. And if in all this at the same time it is always about my being a person, what role then has my conscience in the justification event? Does it have a say? If it does, just how does it have a say? My conscience is that odd personal court of law where the question has to be decided. And the question to be decided is whether I have to live in contradiction to myself or am able on the contrary to live at peace with myself. Can one's conscience be silenced? If so, how? Can a person who is accused and judged by his conscience be justified?

III. Justification – its use in everyday language

Although the theological concept of justification is not incomprehensible, it does present people of today with not insignificant problems of understanding. A glance at daily life will give us some sense of orientation to the question.

To justify something, to have to justify oneself, to be justified – these are basic procedures in secular life. They happen daily. Although they have nothing immediately to do with the central mystery of Christian faith, they afford a premonition of what occurs in the justification of the sinner.

Normally we try *to justify something* when it is not self-evident. For example, people justify their behaviour, their actions, because they are hard to explain or just downright annoying. We justify above all our inappropriate behaviour, which we try to *de-fault* as somehow being necessary behaviour, so that we do not have to *fault* ourselves for our inappropriate behaviour. Rather, we acquit ourselves by *de-faulting* our behaviour as being necessary.

Quite often people will even justify their own existence: that they are here now where they – at least for the moment – seem to be out of place. However, the justification of my own existence can be based, beyond such special situations, much more simply on the plain fact that I *am* rather than *am not*. Then I am no longer justifying something or my particular existence in specific situations; I am, in the original sense of the words, justifying myself. But those who justify their life, their very existence, that is justify themselves, are also making the assertion that their life has a meaning. They are justifying with their existence the meaning of their existence. Meaningless existence cannot be justified. Only *apparently* meaningless existence can be justified – that is, justified as being nevertheless meaningful. But justified *before whom?*

Justifications always occur before *some authority*. I justify myself to other people, to a human institution (for example, to a court) or to myself. These are *secular* occurrences in life, by which I am justified *before the world*. Not totally separate from these, but going beyond them and qualifying their importance, is the justification of a person *before God*. However, in all cases the process of justification is an event which summons me to appear *before a court or forum*. We exist at all times before some forum or other, occasionally before several simultaneously: a child before its parents (and vice versa!), a friend before a friend, a worker before his workmates or the boss, a patient before the doctor, a minister before Parliament, a suspect before the police officer, an accused before the court, and so on. In the process of justification this *existence before. . .* becomes explicit. That is when I experience myself as a self who has to appear before someone. It can also come down to my having to appear before myself. If this occurs, if I am justifying myself *before myself*, then the forum before which I am summoned is my *conscience*.

Wanting to justify yourself is one thing; *having* to justify yourself is quite another. The fact that people want to justify their conduct, their behaviour, their past life and their claim to a future life is linked with the fact that people require recognition. It is essential for people to be recognized. Their personhood depends on it. As human beings we demand recognition of ourselves. The wish for justification has its source in this basic human need for *recognition*.

The fact that people *must* justify themselves, that they can be *compelled* to do so, points to a further basic human requirement: to be human means *the necessity of being accountable*. This is because no human beings live for themselves. They exist only in relationship to others, even when they are relating to themselves. As beings who are relational in every aspect, human beings exist *in a state of accountability* to others. That is why they can, when the need arises, *be brought to account*. At that time they *must* justify themselves.

If I *have* to justify myself, I then appear to be *in the wrong*. If I am in principle living accountably, I am normally only brought to account when I am in some way at fault or appear to be so, that is, when I am *blamed or accused*. If I can justify myself, I am put in the right. If I cannot, I am considered guilty. If I can justify myself, I am declared innocent and set free. If I cannot, I am condemned.

However, it can also happen that I am unable to justify myself, even though I am in the right. This can lead to bizarre miscarriages of justice in normal courts of law, not to mention in kangaroo courts. Later events and clearer insights or simply a fairer system of justice can put the accused and the guilty in the right, quite often in fact without their being able to contribute anything more to their own defence. Then, without their having anything to do with it, they *have been justified*. But they were justified because they were in the right.

Is it possible to justify a person who is *in the wrong*? Is it possible, without perverting justice, to set the guilty person free?

The gospel of the justification of sinners asserts that God has done exactly this. At the heart of the Christian faith stands the tremendous assertion that human beings, rightfully accused – absolutely in the wrong before God and therefore deserving to be called *sinners* or even *ungodly* – are justified by God. That is, they find acceptance with God. Now, if I find acceptance *with God*, I am accepted *irrevocably, once and for all*. I have the right in the fullest meaning of the term to live and to *live together* with others.

IV. Without this article the world is nothing but death and darkness

'Without this article the world is nothing but death and dark-ness.'[2] What was Luther saying by this apparently exaggerated expression about the justification article? We shall make this clear by looking at the story of Cain, the murderer of his brother, which, from the standpoint of the New Testament gospel, may be read as the first story of justification in the Bible.

1. Remembering Cain

Even those who have until now mostly been spared such experi-ences will not dispute the fact that the world is full of death and of all possible kinds of darkness. These precede or follow death as the sign of death. No doubt there is nobody who is com-pletely spared such experiences. Who has not at least had the experience of seeing a human face cloud over – as did the face of Cain according to Genesis 4:5? But it is not only human faces which can cloud over, but whole eras of time, as for example Martin Buber[3] showed so impressively when, speaking of our own time, he called it 'the eclipse of God'. Now, these days anyone can observe that the world is full of death and darkness. In that respect we are better informed today than any previous generation. The media keep us up to date every day. The extent of death and darkness is enormous.

---

[2] M. Luther, *Die Promotionsdisputation von Palladius und Tilemann*, 1537, WA 39/I, 205, 5: 'Sine hoc articulo mundus est plane mors et tenebrae.'

[3] M. Buber, *The Eclipse of God: Studies in the Relation Between Religion and Philosophy*, London: Gollancz, 1953.

And yet it cannot be said that the world is nothing but death and darkness. There are glimpses of light. We are still alive! Luther's assertion that without the article about justification of the ungodly the world is nothing but death and darkness is one of two things. Either it is unreasonable exaggeration, theological hyperbole, or it expresses an experience which is not satisfied by statistics about deaths and by analysing subjective and objective darkness. Here I am thinking of the darkening of the human spirit, of the world spirit, of the light of reason, in short, of the light of life. There is ground for accepting the second of these two alternatives. We may clarify what is meant by a few biblical considerations.

The myths of many religions recall a darkness that threatened the world in its entirety as well as a corresponding threat of death. The Bible, with its story of the Flood, recalls this universal threat. Going back even further, however, the creation story commemorates this threat by having the world in the beginning *tohu wabohu*, desolate and (deathly) empty, chaotic and covered with darkness: 'In the beginning when God created the heavens and the earth, the earth was a formless void and darkness [*tenebrae*] covered the face of the deep.' Only then did God speak: '"Let there be light"; and there was light' (Gen. 1:1–3). This is the Bible recollecting an original threat to everything that exists. It has parallels in other legends of the beginnings of things, and is there to help the reader understand this: everything that is, comes from that darkness and remains under the threat of its origin. But the creation story is also meant to remind us that the definitive difference and contrast between light and darkness is the work of God alone: 'And God saw that the light was good; and God separated the light from the darkness' (Gen. 1:4). It is evidently not given to human beings to make that definitive separation of light from darkness. Rather, in humans the darkness can at any moment win the upper hand; it can win power over us.

Cain, who murdered his brother, is a symbol of this. In him we see clearly what a life without justification is like, and what justification means for a life that has become meaningless.

When Luther translates: 'Cain's face became darkened',[4] we think of the darkness that covered the earth at the beginning of creation. At the murder of Abel, this darkness breaks out again in God's ordered creation. And with it all hell breaks loose in the life of Cain, the tiller of the soil – the murderer. 'Cain rose up against his brother Abel, and killed him' (Gen. 4:8). And the ground 'opened its mouth to receive' his brother's blood from his hand (Gen. 4:11). The result was that Cain was accursed. By his own judgement his sin was greater than could be forgiven. This is exactly what is meant by *a life without justification: falling back into chaos*. In Cain's eyes the world has now *really* become nothing but death and darkness: 'Today . . . I shall be hidden from your face; I shall be a fugitive and a wanderer on the earth, and anyone who meets me may kill me' (Gen. 4:14). This is where the world with all its life and its bright side moves completely into the shadow of that death which Cain's murder has brought into the world. The shadow of death now seems to confront Cain on every side. 'And anyone who meets me may kill me.' From now on the world for Cain is nothing but death and darkness.

Cain represents a possibility within each person. And if you don't want to be a murderer, if you don't have to be a murderer, you can still be the victim. Abel does nothing wrong, yet he is killed. He is struck down by his own brother, simply because Cain does not think he is as accepted (by God) as is his brother. Cain does evil. He kills and is in turn to be killed. According to his own judgement, his life has become meaningless. The meaning of Cain the murderer can no longer be found in this life. His life would no longer have any meaning even as some sort of compensation. Life which is killed does not come back; a murder cannot be compensated for. According to the rigorous logic of human life and its acts, this crime is in fact too great to be forgiven. The consequence of such a murderous life can only be death. Such a death is not to be seen as repentance,

---

[4] In Hebrew: to turn one's face towards the ground, so that others cannot look you in the face. The opposite is Genesis 4:7: to lift one's face.

which would then give some sort of meaning to this life. No, this is the murderer being struck dead, as a sign that his life is meaningless and flies in the face of meaning. This is something along the lines of the reasoning of those people and countries today who defend or argue for the reintroduction of the death penalty.

But God said to Cain: 'Not so!' (Gen. 4:15). This 'No' from God is, in the biblical scheme, the first word of justification, the first text that deals with the justification of the sinner. It gives us a feeling for what it means, in a world full of death and darkness, to be dealing with a God who justifies sinners.

Only a court sitting on the other side of such a murderous life can justify that life, restoring its legitimacy, so that it can continue as life (and not only as a flight from death and consequently a flight into death). 'And the Lord put a mark on Cain, so that no one who came upon him would kill him' (Gen. 4:15). This is the first sign of justification, an effectual sign of grace, a *signum efficax gratiae*: Cain is not killed; his life certainly does go on: 'Cain knew his wife, and she conceived and bore Enoch' (Gen. 4:17). Because of God's sign, Cain's life has regained a future and a meaning.

Now he was even able to build a city, naming it after his son Enoch (Gen. 4:17). It is impossible to express any more strikingly the justification of Cain, the murderer of his brother. The one who killed his neighbour and now must normally expect to be killed by anyone who comes across him – this antisocial person, of all people, becomes the founder of a city. He is the builder of a city, a *polis*, in which no person exists except jointly with another person. In the *polis* the human being becomes a social being. We recognize just how completely Cain's life has been justified when we see that the man who murdered his brother has become the founder of the *polis*, that is, of a society in which a person is by definition a social being. The justification of this antisocial person makes more of him than he was before; it makes him a political being, a ζῷον πολιτικόν.

2. Jesus Christ crucified

Let us now turn from the Old to the New Testament in an attempt to clarify, in the decisive figure of Jesus, Luther's claim that the world without the justification article is nothing but death and darkness. For this claim draws its strength from its interpretation of the life and passion, the death and resurrection of Jesus Christ. Without Jesus the world would be, in the eyes of the Christian faith, *in fact* nothing but death and darkness.

In this regard, the New Testament narratives of Jesus' death speak in a language rich in allusions. It should be noted particularly that the Synoptic Gospels (not John!) report a darkness that immediately preceded Jesus' death, a darkness which, from the sixth to the ninth hour, covered the whole face of the earth: 'darkness came over the whole land' (Mark 15:33; Matt. 27:45; Luke 23:44). Luke increases the force of the whole statement by adding that even the sun was darkened (Luke 23:45, KJV). Obviously the emphasis is meant to be on the hour of Jesus' death being the eschatological hour, in which the darkness that reigned at the beginning of creation moves in again – not only over the scene of what is happening, Jerusalem, but over the whole land. The darkness that covered the earth at the beginning has come back. The historical event of the execution of one man, Jesus of Nazareth, may be seen as an event that leaves the whole world as nothing but darkness.

If, in addition, you take the Synoptic Gospels' suggested linking of darkness with the death of Jesus as recounting the fulfilment of prophetic pronouncements, then the point becomes even clearer. Amos 8:9–14 is relevant here: 'I will make the sun go down at noon and darken the earth in broad daylight. I will turn your feasts into mourning and all your songs into lamentation. I will bring sackcloth on all loins, and baldness on every head; I will make it like the mourning for an only son, and the end of it like a bitter day . . . In that day the beautiful young women and young men shall faint for thirst . . . they shall fall, and never rise again.' The Gospels appear to understand the universal darkness accompanying Jesus' death as the fulfilment of the eschatological prophecies of Amos 8:9–14. If this is the case, then Jesus' dying brings, in the eyes of the evangelists, nothing but death. But the death of Jesus ends this apocalyptic darkness. In this regard it is important to note that the ancient writers reported darkness *following* the death of great men, while the universal darkness recorded in the Gospels immediately *precedes* the death of Jesus. In his dying the darkness of the original chaos came again to the fore in its most intense form. *But his death conquers the darkness!*

So the death of Jesus is seen in the Gospels from the point of view of his resurrection. Seen as victory over darkness, as the death of death *(mors mortis)*, the cross of Jesus is the justification of the world. There is no doubt that this is how Christian preaching, teaching and devotion have seen it. Without *this* person, without the crucified Jesus, the world would be nothing but death and darkness. Without him chaos and death would triumph. The Easter hymn summarizes it most powerfully and profoundly: If he had not risen, the world would have perished.[5] If you have grasped that, you have grasped the doctrine of justification.

---

[5] Cf. The *Evangelisches Gesangbuch*, No. 99: 'Wär er nicht erstanden, so wär die Welt vergangen' (Tr).

2

HOW JUSTIFICATION WORKS
THEOLOGICALLY

At the heart of the Christian faith lies a declared belief in Jesus Christ. This confession, however, also has a centre, a living focal point, which turns the confession of Christ into something that vitally concerns my own existence. This heart of the heart of Christian faith is the belief in the justification of the sinner through the one who 'was handed over to death for our sins and was raised for our justification' (Rom. 4:25).

I. The Reformers' high view of justification

When we believe in the justification of sinners, our declaration of faith in Jesus Christ becomes a truth that sheds light on the whole of human existence. It becomes a critical truth, bringing human self-understanding and all of our existence to a point of fundamental, life and death crisis. Because it is so very critical, the truth of the gospel of the justification of sinners has caused offence from the beginning. And it continues to do so. If you try to avoid this offence, you play down the seriousness and trivialize the joy of the biblical good news. This continues to happen, both within and outside the Christian church. To that extent it was true from the beginning of Christianity and remains true today that the spirits divide over confessing the God who justifies sinners.

'I believe in the forgiveness of sins.' In the Apostles' Creed, of course, justification appears to be only one of many truths of the faith. It is not immediately obvious in the Creed that belief in the justification of sinners is the living focal point at the heart of the Christian faith. But confessions of faith have a tendency to turn the great truths of a religion into a list. These truths are so lineally organized that it is difficult to claim the contents of the great statements about God the Creator, Jesus Christ and the Holy Spirit to be formally correct statements which can only be brought to life by the doctrine of justification. Rather, the good news of justification is based on the fact that there is a creatively active God, who became a human being in the person of Jesus Christ, lived a distinctive human life, for our sakes died the death of a criminal on the cross and was raised from the dead, in order to work among us from then on through his Word and Spirit.

However, in the justification article all these statements come to a head. The decision is made here first of all as to who this God is, and what it really means to be creatively active. Next, it says what it means to die for others and to bring forth new life in the midst of death: a life that imparts itself through the power of the Spirit to our passing world in such a way that a new community arises – the Christian church. The justification article brings out emphatically the truth of the relationship between God and people and in so doing the correct understanding of God's divinity and our humanity. And since the Christian church draws its life from the relationship between God and people, and only from that relationship, the justification article is the one article by which the church stands and without which it falls. So every other truth of the faith must be weighed and judged by that article.

For this reason, the doctrine of justification was considered the 'centre and boundary'[1] of all theology. The best-known expression for this high view of the doctrine is found in its description as 'the article, by which the church stands or falls' (*articulus stantis et cadentis ecclesiae*). Of course, that particular expression does not actually occur in the Reformers' writings. However, the fact remains that it is genuinely reformed in its content.

---

[1] E. Wolf, 'Die Rechtfertigungslehre als Mitte und Grenze reformatorischer Theologie' in *Peregrinatio*, vol. 2, *Studien zur reformatorischen Theologie, zum Kirchenrecht und zur Sozialethik*, 1965, 11–21.

A large number of related expressions are found in Luther. In the *Smalcald Articles* of 1537, in regard to Christ's work and our justification by faith alone – typically, both of these form a single article – he speaks of 'the first and main article': 'Nothing in this article can be given up or compromised, even if heaven and earth and things temporal should be destroyed.'[2] In his exposition of Psalm 117 Luther declares: 'If this one teaching stands in its purity, then Christendom will also remain pure and good, undivided and unseparated; for this alone, and nothing else, makes and maintains Christendom. Everything else may be brillliantly counterfeited by false Christians and hypocrites; but where this falls, it is impossible to ward off any error or sectarian spirit.'[3]

In the *Warning to His Dear German People* in 1531 it is absolutely striking: 'This doctrine, I say, they will not tolerate under any circumstances. We are able to forgo it just as little; for if this doctrine vanishes, the church vanishes. Then no error can any longer be resisted.'[4] In the same year, Melanchthon's *Apology of the Augsburg Confession* IV describes the justification article as the 'highest and most excellent article of the whole of Christian teaching', and explains that 'a great deal hangs on this article, which serves principally to give a clear and right understanding of the whole of the Holy Scriptures, and which alone shows the way to the inexpressible treasure of the right

---

[2] *The Smalcald Articles, BC,* 292

[3] Luther, *Exposition of Psalm 117, LW* 14, 37.

[4] Luther, *Warning to His Dear German People,* 1531, *LW* 47, 54. Similar formulas are to be found in his commentary on Galatians: 'for if the doctrine of justification is lost, the whole of doctrine is lost' (*LW* 26, 9); 'for if we lose the doctrine of justification, we lose simply everything' (*LW* 26, 26); 'therefore the doctrine of justification is nothing to be trifled with' (*LW* 26, 112). And: '. . . if this article stands, the Church stands; if it falls, the Church falls' (*In XV Psalmos graduum* 1532–33, *WA* 40/III, 352, 3). Examples could be multiplied. According to T. Mahlmann (article entitled: 'Articulus stantis et [vel] cadentis ecclesiae *RGG* 4th edn, vol. 1, 1998, *Colossians,* 799f.), the expression 'articulus stantis et cadentis ecclesiae' is traceable to Franz Turrettini. Mahlmann says that the extraordinary spread of the expression was contributed to by Friedrich Loofs' 'failed attempt at finding the origin of this expression'. Cf. F. Loofs, 'Der "articulus stantis et cadentis ecclesiae"', *ThStKr* 90 [1917], 323–420.

knowledge of Christ; it alone opens the door to the whole Bible. Without this article no poor conscience may have a right, lasting and certain consolation or recognize the riches of the grace of Christ'.[5] Melanchthon's comment is important because it gives a double significance to the justification article: firstly as a hermeneutical key to understanding the Bible, but also as a word to console the human conscience and open the door to the possibilities of theological knowledge.

A few years later, at the beginning of a Wittenberg disputation, Luther describes the justification article in the same way. This is the often quoted claim: 'The article concerning justification is the Master and Prince, Lord, Leader and Judge of all kinds of doctrine. It preserves and steers every church doctrine and allows our conscience to stand before God. Without this article the world is nothing but death and darkness.'[6]

II. Theological reservations: an analysis of Karl Barth

Objections have frequently been raised against the Reformers' high opinion of the justification article. Clear positions were taken against the doctrine of justification, even in its original Pauline form, both from within and outside the discipline of theology. We shall need to examine these. But first we must mention an objection that draws its validity from the fact that it is close to the theology of the Reformers.

It was Karl Barth, who, in the context of his own exposition of justification in the first part of his Doctrine of Atonement, made the claim: 'The *articulus stantis et cadentis ecclesiae* is not the doctrine of justification as such, but its basis and culmination: the confession of Jesus Christ, in whom are hid all the treasures of wisdom and knowledge (Col. 2:3).'[7] An analysis of

---

[5] *BSLK* 159, 1f. 4–15. [The version in *BC* is translated from the Latin (Tr).]

[6] M. Luther, *Die Promotionsdisputation von Palladius und Tilemann*, WA 39/1, 205, 2–5. Examples could be multiplied.

[7] K. Barth, *CD* IV/1, 1956, 527. Barth's reservation was repeated by J. Moltmann, 'Ökumene unter dem Kreuz. Evangelische Sicht auf die katholische Kirche', *EK* 31 (1998), 446–8, and E. Busch, 'Ein Wort zur Versöhnung. Die Debatte um die

Barth's claim and its bases is appropriate in order to clear some persistent misunderstandings and to further the awareness of the problem that is essential if we are to make an appropriate judgement about the function of the doctrine of justification.

Barth developed his thesis 'in implicit discussion' with the essay we have already mentioned by Ernst Wolf, who was particularly close to him. Wolf had attempted to clarify the 'doctrine of justification as the centre and boundary of reformation theology'.[8] And so quite a few statements occur in Barth which closely resemble those of Wolf. Barth also says 'there can be no question of disputing the particular function of the doctrine of justification'.[9] Barth also asserts: 'There never was and there never can be any true Christian Church without the doctrine of justification. In this sense it is indeed the *articulus stantis et cadentis ecclesiae*. There is no Christian Church without the truth of what God has done and does for man in virtue of its witness, without the manifestation of this truth in some form in its life and doctrine.'[10] There we have it! These are statements which contain not a whiff of criticism of the Reformers' high opinion of the doctrine of justification.

That is why it is so surprising to read Barth's opinions which run contrary to this. First, there is the exegetical note saying that not only the message of James, but also 'the Synoptics and the Johannine writings . . . cannot be simply equated with this doctrine, even though it is not excluded by but included in them'.[11] Indeed! The witness of James most definitely cannot be simply equated with the Pauline doctrine of justification; and the witness of Matthew only with the greatest difficulty. But even if it were valid for the other elements of the New

---

Rechtfertigungslehre aus reformierter Sicht', *NZZ* No. 199, 29/30 August 1998, 33. Neither Moltmann nor Busch takes the trouble to compare Barth's thesis with the Reformers' understanding of the doctrine of justification, and so they remain miles behind Barth's own expositions.

[8] See above, note 1.

[9] Barth, *CD* IV/1, 522.

[10] *CD* IV/1, 523.

[11] *CD* IV/1, 524.

Testament witness, there remains the question whether such a statement can be considered an *argument*. In any case, it is even less possible to reconcile the New Testament witness to Christ with the Old Testament witness that Barth values so highly. Yet it is for Barth the *articulus stantis et cadentis ecclesiae*, and so it must have a unique hermeneutical function for the Old Testament as well. In that case, it must also be true that although the Pauline doctrine of justification cannot easily be reconciled with the rest of the New Testament witness, nevertheless that doctrine is able to be the *articulus stantis et cadentis ecclesiae*.

For his argument to have any credibility, Barth would have to dramatically relativize the unique claim raised by Paul's gospel of justification which places a curse on anyone preaching another gospel, even an angel from heaven! If you take this exposition of Paul seriously, you will not be troubled by the question whether the rest of the New Testament witness can be reconciled with the Pauline doctrine of justification. Such a question presupposes a ban on any internal criticism of biblical material. It smoothes over what must never be smoothed over.

It is advisable to consider more closely in this context one of the frequently raised objections to the Reformers' evaluation, one that has much in common with Barth's reservations. The objection is that the Scriptures know of 'other images and concepts than the word "justification" to describe the once and for all saving act of God in Jesus Christ – for example, liberation into freedom, atonement, peace, a new creation, life, sanctification'. For this reason we cannot talk of an 'exclusive importance'[12] for the criterion of justification. Nobody doubts that the Bible knows of 'other images and concepts' by which the 'once and for all saving act of God in Jesus Christ' may be described. Even the Reformers confirm it, yet their evaluation

---

[12] W. Kasper, 'In allem Christus bekennen. Einig in der Rechtfertigungslehre als Mitte und Kriterium des christlichen Glaubens?', *Katholische Nachrichten-Agentur – Ökumenische Information* 32 vom 12, August, 1997, 5–7 (p. 6).

of the doctrine of justification remains sound. For example, Luther avoided justification terminology in both his catechisms and spoke instead of *sanctification*. However, he meant 'nothing other than what is called in theological language "justification by faith alone" . . . This is an impressive illustration that the content of the doctrine of justification may be expressed without its terminology'.[13] What is decisive is *how* such other images and concepts express God's saving act in Jesus Christ. And the justification article will be the decisive point. As we have seen, even Karl Barth does not question that.

There is a particularly noteworthy argument which Barth begins by stating that Christianity in the first centuries between Paul and Augustine 'did not know any explicit doctrine of justification'. It 'lived in a naive Pelagianism (as also in a naive Adoptionism or Sabellianism)' and was nevertheless the 'Christendom of the martyr-centuries, which obviously, without the doctrine of justification, knew what their faith was all about, and for which the truth of the doctrine was not in question, although they did not clearly understand it'.[14]

Barth pointed out correctly that the teaching of the doctrine of justification in the church, introduced by Augustine, has remained a specific concern of *western* Christianity, with its particular interest in law, both in the Roman and the Germanic realms of the west. On the other hand, eastern Christianity, with its far greater interest in the contrast between the temporal and the eternal, between life and death, rather than in guilt versus grace, 'contented itself with the bare minumum'.[15] Ernst Wolf noted that even in western theology 'the dogma of medieval scholasticism (despite its Augustinian and Anselmian

---

[13] G. Ebeling, 'Luthers Ortsbestimmung der Lehre vom heiligen Geist' in *Wort und Glaube*, vol. 3: *Beiträge zur Fundamentaltheologie, Soteriologie und Ekklesiologie*, 1975, 316–48 (p. 335). Cf. E. Jüngel, 'Um Gottes willen – Klarheit! Kritische Bemerkungen zur Verharmlosung der kriteriologischen Funktion des Recht-fertigungsartikels – aus Anlaß einer ökumenischen "Gemeinsamen Erklärung zur Rechtfertigungslehre"', *ZThK* 94 (1997), 394–406.

[14] Barth, *CD* IV/1, 524.

[15] Ibid.

heritage) does not specifically treat of a *locus de iustificatione impii*, but rather taught the matter in other contexts, within christology and the doctrine of the sacraments' (Thomas Aquinas also treats it in his doctrine of grace). It is taught 'against the background of anthropology' or in answer to specific anthropological questions,[16] so that the importance of the doctrine of justification for a doctrine of God has become scarcely recognizable, if at all. According to Barth, 'In the West it was only at the time of the *Reformation* that the doctrine of justification became a burning issue, or, to put it more exactly, it was only in the questing German spirit of *Luther*'.[17]

From these indisputable historical references, Barth then draws what is for systematics a very strange conclusion. He has admitted that there is a 'particular function of the doctrine of justification', which 'at certain periods and in certain situations', that is when a 'definite opposition and obscuration' gives it the impetus, can and must be asserted as '*the* Word of the Gospel' and be adopted as '*the* theological truth. There have been times when this has been not merely legitimate but necessary'.[18]

There were and are, however, other times when 'the in a sense, innocent righteousness of works' has not yet 'ceased to be innocent'.[19] Times when the 'formulated recognition and attestation' of the truth of the doctrine of justification cannot only 'withdraw ... behind other aspects of the Christian

---

[16] Wolf, 'Die Rechtfertigungslehre als Mitte und Grenze reformatorischer Theologie', 12.

[17] *CD* IV/1, 524.

[18] *CD* IV/1, 522–3. Barth gives as examples of such occasions: When Augustine was combating Pelagianism; the Reformation and its struggle against 'the sacramentalistic and moralistic misunderstanding of the much cited "grace"'; the time of the 'awakening' with its necessary 'reaction against the secularization of the understanding of salvation in the Enlightenment'; but 'another such time may well be our own day', so that we must be happy 'to find in the doctrine of justification a fully developed weapon with which to meet' the theological aberrations of the twentieth century (p. 523). His examples make clear that Barth defines the 'particular function' of the doctrine of justification as a doctrine of battle (he himself speaks of attack and defence [p. 522]).

[19] *CD* IV/1, 523.

message' but indeed be 'hidden'[20] – obviously so, without the church being called into question. Such times, according to Barth, alert us to the fact that the doctrine of justification 'relates only to one aspect of the Christian message of reconciliation' and that we may understand, in fact 'have to understand this aspect with others'. And that is why 'it would be an act of narrowing and unjust exclusiveness to proclaim and treat' the doctrine of justification everywhere and on every occasion as '*the* word of the gospel'.[21] For a church dogmatics 'which is ecumenical at least in prospect'[22] we must particularly rule out attributing everywhere and on every occasion that 'particular function' to the doctrine of justification which it no doubt had at specific times, as Barth has also said.

Barth continues: 'our very confidence in the objective truth of the doctrine of justification, which forbids us to postulate that in the true Church its theological outworking must *semper, ubique et ab omnibus* [always, everywhere and by everyone] be regarded and treated as the *unum necessarium*, the centre or culminating point of the Christian message or Christian doctrine'.[23] The theological laurel of being the *articulus stantis et cadentis ecclesiae* is to be given always, everywhere and by everyone not to this doctrine, but to confessing Jesus Christ. For this confession is according to Barth both the foundation and the pinnacle of the doctrine of justification.[24]

What shall we say, then? No doubt Barth's exposition is extremely worthwhile in many aspects, but it is difficult to evaluate when he insists on using the very same arguments against quite different understandings and misunderstandings of the function of the doctrine of justification. As an inevitable consequence his argument becomes tenuous.

---

[20] Ibid.

[21] Ibid.

[22] Ibid.

[23] *CD* IV/1, 523–4.

[24] *CD* IV/1, 527. [Bromiley renders 'Grund' and 'Spitze' as 'basis' and 'culmination'. In this rare departure from the official translation I have attempted to reproduce the building idiom of the German as being more consistent and more powerful (Tr).]

Doubtless Barth will enjoy widespread support for his reminder to 'be constantly aware of the limits of the ruling trend (however true and well-founded it may be)'.[25] But can we seriously put the doctrine of justification under the heading of the 'ruling trend'? If we did that we would show that we had understood nothing of the 'particular function' that even Barth grants to this article. And so it cannot be objected against any insistence on this function that it is good for theology 'to look beyond the needs and necessities of the moment'.[26] It would reduce justification to a sort of *ad hoc* weapon to be used only in short-lived battles if it only responded to the needs of the moment and if any needs beyond that required the quite different tactic of legitimately relativizing the doctrine of justification. This would also mean a challenge to the doctrine's claim to be the 'truth' without which 'there never can be any true Christian Church'.[27] So the unique importance given to justification by the Reformers cannot be what is meant by the quite justified warning against a 'narrowing and unjust exclusiveness'.[28] It is self-evident that any theological utterance must be appropriate to both time and occasion or that it must lead to such appropriateness. And it is no doubt true that the doctrine of justification must be able to bring its particular function to bear on specific situations. But that is valid for any concrete truth. And Barth's worthy reminders in this regard are nothing more than theological platitudes.[29]

Barth's polemic against the definition that ascribes to this article 'the function of a basic and central dogma in relation to which everything else will be either presupposition or consequence, either prologue or epilogue'[30] also misses the Reformers' evaluation of the article. Just read Luther's *Smalcald Articles*, Melanchthon's *Augsburg Confession*, even his

---

[25] *CD* IV/1, 523.
[26] Ibid.
[27] Ibid.
[28] Ibid.
[29] Ernst Wolf's argument is not affected by these platitudes.
[30] *CD* IV/1, 521.

Loci Communes of 1521, and then ask yourself whether what is said in these texts is just a 'presupposition or consequence, . . . prologue or epilogue' to the article of justification. The same can hardly be said for those Lutherans who have proclaimed it the 'basic principle of Protestantism'. And if you take the trouble to study Martin Kähler's *Wissenschaft der christlichen Lehre*, which quite simply presents justification as the 'foundational protestant article', you can see clearly that this article develops its systematic function with no consideration of anything else that might be 'either pre-supposition or consequence, either prologue or epilogue'. Furthermore, Kähler stresses that justification is not 'a so-called principle from which one can logically deduce the whole of Christian knowledge without any specific preceding information'. Rather, for Kähler, justification is a point of departure which must simultaneously be 'a focal point from which the connecting lines to all other points naturally flow'.[31] It should also be noted

---

[31] M. Kähler, *Die Wissenschaft der christlichen Lehre von dem evangelischen Grundartikel aus im Abrisse dargestellt*, 3rd edn, 1905 (reprinted 1994), p. 67. The essay by R. Saarinen ('Die Rechtfertigungslehre als Kriterium. Zur Begriffsgeschichte einer oekumenischen Redewendung', *KuD* 44 [1988], 88–103) does not at all do justice to Kähler's exposition. It is incomprehensible why Saarinen refers to the second and not the last edition, edited by Kähler himself. His interpretation of Kähler goes completely astray. To say that Kähler himself knew of the confessionalistic drift of his method and therefore seriously considered whether, instead of justification, ecumenical confessions could offer a proper central proposition for presenting Christian doctrine (Saarinen, p. 101) is to turn Kähler's argument around completely. Kähler expressly rejected the possible objection that the doctrine of justification could be suspected of being a non-ecumenical measure. He stated that the doctrine led precisely to the appropriate interpretation of the ancient confessions. Saarinen's assumption that Kähler's point of view can perhaps be seen today as old-fashioned leads me to quote Kähler's remark made in this context: 'to a superficial consideration of the procedure, it retains the appearance of one-sided confessionalism . . . Its honesty and carefulness guarantee the ecumenicity of the theology even when it comes to rejecting a direct mistake in a confession' (Kähler, p. 70). Saarinen, who wrote his essay to 'counter appropriately . . . Jüngel's criticism' of his handling of the concept of a criterion in the writings of certain apologists in the *Joint Declaration* [*Gemeinsame Erklärung* = *GE*] (Saarinen, p. 89), refers approvingly to 'a hermeneutical decision' made on *GE* 18 by the Bishops' Conference of the Finnish Evangelical-Lutheran Church (Presentation of the Finnish Bishops'

that Kähler expressly stresses the ecumenical nature of such a teaching and clears up 'the suspicion of a one-sided Paulinism or Protestantism'.[32]

We shall now turn to Barth's definition of the doctrine of justification. In his *Church Dogmatics* he gives this doctrine the task of attempting 'to *see* and *understand* in its positive sense the *sentence* of God which is executed in His judgment and revealed in the resurrection of Jesus Christ'.[33] Thus we are concerned here with nothing less than the right understanding – made possible by his resurrection – of Jesus' death on the cross. And if this is not the centre of Christian theology, what is? Barth stresses: 'It is a matter of the genuineness of the presupposition, the inner *possibility*, of the reconciliation of the world with God'.[34] However, this cannot be said of other aspects of the doctrine of reconciliation. It is surely mistaken on that basis to play off against each other the justification article and

---

Conference No. 1/1997 to the Synod, on 16 September 1997; page 12 of the German translation). This decision stated: 'The Lutheran emphasis on the uniqueness of the doctrine of justification is . . . not to be understood as reducing the content of the Christian faith to that doctrine.' Who would have ever thought that? The Lutheran bishops justify this 'hermeneutical decision' as follows: 'for Lutherans "do not deny the context and importance of all truths of the faith". Thus, in the document, a narrowing which is typical of neoprotestantism is indirectly avoided.' Saarinen also sees such a 'reductionistic . . . perception' – attributable to neoprotestantism – '. . . also represented in the EKU/VELKD negotiations of some Lutheran theologians' (Saarinen, p. 102). I suspect that means me. Isn't it clear to the Finnish bishops and to Saarinen that such a *reduction* would make any functioning of the justification article as a criterion not only superfluous but impossible? For what purpose could it still be used as a criterion if 'the content of the Christian faith is reduced to that doctrine'? I was left speechless at Saarinen's claim (Saarinen, p. 101, n. 71) that I had complained that Luther's familiar statements about the importance of the justification article (see above, note 6) were 'not well enough known in ecumenical circles', while, according to Saarinen, the opposite is the case. I have read over and over the page in my article which he gives as evidence for his claim (E. Jüngel, 'Um Gottes willen – Klarheit!', p. 400) without finding the slightest hint of the complaint which it is implied I made. There is no such suggestion anywhere in the whole essay. This is a strange way to 'counter appropriately Jüngel's criticism'.

[32]   Kähler, *Die Wissenschaft*, p. 69.

[33]   *CD* IV/1, 516.

[34]   *CD* IV/1, 517–18.

confession of Jesus Christ. If the doctrine of justification is really about the inner possibility of reconciliation of the world with God, then at the same time it is about the inner basis of confession of Christ. And so Barth himself expresses it: 'the Christian community and Christian faith stand or fall with the *reality of the fact* that . . . there is a genuine justification'.[35] To quote Barth again: 'What is *God* for sinful man? And what is sinful *man* before the God who is for him? The basis of the community and the certainty of faith stands or falls with the answer to this question. The doctrine of justification undertakes to answer the question of this pre-supposition.'[36] So by that doctrine is decided the theologically appropriate understanding of God, of human beings and of the relationship between God and human beings. And that is why for Barth it has 'the decisive significance of a *leaven*' for *all* other theological questions.[37]

Now, in his *Church Dogmatics*, by no means does Barth consider the doctrine of justification by mentioning only one single soteriological aspect. No, he expressly criticizes the practice, specially prevalent in early Protestant orthodoxy, of having 'a single complete and self-contained chapter on Jesus Christ, the so-called "*Christology*", as the climax in the whole presentation'.[38] For Barth, in such an isolated Christology 'what He is and means and does and accomplishes for man is not yet revealed or revealed only in the far distance', so that this isolated Christology must then 'be completed by a special presentation of the relevance of His existence for us, by a related but relatively autonomous soteriology and ecclesiology'.[39] In accordance with this criticism, in his doctrine of reconciliation Barth then makes use of the doctrine of justification while expounding the person, life [*Weg*] and office of Jesus Christ. Then in the midst of the

---

[35] *CD* IV/1, 518.

[36] Ibid.

[37] *CD* IV/1, 528. Paul's metaphor of leaven (1 Cor. 5:6; Gal. 5:9) is used by the *Formula of Concord*: 'And St Paul says specifically of this doctrine that a little leaven ferments the whole lump. Therefore he stresses the exclusive terms . . . with such zeal . . . in this article . . .' (*FC.SD*, Article III, in *BC*, 540).

[38] *CD* IV/1, 123.

[39] *CD* IV/1, 124.

so-called 'Christology', under the heading 'The Judge Judged in Our Place', the 'act of righteousness' or 'obedience' of Jesus is mentioned, 'in the power of which the vindication of all men was accomplished'.[40] Consistent with these explanations, Barth declared: 'All theology, both that which follows and indeed that which precedes the doctrine of reconciliation, depends on this *theologia crucis* . . . There is no avoiding this strait gate. There is no other way but this narrow way.'[41]

That is exactly how the Reformers also saw the matter. When, concerning the justification article, Luther affirms that it preserves and directs all church doctrine, he means this narrow way, which, as Barth correctly stresses 'will then *further* the free development of the riches of Christian knowledge instead of hindering it'.[42]

Barth proposes an alternative, which is difficult to understand even in the framework of his own argument, that not the doctrine of justification, but rather the confession of Jesus Christ is the *articulus stantis et cadentis ecclesiae*. One can then hardly agree with Barth when he conjectures: 'It could probably be shown that this was also the opinion of Luther.'[43] But with regard to what Barth has so positively expounded concerning the 'particular function' of the doctrine of justification, and to how he has already highlighted justification within Christology, one must say that this was in fact 'also the opinion of *Luther*'.[44]

To return to that unfortunate alternative which Barth offers of making the *articulus stantis et cadentis ecclesiae* not justification, but rather the confession of Jesus Christ – 'the recognition of his being, of his acting for us, to us and with us', as Schwarz puts it[45] – it is appropriate to emphasize that this is precisely the function of the doctrine of justification: to convey the being

---

[40] *CD* IV/1, 272.

[41] *CD* IV/1, 273. Cf. in particular the judgement of human religion by the justification article in *CD* I/2, 352ff.

[42] *CD* IV/1, 528.

[43] *CD* IV/1, 527–8.

[44] Cf. R. Schwarz, 'Luthers Rechtfertigungslehre als Eckstein der christlichen Theologie und Kirche', *ZThK*, Beiheft [Supplement] 10 (1998), 14–46.

[45] Ibid.

and work of Jesus Christ for us, to us and with us. It is only when explained by means of that doctrine that Christology becomes appropriate Christology at all. It is *appropriate* Christology when it is the doctrine of justification. For part of the appropriateness of Christology is not only the subject-matter itself, but also its correct use: that is, the use which the subject-matter itself demands.

As in many other respects, so also with the matter (*res*) of Christology, Luther vehemently insisted that the *use* of the matter is part and parcel of it, that is to say that you are not teaching the *matter* properly if you do not at the same time think of its use. It is in order to quote what the Tübingen theologians later stated in their dispute with the Giessen theologians about the correct understanding of the κένωσις (the emptying of the heavenly attributes of Jesus' divine nature referred to in Phil. 2:7): no possession without use! We may refer to Luther's well-known text from his *Operationes in Psalmos*, when, in discussing the Holy Spirit speaking in Psalm 18, he says:

> He gives utterance not only to things [*res*], but also to the use [*usus*] which things are to be put to. For many preach Christ, but in such a way that they neither recognize nor express his ways and his miracles . . . as do most of those preachers who only preach the stories of Christ, when they are preaching at their best. But it is not Christian preaching when you preach Christ only from a historical point of view; that is not proclaiming the glory of God. But *this* is: when you teach that Christ's story refers to its usefulness for us as believers unto righteousness and salvation. That is [then], that he accomplished all not for himself, but for us by the will of God the Father, so that we may know that everything that is in Christ belongs to us.[46]

---

[46] M. Luther, *Operationes in Psalmos*, 1519–21, WA 5, 543, 13–21; 'non solum res, sed et usum rerum exprimit. Multi enim Christum praedicant, sed ita, ut usum et benefitium eius nunquam intelligant aut dicant, ut facit vulgus illud concionatorum, qui non nisi historias Christi praedicant, dum optime praedicant. At non est christiana praedicatio, si historice Christum praedices, non hoc gloriam Dei praedicare est. Sed si docueris, historiam Christi eo pertinere, ut nobis prosit credentibus ad iustitiam et salutem, ut non sibi, sed nobis omnia fecerit voluntate dei patris, et omnia, quae in Christo sunt, nostra esse sciamus'. Cf. also Luther's, *An Exposition of the Lord's Prayer for Simple Laymen*, 1519, LW 42, 58–9; *The Freedom of a Christian*, in *Reformation Writings of Martin Luther*, 2 vols,

Luther knows a 'Christology' from tradition as a sort of 'factual reconstruction', and he disputes whether this as such is *right* Christology. It is not true that this 'factual reconstruction' *rightly* discusses God and human beings, even though it does discuss God and humans (that is, God and human nature in their personal union). That only occurs when the stories of Christ [*die Historien Christi*] are so taught and preached that they are understood as having happened *for the righteousness* and *for the salvation* of believers. The doctrine of justification makes clear that *nothing* of Jesus' being, works or suffering is irrelevant for salvation. Using the concept of time, we can word it thus: the story of Jesus, the man identical with the Son of God, is no *past* story; rather, as a *past story* it is *present* and effectual *in the present*. The doctrine of justification goes beyond the 'fact' of personal unity of Godhood and humanity in the person of Jesus Christ to make clear the soteriological effectiveness of that unity, an effectiveness which belongs to the *being* of the God-Man. This can also be worded using the concept of time: the justification article applies what happened then and there to the present time. Accordingly, in his *Small Catechism*, Luther explained faith in Jesus Christ as faith in his person *affecting me here and now*: 'I believe that Jesus Christ, true God . . . and also true man . . . is my Lord.'[47] When the doctrine of justification

---

trans. and ed. by B. L. Woolf, London: Lutterworth, 1952, I, 367–70. Cf. also the *Apology of the Augsburg Confession*, written by Melanchthon: 'Thus the faith which makes us pious and righteous in the eyes of God is not just this, that I know the history, how Christ was born, suffered (the devils know this too); no, faith is the certainty or the sure, strong trust in the heart that with my whole heart I take God's promises to be sure and true, by which are offered to me without any merit of mine forgiveness of sins, grace and full salvation through Christ the Mediator. And so that no-one can say it is simply a matter of knowing history, I will add: faith is this, that my whole heart accepts that same treasure. This is not my doing, nor my gift or offering, not my work or preparation. It is [simply] that a heart takes for its consolation and trusts in the fact that God grants and gives to us, not we to him, that he pours all the riches of grace upon us in Christ' (*ApolCA* IV, *BSLK* 169, 43–170, 11). [Translated from the German paraphrase, used here by Jüngel, which appears in *BSLK*. The English translation from the much shorter Latin original in *BSLK* is to be found in *BC*, 113–14 (Tr).]

[47] *Small Catechism, The Creed, BC*, 345.

says that Jesus Christ is *for us*, it says *who he is*. So it adds nothing new to Christology, but it does go to its very heart and explains what it finds there: the God who justifies and saves, and guilty and lost human beings. And the relationship of God who justifies and saves to guilty and lost human beings is for Luther *the* object of genuine theology.[48]

III. An explicitly low view

The reservations against the Reformers' high view of the doctrine of justification which have been discussed up to this point still attribute to that doctrine a 'particular meaning' for Christian life and teaching. It is important to distinguish such judgements about the doctrine from those that amount to an explicitly low view or disparagement.

In sharp contrast to Karl Barth's judgement that 'the doctrine of justification became a burning issue . . . only in the questing German spirit of Luther',[49] is the judgement of those who are no less German and who contest the special value of the doctrine of justification. They describe it and not infrequently have felt bound to discredit it as being a product of a specifically *Jewish* spirit.

There is, for example, Fichte's reproach[50] that Paul with his doctrine of justification – apparently in contrast to John's Gospel – led Christianity back to the bondage of the Jewish spirit.[51] According to Fichte, this occurred through the Pauline fiction of Jesus' messianic elevation. Jesus was to be believed on as the Christ. This meant the justification of human beings

---

[48] Cf. Luther, 'The proper subject of theology is man guilty of sin and condemned, and God the Justifier and Savior of man the sinner', 'Psalm 51', *LW* 12, 311 = 'Enarratio des 51. Psalms', *WA* 40/II, 328, 1f. 'ut proprie sit subiectum Theologiae homo reus et perditus et deus iustificans vel salvator'. For an explanation, see G. Ebeling, 'Cognitio Dei et hominis' in his *Lutherstudien*, vol. 1, 1971, 221–72.

[49] See note 17 above.

[50] Cf. J. G. Fichte, *The Characteristics of the Present Age* in *The Popular Works of Johann Gottlieb Fichte* I, trans. W. Smith, London, 1849, pp. 96–112.

[51] E. L. Schaub opposed any anti-Semitic use of this or other parts of Fichte's work in 'J. G. Fichte and Anti-Semitism', *The Philosophical Review* 49 (1940), 37–52.

before God, who makes covenants with humans. Christology appears here as a Jewish construction that became necessary because of the doctrine of justification. To a doctrine of justification proceeding from a Jewish belief in God and giving birth to a fundamentally Jewish Christology, Fichte objects that it is a 'departure from the simplicity of Christianity for the purpose of gaining the good graces of Judaism'[52] and that such a departure, not unknown in the history of the church, represents the 'true source of the evil'[53] of Christian dogmatic education and dogmatic quarrels. This 'degenerate form of Christianity', whose originator was Paul, was 'also a necessary product of the whole spirit of that Age' so that Paul's role as originator was considered as 'accidental': 'for had he not done so . . . some-one else . . . would have done the same' unless he – like John – 'had . . . risen superior to his Age'.[54] But in the nature of things, as Fichte said, 'Christianity . . . is no method of atonement and expiation'.[55] For, and this is Fichte's real argument – 'man can never disunite himself from the Godhead – and in so far as he *desires* to do so, he is a *Nonentity*, which on that very account cannot sin, but on whose forehead the imaginary brand of Sin is placed, that he may thereby be directed to the True God'.[56] Or, as he puts it more positively: 'According to the meaning of True Religion, and in particular of Christianity, Humanity is the one, visible, efficient, living and independent existence of God; or . . . the one manifestation and effluence of that Existence – a beam from the Eternal Light, which divides itself, not in reality, but only to mere earthly vision, into many individual rays.'[57] Humans are not created by God from nothing, but are an emanation of God. And an emanation of God cannot be separated from God by something like sin. Since the time of Fichte at the very latest, humans have existed *etsi peccatum non daretur* – as though sin did not exist.

---

[52] Fichte, *The Characteristics of the Present Age*, 101.
[53] Ibid.
[54] Ibid., Lecture 13, 201.
[55] Ibid., 200.
[56] Ibid.
[57] Ibid., 198.

So according to Fichte, the 'true Christian knows no Covenant or Mediation with God, but only the Old, Eternal and Unchangeable Relation, that in Him we live, and move, and have our being'.[58] Against the background of such a verdict, then, he sounds triumphantly smug about the victory of progress when, in considering the church's proclamation of justification and its effects, he declares 'the Church has indeed almost ceased to preach this doctrine; and even where it still does so, it is without fruit, for no one lays it to heart'.[59]

Well, that is what Fichte the Saxon says. There is not much of the 'questing German spirit' of a Luther to be found here as far as justification goes. In fact, a representative of the Jewish people is made responsible – Paul, who is set up in opposition not only to John the Gospel-writer, but to Jesus himself. The dispute about justification is becoming a dispute about 'Paul and Jesus'.

Fichte became the flavour of the month. His objections to the doctrine of justification turn up in many variations, guided by two premises. It is asserted that the doctrine of justification is the genuine work of the apostle Paul and must therefore be judged in the context of his theology, but at the same time it must be judged together with (that is, critically) in its relation to Jesus' preaching. Justification, it is further asserted, is to be explained and judged as the theological expression of a certain human – specifically a Jewish – understanding of self and God. But at the same time, on closer examination, not only the preaching of Jesus, but far more powerfully, the critics' own understanding of God, the world and themselves function as a criterion of judgement. We shall discuss the various objections – which partly eclipse, partly contradict each other – so as to name the most important of them as they are based on the premises mentioned. We shall then examine them meta-critically.

First, it is asserted that within Paul's theology his doctrine of justification is not objectively connected with the other parts of

---

[58] Ibid., Lecture 7, 105.
[59] Ibid., Lecture 13, 203.

that theology. For Fichte, Paul's doctrine of justification is an expression of 'the great problem of his life'. Beside it there are, however, other expressions of Pauline piety that articulate 'the True God of Jesus' so strikingly 'that we seem to listen to another man altogether'.[60] Paul Wernle's opinion is similar. He describes Paul's doctrine of justification as 'one of his most disastrous creations'; everything about it is 'ambiguous', 'confusing', 'fraught with evil consequences', 'arbitrary and artificial'.[61] He goes on to say 'it is as though one stepped out of the dark night into the bright light of day', when you turn from Paul's teaching on justification to the 'marvellous and simple sentences'[62] of the apostle about the freedom of Christians. According to William Wrede,[63] Paul's doctrine of justification is nothing but a 'polemical doctrine' against Jews and Jewish Christians. As such they have no central function within Paul's theology or religion. 'In fact, it is possible to portray the whole of Pauline religion without taking any notice of it at all . . .'[64] Albert Schweitzer traced the apparent disparity between Paul's doctrine of justification and the rest of his theology to the difference between juridical thinking and mysticism. Paul, he affirmed, offered *three* different conceptions of redemption: 'an eschatological, a juridical, and a mystical'[65] doctrine of redemption. Of these, Paul's mysticism is the one which is central to his theology. Compared with that, the juridical 'doctrine of righteousness by faith is . . . a subsidiary crater, which has formed within the rim of the main crater – the mystical doctrine of redemption through the being-in-Christ'.[66] Paul, says Schweitzer, inserted the doctrine of justification into this, his

[60] Ibid., Lecture 7, 100.
[61] P. Wernle, *The Beginnings of Christianity*, trans. G. A. Bienemann, London: Williams & Norgate, 2 vols, 1903–4, vol. 1, 309.
[62] Ibid., 311.
[63] Wrede, *Paulus*, 2nd edn, 1907, 72ff.
[64] Ibid., 72.
[65] A. Schweitzer, *The Mysticism of Paul the Apostle*, trans. W. Montgomery, London: A&C Black, 1931, 25.
[66] Ibid., 225.

main teaching, 'by means of logical ingenuities'; but even taken by itself, justification is quite simply 'an unnatural construction of thought'.[67]

Second, it is asserted that the doctrine of justification is an expression of a misunderstanding of Jesus by Paul and thus the expression of a self-misunderstanding by Christianity. According to Fichte, Paul, 'having become a Christian, did not wish therefore to be in the wrong in having once been a Jew'.[68] As a consequence he had to link the revelation of the true God in Jesus with his *Jewish* faith in God.

According to the third objection, the doctrine of justification has elevated (or reduced) the person of Jesus, by a problematic interpretation of his death, to being the Jewish Messiah and has thus given birth to a Christology which does violence to the historical Jesus. This would make Christology, as a product of the doctrine of justification, the specifically Jewish consequence of specifically Jewish premises.

For Fichte the doctrine of justification compels us to ask who Jesus himself was, and what was the meaning of his person. Only the doctrine of justification offered a *Christological* answer to this question about the person of Jesus. But in doing so the gospel of Jesus was twisted and Christianity robbed of its purity. The 'true Christian', he said, asks 'not *who* has said this, but *what* has been said'.[69] If this impression were valid, there would be virtually no 'true Christians' in the emerging early church. Nonetheless, it remains noteworthy how clearly Fichte recognized that Paul's doctrine of justification implies how the preached Christ could come from Jesus the preacher. Ferdinand Christian Baur made a similar judgement, though

---

[67] Ibid., 224–5. It is strange that such a reflective Catholic theologian as Eugen Biser brings up all these arguments again without mentioning a word about their rebuttal in recent exegetical research. See E. Biser, 'Das Spiegelkabinett. Wohin führt die Rechtfertigungsdebatte?' *StZ* 123, vol. 216 (1998), 375–85.

[68] Fichte, *The Characteristics of the Present Age*, Lecture 7, 99. [Translation amended (Tr).] As a consequence he had to link the revelation of the true God in Jesus with his *Jewish* faith in God.

[69] Ibid., 105.

with a positive purpose, that Paul placed the 'substantial central point', on which everything rests, moving from Jesus' *teaching*, 'onto the absolute importance of his person'.[70]

The truth of the belief in justification made it necessary that Jesus 'live as the one who had died'.[71] In this way the person of Jesus Christ was brought into the centre of theology. In bringing out the discrepancy between Jesus and Paul, even William Wrede notes 'Jesus knows nothing of what for Paul is the one and only thing'.[72] In Paul we find, instead of the earthly Jesus, a basically heavenly being. Paul applies to Jesus 'ideas of Christ that had arisen quite independently of the person Jesus',[73] so that it is 'really not at all the historical person Jesus, but someone else'[74] on whom Paul depends. According to Johannes Weiss, even just before his conversion to the Christian faith Paul was making use of his originally Jewish Christology to make the human Jesus of Nazareth unfamiliar: 'We can construct not only an eschatology, but also a Christology antecedent to Christ in time.'[75] Paul's conversion stirred the greater part of the messianic, that is, Christological conceptions which he had already discovered 'to fresh energy, rearranged them and became a nucleus around which they crystallized afresh',[76] to the extent that *Jesus* now became the object of Christological veneration. But 'as compared with the preaching of Jesus, this practice is a complete innovation . . . Here there appears to my mind a discrepancy which no theological device can bridge'.[77]

It is asserted, fourthly, that the doctrine of justification is a purely *theological construction*, which emerges in Paul in place of

---

[70] F. C. Baur, *Vorlesungen über neutestamentliche Theologie*, ed. F. F. Baur, 1864 (repr. 1973), 123.

[71] Ibid., 126.

[72] Wrede, *Paulus*, 94.

[73] Ibid., 96.

[74] Ibid., 95.

[75] J. Weiss, *Paul and Jesus*, trans. H. J. Chaytor, London and New York: Harper & Brothers, 1909, 14–15.

[76] Weiss, *Paul and Jesus*, 15.

[77] Weiss, *Paul and Jesus*, 5.

the simple and immediate *religion* of Jesus. The polemic against justification is guided here by the contrasting of *religion* and *theology*, which is the trademark of the 'history of religions' (*religionsgeschichtlich*) school of thought. In place of a *religious*, that is an immediate practical relationship of humans to God, has come a contact between humans and God which is only able to be brought about by theoretical, in fact, *theological* mediations. In the front line of this polemic they privilege the simplicity of Jesus' religion against the complicated doctrine of justification. They express Paul's doctrine of justification in simplistic words and are influenced by what it has become over the course of history.

The fifth claim is that the doctrine of justification is Christianity becoming fixated on Judaism. Fichte interpreted justification as a projection of the simple 'gospel of Jesus' and 'true Christianity' back onto a limited Jewish piety. This was also the opinion of Paul de Lagarde.[78] According to William Wrede, with the 'polemical doctrine' which was specifically *anti-Jewish* and therefore worked with Jewish methods of arguing, the apostle was wanting to safeguard the 'superiority of the Christian redemption faith over the whole of Judaism'.[79] In so doing, the doctrine of justification, based on the historical success over Judaism which it then came to enjoy, 'had the not inconsider-able effect of making itself superfluous'.[80]

The sixth objection says that justification is the expression of a belief in an arbitrary God and thus is an expression of superstition. Fichte's talk of a Pauline 'leading error' refers when all is said and done to the *concept of God* in the doctrine of justification. Fichte claims that this implies 'the great leading error of an arbitrary God, now making Covenants, and now abolishing them, according to time and circumstances'.[81]

---

[78] Cf. P. de Lagarde, 'Über das Verhältnis des deutschen Staates zu Theologie, Kirche und Religion. Ein Versuch, Nicht-Theologen zu orientieren' in idem, *Schriften für das deutsche Volk*, vol. 1, 1937 (3rd edn), 45–90.

[79] Wrede, *Paulus*, 74.

[80] Ibid., 100.

[81] Fichte, *The Characteristics of the Present Age*, 103–4.

Such a God cannot, according to Fichte, be understood as *just* or *faithful* or *humane*. To worship him is 'religious super-stition'.[82] As is so often the case, Nietzsche's polemic against the God who chooses the weak and justifies sinners is most perspicacious when it asserts that Paul's idea of God destroys the received idea of God – 'deus, qualem Paulus creavit, dei negatio'[83] – so that the apostle's whole theological conception, which is bound up with the doctrine of justification, signifies a 'revaluation of all antique values'.[84]

According to the seventh claim, justification presupposes an overly developed consciousness of sin and guilt, which it projects onto human beings. Nietzsche radicalized and in numerous respects developed Fichte's theory that to see *humans* as *sinners* is unacceptable from an anthropological point of view and must be resisted as a religious delusion.

The eighth and final claim is that the doctrine of justification no longer has any decisive influence for human beings. It is claimed that modern people no longer ask: 'How can I find a gracious God?'[85] They are asking, apparently far more radically, about God in general.[86]

If we gather together the objections against justification which I have summarized briefly above, we shall need to differentiate between those that question the doctrine itself, and those that question its central theological function while still affirming its conditional relevance. In doing this, we must not neglect to note that the fundamental objections against justification itself recur within the framework of particular conceptions of that doctrine and lead to a mis-conception, so that the disagreement about justification

---

[82] Ibid., Lecture 13, 203.

[83] 'God, as Paul created him, is a denial of God' (F. Nietzsche, *The Anti-Christ* in idem, *Twilight of the Idols and the Anti-Christ*, trans. R. J. Hollingdale, Harmondsworth: Penguin Books, 1990 [1968], 175.

[84] Idem, *Beyond Good and Evil*, 75.

[85] Luther, *Von der heiligen Taufe Predigten*, 1534, WA 37, 661, 22–4.

[86] Barth says that this is 'of all the superficial catchwords of our age, surely one of the most superficial' (*CD* IV/1, 530).

becomes a disagreement about the *correct* doctrine of justification. The three objections which we listed last are objections
to the doctrine itself, and it is on these that we shall concentrate
our metacritical examination. We are assuming here that to
describe justification as a polemical doctrine is quite correct,
although in a very different sense from that of Wrede. For this
doctrine of itself forces disagreement. It forces into opposition
on the one hand a faculty of judgement that has learnt its skills
in the plausible school of worldly wisdom and on the other
hand an ego that is marked by religion and morality. Those
agreeing with this doctrine can boast only of their weakness (2
Cor. 12:5). And, in contradistinction to those who are
considered clever and wise, they are out-and-out fools (cf. 1
Cor. 3:19; 4:10). What justification is in itself is a thoroughly
contentious issue that forces us to take sides.

1. The concept of God

Criticism of the concept of God in the doctrine of justification
is in order only in so far as God, as he is assumed to be in that
concept, is in fact understood as a 'God who makes covenants',
or more exactly, as the *God of the Covenant,* that is, the God of
the Old Testament. The doctrine of justification is unthinkable
without God as the God of the Covenant. It is precisely in his
Covenant that this 'God who makes covenants' reveals himself
to be the complete opposite of an arbitrary God. This is demonstrated in Paul's legitimization of the *New Covenant* by the use
of texts from the *Old Covenant.* An arbitrary God does not need
to be legitimized by his earlier words and deeds. The accusation
that the doctrine of justification has to operate with the concept
of a God who acts arbitrarily is to that extent totally wrong. God
is sovereign, but not arbitrary.[87] And his sovereignty shows itself
in the fact that, far from being arbitrary, he remains faithful to

---

[87] Fichte's concept of arbitrariness had an element of unpredictability which is
characteristic of modern linguistic usage. For Kant the concept still served to
describe the freedom of practical reason.

himself. What the doctrine of justification has to demonstrate is that God, in pronouncing the ungodly righteous, is himself righteous, and that means that 'God is just in Himself'.[88] Its task is to demonstrate that God in his freedom remains faithful to himself, in that he remains faithful to human beings, whom he created *good*.

2. The concept of sin

It is even fair to say that the doctrine of justification 'makes' a person into a sinner. Proof enough of this can be found in Luther's extremely offensive sentence, with which he began his Lecture on Romans in 1515/16: 'The chief purpose of this letter is to break down, pluck up, and to destroy all wisdom and righteousness of the flesh ... [and] to affirm and state and magnify sin.'[89] In such magnification of sin could be seen what a large shadow was thrown onto humanity by the high estimation of the doctrines of *solus Christus* and *sola gratia*. In a letter dated 22 June 1781, Goethe felt compelled to say it was 'unfair, a robbery ... which ill befits your affair, that you should pluck out all the finest feathers of the thousand kinds of bird that there are under heaven, as though they had no right to them, in order to adorn your bird of paradise exclusively with them'.[90] And in fact the Augustinian version of justification with its hamartiological argument about the unavoidability of sin brought forth a 'Christian ... inconsistency with the natural',[91] whose devastating consequences cannot be exaggerated. 'A dreadful melancholy spread from this anthropology over the whole mood of Augustinian theology. The serene world-view of

---

[88] Barth, *CD* IV/1, 530–1.

[89] Luther, 'Lecture on Romans', 1515/16, *LW* 25, 135.

[90] J. W. von Goethe, letter of 22 June 1781, *Goethes Werke* (Weimar Edition), ed. for Duchess Sophie of Saxony, vol. IV/5, 1889 (repr. 1987), 147f. Cf. E. Hirsch, *Die Umformung des christlichen Denkens in der Neuzeit*, 1938 (repr. 1985), 126.

[91] J. Baur, *Salus christiana. Die Rechtfertigungslehre in der Geschichte des christlichen Heilsverständnisses*, vol. 1: *Von der christlichen Antike bis zur Theologie der deutschen Aufklärung*, Tübingen: Mohr Siebeck, 1968, 25.

the ancients . . . was dealt its final blow.'[92] In place of the regime of the gods of Greece, people's self-understanding started to be characterized by a deep pessimism. 'In Adam's fall is ruined all our human kind and being',[93] as it says further on. And we cannot be asked too often whether we have sufficiently considered the weight of our sins.[94]

Even in this objection it is true that justification means in fact the justification of the unrighteous (and not of the righteous), that is, the justification of sinful people. It is also true that, when treating forgiveness of sins, it takes people seriously, both as subject of their sins and as subjects who are under the compulsion of sin.

Nevertheless, significant corrections must be made to the way in which we in the church have come to speak of human sin. No doubt we cannot overemphasize Anselm's warning about the weight of sin. Yet this insistent reference by Christians to human sin becomes *fatal* when it discredits in a total and abstract manner the *natural* life of human beings in order to privilege the total depravity of human nature in the whole work of redemption. The Danish theologian Grundtvig was right to protest that, for the sake of the doctrine of justification by faith alone, natural life 'must be destroyed at all costs and rooted out'.[95] And Dietrich Bonhoeffer[96] was right to denounce the 'religious method' that gives theological consideration to the *negative* qualities of human beings, *before* talking of the relational

[92] A. Adam, *Lehrbuch der Dogmengeschichte*, vol. 1: *Die Zeit der Alten Kirche* (3rd edn), 1977, 270.

[93] *EKG* 243, 1. Cf. P. Wackernagel, *Bibliographie zur Geschichte des deutschen Kirchenliedes*, vol. 3, 1850, No. 71, 48.

[94] 'You have not yet considered what a heavy weight sin is. (Nondum considerasti, quanti ponderis sit peccatum)' as Anselm of Canterbury objected to Boso (Anselm of Canterbury, *Cur deus homo?* in *A Scholastic Miscellany: Anselm to Ockham*, trans. and ed. by E. R. Fairweather [Library of Christian Classics], London: SCM Press, 1956, 138).

[95] N. F. S. Grundtvig, *Das christliche, geistliche und ewige Leben*, 1857, in Börnelaerdom, 3rd edn, 1883, quoted by J. Baur, *Salus christiana*, 26, n. 50.

[96] D. Bonhoeffer, *Letters and Papers from Prison: The Enlarged Edition*, ed. E. Bethge, trans. R. Fuller et al., London: SCM Press, 1971 (1967), 362.

link between us and God. Similar methods evidence the supreme theological lack of identifying, recognizing and understanding sin in people and people as sinners *before* acquainting people with the God who justifies. Such a procedure appears to be logical, but in fact totally contradicts what the doctrine of justification means to say. The logic of justification demands rather that sin be recognized *as already overcome*. This is the only way it can be adequately recognized *as sin*. Sin is recognized *as sin* when it is forgiven. Only in the fact of forgiveness does it appear in all its loathsomeness; only then does all its 'dialectic' become apparent, that is: (1) the realization that it really did not have to be and certainly should not have been allowed to be like this, and (2) the realization that if we were dependent only on our own strength, what should not have been allowed would only have become worse and worse. Luther deliberately put this *retrospectively*: 'And deeper, deeper still I fell, / My life became a living hell, / For sin enslaved me wholly.'[97] We need a theologically adequate definition of the relationship between law and gospel, to prevent *false* appraisals of human sin which in fact discredit the doctrine of justification.

3. The modern understanding of freedom

The third objection, which questions the doctrine of justification itself, is also in present-day theology a major objection against the central theological function of justification. According to this objection, the doctrine of justification no longer has any decisive influence for human beings. It cannot be denied that this objection only balances out the two views already discussed. That is, in a sense it paves the way for talk of God – talk that sees God as arbitrary – and for talk of humans as beings completely labelled by our sin. This is what modern people see as fundamentally unacceptable: that they should be subject to a capricious God and that their very selves should be labelled

---

[97] *Lutheran Hymnal*, Adelaide: Lutheran Publishing House, 1973, 322.2. Cf. Luther, 'Nun freut euch, lieben Christen g'mein', 1523, *WA* 35, 423, 10–12.

negatively. That is, modern people cannot see themselves as slaves either to God or to themselves. They see themselves as basically *free* in every respect. And the justification article can only be applied superficially, 'as a foreign ingredient'[98] to people who are in charge of their own destiny. It is not possible to impress this article on people who are concerned with freedom in such a way that it can say anything essential about them. So, in the words we have quoted above, Fichte would seem to have managed a description of the status quo which applies to our time: that the church itself has already 'almost ceased to preach this doctrine; and even where it still does so, it is without fruit, for no one lays it to heart'.[99]

Of course, the facts as I have portrayed them are not without some historical paradoxes. It was the Reformation, with its zealous campaign for justification, which founded or at least partially founded the modern freedom consciousness on which that same doctrine of justification was later supposedly to founder, so that today it is considered a total loss. One somewhat unexpected witness in this respect is Karl Marx, who expressed it very clearly: 'Germany's *revolutionary* past is theoretical – it is the Reformation. In that period the revolution originated in the brain of a monk, today in the brain of the philosopher. Luther, without question, overcame servitude through devotion but only by substituting servitude through conviction. He shattered the faith in authority by restoring the authority of faith.'[100]

Despite Marx's objection to Luther's historical achievement, it is clearly no exaggeration to say that the Reformers' re-discovery of the doctrine of justification was a decisive basis for the modern age, given over as it is to the concept of freedom – a freedom which at the same time wreaks havoc on our age as

---

[98] Fichte, *The Characteristics of the Present Age*, Lecture 13, 203.

[99] Ibid.

[100] K. Marx, 'Contribution to the Critique of Hegel's Philosophy of Right: Introduction', in *The Marx-Engels Reader*, ed. R. C. Tucker, New York: Norton, 1972, 18.

never before. Famous statements like Luther's: 'A Christian is a perfectly free lord of all, subject to none',[101] were more than academic pronouncements. They were a signal. Across the whole of the realm Luther's statement was heard, understood – and misunderstood. But even when misunderstood, such a statement took effect. We shall need to remember this when it is claimed that modern people are unresponsive to the doctrine of justification – modern people who are convinced of their freedom, whether a present freedom, or one still to be earned. It is, of course, true that Luther did not wish to have the freedom of a Christian identified – at least not directly – with the freedom of a 'person of the world'. You can in fact be free *before God*, even when you are robbed of your freedom in the world. But you cannot accept lack of freedom in the world if you are free *before God*. No, as someone set free by God and free before God, you will quite naturally (Luther used to say 'spontaneously' and 'joyfully')[102] fight for worldly freedom. Thus those claims and theories are superficial which demand we set the doctrine of justification aside as irrelevant to our times because supposedly inimical to freedom.[103] The doctrine of justification is just as relevant today as ever. Nor is it by any means inimical to freedom. Rather, it is an enemy to all enemies of freedom.

4. The question of the existence of God

A Christian church must be very superficial indeed if it declares irrelevant the search for a gracious God as the basic problem of the doctrine of justification, simply because modern people are concerned with a much more radical question – that of the

---

[101] Luther, *The Freedom of a Christian*, *LW* 31, 344.

[102] Cf. *LW* 31, 359 with idem, *Tractatus de libertate christiana*, 1520, *WA* 7, 64, 36.

[103] On this whole issue see O. Bayer, 'Marcuses Kritik an Luthers Freiheitsbegriff', *ZThK* 67 (1970), 453–78 (also in idem, *Leibliches Wort. Reformation und Neuzeit im Konflikt*, 1992, 151–75; W. Maurer, Autorität in Freiheit. Zu Marcuses Angriff auf Luthers Freiheitslehre [*CwH* 111], 1970; E. Jüngel, *The Freedom of a Christian*, trans. R. A. Harrisville, Minneapolis: Augsburg, 1988; U. Liedke, *Freiheit. Amerkungen zu Herbert Marcuses Lutherkritik*, *NZSTh* 40 (1998), 197–213.

search for 'God Himself and as such'. Karl Barth rightly objected to this: 'As though grace were a quality of God which we could set aside while we leisurely ask concerning His existence! As though the Christian community and Christian faith had any interest in the existence or non-existence of this God Himself and as such! As though 16th-century man with his concern for the grace of God and the right of His grace were not asking about God Himself and His existence with a radicalness compared with which the questioning of modern man is empty frivolity!'[104] This very matter-of-factness is where the *radical* question is first of all asked about God. And without this matter-of-factness, to ask *whether* God exists at all is to ask about the *existence* of an unknown being, so that here 'man . . . asks concerning the existence of God without' *really* 'knowing for what he asks'[105] and without knowing, when denying or affirming God's existence, *what* is really being denied or affirmed.

This fact can also be explained by saying that the supposedly more radical modern search for any existence of a God always presupposes a certain concept of God as an answer to the question of *what* God is. This is true, whether, on the one hand, it is the concept of an almighty being, which brought Nietzsche to the immodest but understandable conclusion: '*If* there were gods, how could I endure not to be a God? *Therefore* there are no gods.'[106] It is equally true if, on the other hand, it is the concept of a God who, in his omnipotence, compels people to be righteous – a concept which caused Dostoevsky, and, if the truth be known, not only him, to raise the issue of theodicy. It is just this fundamentally most extraordinary of questions about God which makes modern people wonder whether there is a God at all. It makes them wonder to such an extent that clearly we need first to shed some light on the concept of God so that the question *of God's existence* can even be raised.

---

[104] Barth, *CD* IV/1, 530.
[105] Ibid.
[106] F. Nietzsche, *Thus Spake Zarathustra*, Harmondsworth: Penguin, 1969, 110.

Regardless of this logical problem, however, Christian theology cannot ask the isolated question about the *existence* of God. For Christian theology is the explanation of what faith sees itself to be. So it presupposes faith in God and, of course, the existence of God. That is what distinguishes it from philosophy. Schleiermacher was right in demanding that dogmatics match the Scripture and the symbolical books, which 'do not prove, but simply assert' the existence of God. 'Dogmatics must therefore presuppose intuitive certainty or faith; and thus, as far as the God-consciousness in general is concerned, what it has to do is not to effect its recognition but to explicate its content.'[107] The faith which is presupposed by dogmatics is, however, by definition faith in God, revealed in Jesus Christ and revealed as a gracious God.

So for Christian faith the question of the existence of God is in any case identical with the question of a *gracious* God. For when he justifies the godless by grace alone through faith alone, at the same time God justifies himself. In remaining faithful to himself as the God of the Covenant, he justifies his own *being*. And with the justification of his being, his existence *is* justified. In the doctrine of justification the determination is made that God's existence cannot be recognized apart from God's self-justification. Concerning God's *existence*, it cannot be argued whether it may be 'proved' – it cannot be proved – but only whether it may be justified. However, the *existence* of something can only be justified on the basis of *what* that something whose existence is questioned *is* and *does*. The question 'How can I find a gracious God?' is framed in a dangerously individualistic way. But as regards God himself it points to the most decisive issue: God exists as the *gracious* one and justifies himself in the fact of his existence. And that means: God, as the one who justifies human beings, is justified in his own existence. To that extent the doctrine of justification is an extremely radical question about God himself.

---

[107] F. D. E. Schleiermacher, *The Christian Faith*, H. R. Mackintosh and J. S. Stewart, eds, Edinburgh: T&T Clark, 1968 (1928), 136–7.

In summarizing the metacritical content of the most important objections to the doctrine of justification, we shall be alerted to dangers and mistakes that threaten discussion of God's freedom and of human bondage. Such discussions are basic to the doctrine, but only in order to allow us to speak more clearly of the God who sets free and of humans who are to be set free. If the church wished to be dissuaded from concentrating on these matters, it would have to stop talking of God and people altogether. Then whatever it had to say about God and people, no matter how insightful, thoughtful, profound, revolutionary or edifying, it would have to say in a way that said nothing. The church would have nothing to say. And when one has *nothing* to say, it is best to remain silent – not, smitten by one's own powerlessness, to coin endless new ways of saying that one has *nothing* to say. This is not the way theology will drag itself out of its own bog. What it does by such Münchhausen-like behaviour is to make it obvious how far down in the slough it has gone, and that it lacks even the hair necessary for dragging itself out again. The church would have to pull itself by its own bald head out of the slough that it made for itself.* *Quod deus bene vertat!*

IV. Justification as a hermeneutical category

The best way to express the central function of justification is to highlight its hermeneutical significance for the whole of theological knowledge and (with Gerhard Gloege)[108] to see it accordingly as *the* 'hermeneutical category' of theology: 'With the doctrine of justification we do not simply have a doctrine handed down to us along with other doctrines, but the "category" has been entrusted to us which determines "before

---

* For the allusion, see G. A. Bürger, *Wunderbare Reisen zu Wasser und Lande, Feldzüge und lustige Abenteuer des Freiherrn von Münchhausen*, Stuttgart: Reclam, 1969, 36 (Tr).

[108] G. Gloege, *Gnade für die Welt. Kritik und Krise des Luthertums*, 1964. See especially 26.34–54.

God" all our thinking, speaking and acting'.[109] It is 'the ongoing structure for understanding which gives shape to theology's pronouncements and their content. It is theological knowledge as a category of reality all in one. As such it sharpens all statements by directing and defining them from their premises toward their goals. In a manner of speaking, it steps back into the shadows terminologically, to give all statements form and lustre, clarity and strength'.[110] It does this by also, in fact *even* by 'removing the absence of the "thing" (*sc.* justification), by removing the silence about it'.[111] In that sense, it functions as a catalyst.[112] By using the doctrine of justification, all theological statements gain their distinctive image, focus and character, as does all of theology. And conversely, all theological statements that slip past it betray, viewed from the perspective of justification, their lack of distinctive theological image, their dullness, their lack of doctrinal character.

The doctrine of justification has this strength of a hermeneutical category because it brings all of theology into the dimension of a legal dispute: that is, the legal dispute of God about his honour, which is at the same time a legal dispute about the worth of human beings. This is the central function of justification that is highlighted in all theological writings: to see God's honour and our human worth as issues to be defended and to bear witness that the meaning of God's honour and our human worth is *we must be saved by God himself alone* and *we are saved in Jesus Christ alone.* It is proper and no exaggeration to describe it as the doctrine that proclaims 'the whole of the life-bringing Word of God'.[113]

In its resemblance to a *law case*, the doctrine of justification is in fact by nature polemically oriented. It is definitely a contentious doctrine, but not only over against what has been

---

[109] Ibid., 26; cf. 35.
[110] Ibid., 37f. Cf. the similar statements in W. Härle and E. Herms, *Rechtfertigung. Das Wirklichkeitsverständnis des christlichen Glaubens*, 1980, 10.
[111] Gloege, *Gnade für die Welt*, 38.
[112] Cf. ibid., 39.
[113] Wolf, *Die Rechtfertigungslehre als Mitte und Grenze*, 14.

described – in a terrible generalizing summary of the Old Testament – as Jewish legal piety. It must of course be precisely defined what is meant by 'polemic' and 'contention' [*Kampf* (Tr)]. To contend in a law case means to exchange arguments, to argue. The doctrine of justification is, like all good law cases, eminently argumentative. Its argument is, of course, not only used to *defend* the truth (of the gospel), but more for the *expansion* of this truth, an *expansion* that operates as an *expulsion* of untruth (or, as John puts it, of lies). In that way it strengthens the ability of the Christian faith to contradict and thus fulfils a basic task of all theology.[114] *This* is what makes justification into a contentious doctrine. And in that sense it *remains* a contentious doctrine, quite independently of the historical circumstances in which Paul once formulated it. *This* is what makes first-rate polemicists of its hitherto greatest teacher Paul and his expositor Luther. However, their polemics are not facts to be judged psychologically. In their polemics they are advocates of God's dispute with human beings concerning the honour of God and the worth of human beings. The *doctrine* of justification necessarily leads to this dispute about how to speak properly of God and humans. The evidence and criteria for this dispute are the exclusive terms employed by the Reformers: Christ alone (*solus Christus*), by grace alone (*sola gratia*), by the Word alone (*solo verbo*), through faith alone (*sola fide*). Where the word 'alone' is mentioned, there is and must be a legal dispute[115] – about the truth of life.

However, this is not a lawsuit for its own sake. It is one of arguments! And arguing has agreement as its goal. The legal dispute aims at a legal peace. The doctrine of justification is the hermeneutical category of theology because it combines

---

[114] Cf. J. Fischer, 'Die Theologie und die Wissenschaften. Untheologische Betrachtungen zum Ort der Theologie' (post-doctoral [Habilitation] thesis), 1987, 54f.

[115] Does the phrase *rabies theologorum* – which is oft-lamented, and often assumes intolerable forms – have its legitimate roots in these *particulae exclusivae* that denote the doctrine of justification? Does it have its roots in the necessity of saying 'alone' without compromise?

both elements. It refuses to compromise in the dispute about the truth of faith. But in addition, where this truth takes its rightful place is where agreement also occurs. In its polemic, which draws the shape, sharpness and character of all its theological sentences from its being based on Jesus Christ alone, the doctrine of justification ensures that theology makes no compromises. In its *purposefulness*, which forces all *theological* statements to become *proclamation* and *confession*, the doctrine of justification aims at *a growing agreement* – growing in respect of the *number* of those who understand, and even more in the sense of the *understanding* reached by those people. It is not a matter only of the *increasing number* of those who see themselves as justified sinners; just as important is their *growing understanding* of what has happened to them. We are not only talking about the spread of the faith, we are talking even more about a deepening understanding of the faith, that is, about a deepening understanding of the truth of the gospel. Only through such a deepening understanding of the truth of the gospel can (and, it is to be hoped, *will*) there also come agreement between Christian denominations and churches that once split because of their different understanding of the justification article.

Thus the dispute connected with the doctrine of justification aims at a peace which is also an integral part of that doctrine. The dispute is about the peace whose heart is the truth of the Gospel. For, as C. F. von Weizsäcker has so accurately said, when all peace is the 'body of a truth' and all peace is possible 'as far as the truth that brings it reaches',[116] then truth is the 'soul' of peace. The truth of the gospel can rightfully count as the soul of peace. The dispute goes on about it, within the doctrine of justification and using that doctrine.

---

[116] C. F. von Weizsäcker, *Der Garten des Menschlichen. Beiträge zur geschichtlichen Anthropologie*, 7th edn, 1980, 40f.

3

THE JUSTIFICATION EVENT:
THE RIGHTEOUSNESS*
OF GOD

The doctrine of justification is the theological exposition of an *event*. It is vitally important to analyse the concepts in the context of the *doctrine* in order to arrive at a better understanding of *this event*. Definitions are essential, but have no intrinsic value in the context of this doctrine. We shall need to bear this in mind in view of the 'whole secret body of knowledge'[1] which has come to surround the article over the course of the history of theology. If the church really stands and falls by this doctrine, it must be understandable at a very basic level. The essential 'teasing out the idea' – which, as everywhere in theology, is not to be neglected – must on no account lead to us being unable to understand the central event because of a plethora of ideas. With this reservation, let us now proceed to analyse the concept that is vital for a theological exposition of the justification event: *the righteousness of God*. This concept is of paramount importance for the understanding of the justification event, but not in itself or in any abstract way. Rather, it is important in its *biblical* and specifically in its *Pauline* use. What then do we mean by *the righteousness of God*?

Are we to think of a *corrective* justice† (iustitia *commutativa*, which has to do with the exchange of goods and with treaties),

---

[1] E. Wolf, *Die Rechtfertigungslehre als Mitte und Grenze*, 12.

* The German word *Gerechtigkeit* can yield in English either *justice* or *righteousness*, as indeed can the biblical words for the concept. Throughout this translation, a necessary choice will be made in every case between the two terms (Tr).

† The German term *ausgleichende Gerechtigkeit* is used as an everyday idiom to express what English would call *poetic justice*. However, this English term would take us too far away from both Aristotle's sense and Jüngel's examination of the words

or of a *distributive* justice (iustitia *distributiva*, which has to do
with dividing something *among the members of a society*)? Is it a
question of an active righteousness of God (*iustitia dei activa*),
that is, of a God who acts justly, or perhaps of something like
a passive righteousness of God (*iustitia dei passiva*)? And what
does that mean exactly?[2] Furthermore, how do we interpret the
genitive in the expression 'righteousness of God'? Is it *genitivus
possessivus, genitivus subiectivus, genitivus obiectivus, genitivus
auctoris*? How are we to understand the biblical expression
righteousness of God? And how do we differentiate righteousness
when talking of God from what is normally called justice and
deserves so to be called?

I. The traditional concept of justice

1. In praise of law and justice

'Neither evening nor morning star is so wonderful'[3] as justice.
It is considered the highest of virtues, the perfect virtue. For
those who have it possess it not only as a personal virtue, but
also in relation to others. And among human beings, 'the best
man is not he who exercises his virtue towards himself but he
who exercises it towards another; for this is a difficult task'.[4]
This panegyric for justice was composed by Aristotle,[5] quoting
Euripides and Theognis. Melanchthon quoted it in his *Apology
of the Augsburg Confession*,[6] and many important thinkers would
agree. Not only great thinkers, but also so-called ordinary folk

---

themselves. Here, then, as elsewhere in this chapter, we have instead used the
translation of Aristotle's Greek terms found in the Loeb edition (Tr).

[2] To my knowledge, the grammatical or categorical sense of the opposition of
'active' and 'passive' has not yet been clarified, despite E. Hirsch's study 'Initium
theologiae Lutheri' (repr. in idem, *Lutherstudien*, vol. 2, 1954, 9–35). See below,
note 41.

[3] Aristotle, *Nicomachean Ethics* in *Aristotle*, vol. II [*Great Books of the Western World*],
W. D. Ross, ed., Chicago: Encyclopaedia Britannica, 1952 (E, 1129b 28f.), 377.

[4] Ibid. (1130a 7f.).

[5] Ibid. (1129b 25 – 1130a 8).

[6] *BC*, 110.

with their ordinary common sense go along with it: a just people, a just society – those are grander things than the evening or the morning star. It will no doubt be easy to reach agreement with the philosophers of old as well, that a just person is one who obeys the law. From this Aristotle concludes: 'evidently all lawful acts are in a sense just acts'.[7] Thus, further praise could be added to the hymn that extols the law so highly. Instead, let us recall here Immanuel Kant's famous apostrophe to duty, which also applies to the law:

> Duty! Thou sublime and mighty name that dost embrace nothing charming or insinuating but requirest submission and yet seekest not to move the will by threatening aught that would arouse natural aversion or terror, but only holdest forth a law which of itself finds entrance into the mind and yet gains reluctant reverence (though not always obedience) – a law before which all inclinations are dumb even though they secretly work against it: what origin is there worthy of thee, and where is to be found the root of thy noble descent which proudly rejects all kinship with the inclinations and from which to be descended is the indispensable condition of the only worth which men can give themselves?[8]

The Bible, too, praises justice, or righteousness. In the Old Testament, this takes the form of praising love for the law. For life's relationships are so ordered through the law and justice, that all people included in these relationships come into their rights without having to *take* them (which is usually at the cost of the rights of others). Justice here means guiding the wealth of life's relationships in such a way as to guarantee that people's lives are successful. Where justice rules, peace – *shalom* – flows forth.

So the word *just* is used to describe that ordering of life's relationships without which creaturely life finds no peace. This view is shared by the New Testament, which, when talking of basic life-defining relations and connections, means (1) the relation of human beings to God, (2) our relation to our social

---

[7] Aristotle, *Nichomachean Ethics* (E, 1129b 11f.), 377.
[8] *Immanuel Kant: Critique of Practical Reason*, trans. L. W. Beck, Indianapolis and New York: Bobbs-Merrill, 1956, 89.

and natural environment and (3) the relation of a person to himself or herself. These are basic relationships within which an enormous number of life relationships are built. This immensely rich tapestry of relationships thrives in turn on the fact that God remains creatively and affirmatively devoted to it. That is when justice and peace rule.

The opposite occurs when the fundamental relationships of life, instead of being mutually encouraging, start to compete and damage each other and bring about mutual destruction. This happens when a person furthers the relationship with himself or herself to the point of *reckless self-actualization,* subordinating or even sacrificing the relationship to God. Idols are then worshipped, which are idols for the reason that people can *use* them for their own advantage. And in the very use of them for their own purposes they become addicted to them. Idols are never interesting for their own sake. But God *is* interesting for his own sake. When he is no longer present, the worship of idols begins, and that is simply a tool of humans' reckless self-actualization.

In the same way that reckless self-actualization perverts our relationship to God, it also perverts our relationship to our social and natural environment. Other persons, made in the image of God, instead of being interesting for their own sake and thus a goal in themselves, now become simply a means to achieve our own interests and purposes. The Thou becomes an It. And the I–It relationship,[9] which is our connection to the natural environment, becomes such a master–servant relationship that non-human creatures in our hands turn into mere things. Nothing is any longer important *for itself.* The only importance is what we can get out of something. In relationship to our natural environment, *being human* is reduced to *being manufacturers.*

So the rich network of relationships of created life is destroyed by this reckless self-actualization on the part of humans; in fact it is twisted, so that justice becomes injustice,

---

[9] Cf. Buber, *The Eclipse of God,* 165–7.

and in place of that wealth of relationships comes a growing lack of relationships. The compulsive urge towards such a lack of relationships, when self-actualization becomes an absolute, is what the Bible calls *sin*. And because, when relationships *die*, life dies too, the Bible sees *death* at work wherever relationships break down and are replaced by a relational void: 'The wages of sin is death' (Rom. 6:23). Even life itself is marked with the sign of death.[10]

That is the verdict of the Bible, and quite a few non-biblical sources agree. That is also the verdict of the New Testament. But, *in contrast to* the Old Testament and to a great number of non-biblical sources, the New Testament claims that we cannot escape this situation through any *deed* required by the *law*, or by anything we are able to do. Even though it is normally asserted by everyone that the law is the basis for righteousness, Paul says that obedience to the law cannot bring about our righteousness before God. For the law makes *demands* of us, it demands *deeds* of us and sends us with our deeds *to the world*. It is in the world that we have to do our work. We are to act and have our dealings in the world. But as regards God, we cannot be simply *doers*. With God, we are always *receivers, non-actors* (Rom. 4:5).

That is why Paul claims that no one can become righteous through the works demanded by the law (Rom. 3:20). We *cannot* do it. And we do not *need* to do what we cannot do. For now the righteousness of God is revealed, *in the gospel* (Rom. 1:16f.). We can see the importance of the contrast between law and gospel even in Paul's writings – that contrast which became so decisive for Luther. Which alternative we emphasize as the locus of God's revelation – law or gospel – will decide the importance of the expression *the righteousness of God*.[11]

---

[10] Cf. E. Jüngel, *Death: The Riddle and the Mystery*, trans. I and U. Nicol, Edinburgh: Saint Andrew Press, 1975, 87–9.

[11] On the relationship between law and gospel in Paul and the Old Testament presuppositions for these distinctions, see E. Jüngel, 'Das Gesetz zwischen Adam und Christus. Eine theologische Studie zu Röm 5, 12–21', in idem *Unterwegs zur Sache. Theologische Bemerkungen* (*BEvTh* 61), 2nd edn, 1988, 145–72.

2. Righteousness as an attribute of God

In the following section we shall need to make a special examination of Paul's use of language, since it was he who gave
justification its biblical shape. It is undeniable that Paul can
speak of God's righteousness in the sense that God is *righteous*.
This occurs in Romans 3:5, when 'our righteousness' is compared with 'God's righteousness' and at the same time it is stated
that God is not *unjust* for being angry with us. In Romans 9:14,
any possible *injustice* on God's part is also excluded when God
loves Jacob, but hates Esau: 'Is there injustice on God's part? By
no means!' According to this, the expression 'righteousness of
God' says: God *is* just. Only by being just can he be God. Paul
can even identify 'righteousness' with 'God' (compare Rom. 6:18
with 6:22).[12] We are reminded of this usage in Romans 3:26,
with the expression 'that he himself [*sc.* God] is righteous'.
Admittedly, in its context this is making a specific point, to which
we shall return.

From the texts mentioned so far we could take the genitive
God's righteousness in Paul as a subjective genitive: the righteousness of God, through which God is righteous (*iustitia dei
qua deus iustus est*). In this sense the expression *God's righteousness*
is traditional. Jewish divines also speak in this way. It is well-
known of God that 'his work is perfect, and all his ways are just'
(Deut. 32:4). Here justice is understood as an attribute of God.
God is thought of in the same way as a person who has the
attribute of being just. And a person who acts justly and does
what is right is called just. In this respect it is required of all
people – in a moral sense – that they be just. But justice is the
special attribute of someone acting in a judicial capacity. It is
unreservedly expected of a judge that he be just. Thus *God's
righteousness* or justice is presented here as an attribute of God
as judge.

But what is required of him? What does justice mean when it
is seen as an attribute of a person and particularly of the judicial

---

[12] Cf. E. Käsemann, *Commentary on Romans*, trans. G. W. Bromiley, London: SCM
Press, 1980, 28.

personage of a judge? The point of what the Bible means when it talks of *God's righteousness* has often been summarized by this view of the subjective genitive. So it is important to pursue this issue before we examine how the genuinely Pauline usage of *God's righteousness* is to be understood more precisely. We shall take the common definitions used since Plato and Aristotle as our starting point, since they are of paramount importance for both the philosophical and the judicial meaning of the concept.

3. To each what is due: justice since Plato and Aristotle

Why do we long for justice anyway? And what are we desiring when we call for justice? To answer these questions, it is best to start with the fact that there exists something like *injustice* in the world or that people feel they are *not treated justly*. Generally it is felt in human society that it is *unjust* when someone 'has more' at the expense of someone else.[13] *Having too much*, and thus leaving another or others with too little and 'offending' and harming them, is *unjust*. The 'Pre-Socratic' Anaximander even made the injustice of having too much, *pleonexia*, into the explanation for the source and destruction of existing things: 'the source from which existing things derive their existence is also that to which they return at their destruction, according to necessity; for they give justice and make reparation to one another for their injustice, according to the arrangement of Time'.[14] Here the being of existing things as against the non-being of the non-existent is understood as an injustice, the injustice of having too much. So right consists in evening this out: existing things are destroyed so that the non-existent can come into existence. Time brings about this balance.

With Plato the craving for justice comes under the heading of pastoral care. The latter also refers to community, to the

---

[13] Cf. Plato, *Gorgias* 483c.

[14] Anaximander, in K. Freeman, *Ancilla to the Pre-Socratic Philosophers: A Complete Translation of the Fragments in Diels*, Fragmente der Vorsokratiker, Cambridge, Mass.: Harvard University Press, 1978, 19.

polis, since according to Plato the essence of the human being unfolds in political community. To that extent community may be regarded as an enlarged model of the soul. Accordingly, in his *Republic*, Plato placed the cardinal virtue of justice next to the three other cardinal virtues of wisdom (φρόνησις, prudentia or σοφία, sapientia), courage (ἀνδρεία, fortitudo) and temperance (σωφροσύνη, temperentia) and related all the virtues (ἀρεταί) to both the individual domain of the soul and the political domain. 'Separation and order in state and soul correspond to each other trait by trait.' The correspondence of the life of the soul and political life expresses clearly the fact that for Plato the 'goal of all ethical and political action' is 'pastoral care'.[15] Relating the soul and the *polis* is attained in the case of the three last-mentioned virtues when *individually* the three capacities of the soul and *politically* the three classes of the *polis* are considered as quantities of reference: judgement is assigned particularly to the *rational* (λογιστικόν) in the soul and to the *teaching class* in the community, courage (ἀνδρεία) is particularly assigned to energy (θυμοειδές) in the soul and to defence in the state, and temperance or level-headedness (σωφροσύνη) would then be assigned to covetousness (ἐπιθυμητικόν) in the soul or to nourishment in the community. However, the third virtue is assigned to all classes and parts of the soul as 'a type of harmony'[16] for them. In that respect it is a sort of prelude to the fourth cardinal virtue, that of *justice* (δικαιοσύνη).[17] *Justice* does not allow of its being assigned to any special quality of the soul or specific class of the state. Rather, the virtue of *justice*, for its part, is assigned to the three remaining virtues as the harmonious collaboration of the three. At the same time it is the sum of all virtues. Its most

---

[15] A. Dihle, 'Gerechtigkeit' in *Reallexikon für Antike und Christentum*, vol. 10, 1978, 233–360, 256f. The western concept of pastoral care can be traced to Plato.

[16] P. Friedländer, *Platon*, vol. 3: *Die platonischen Schriften. Zweite und dritte Periode*, 2nd edn, 1960, 91.

[17] It could also be said that 'between σωφροσύνη and δικαιοσύνη an overlap' occurs which 'reveals a certain conflict between the platonic outline and socratic intellectualism' (A. Dihle, 'Gerechtigkeit', 256).

common definition is the 'doing of what is one's own'[18] and not doing many things at once.

Although Aristotle did not exactly repeat the Platonic conception of justice as being a harmonious collaboration of the three classes of the state and of the three capacities of the soul, he did follow his master Plato in seeing justice as the highest of all virtues. Aristotle's definition from his *Rhetoric* has become famous: 'Justice is the virtue through which everybody enjoys his own possessions in accordance with the law; its opposite is injustice, through which men enjoy the possessions of others in defiance of the law'.[19] 'The characteristic' of the just person

---

[18] Plato, *Republic* (Book 4, 433a), in *Great Dialogues of Plato*, trans. W. H. D. Rouse, New York: Mentor, 1956, 233.

[19] Aristotle, *Rhetoric* A, 1366b 9–11 in Aristotle, op. cit., 609. For Aristotle, justice is the κρατίστη τῶν ἀρετῶν and ἀρετὴ τελεία: 'in justice is every virtue comprehended' (Aristotle, *Nicomachean Ethics* E, 1129b 25–30 in Aristotle, op. cit., 601). So Aristotle sees justice as epitomizing virtue, since it is present not only as the merit of the one who has it, but in addition it always exists for the benefit of the other. The virtue of courage can be limited to being an asset of the one who is courageous. However, the virtue of justice is an asset, not only for the just person, but also invariably acts to the advantage of another. In this sense justice, seen as epitomizing virtue, is a relational concept. It is 'related to our neighbour' (πρὸς ἕτερον, ibid., 1130a 2) or 'in a relation to one's neighbour' (ἐν τῷ πρὸς ἕτερον, ibid., 1130b 1). For Aristotle, this justice, conceived of as the epitome of virtue (ὅλη ἀρετή), corresponds in content with *what the law* commands: what is just (δίκαιον) is what is commanded by the law (νόμιμον). 'For practically the majority of the acts commanded by the law are those which are prescribed from the point of view of virtue taken as a whole; for the law bids us practise every virtue and forbids us to practise any vice' (ibid., 1130b 22–4). Here, of course, the main orientation of what is 'positively right' (laws made by the lawmakers) presupposes the 'unwritten law' or the 'naturally just'. Aristotle makes a distinction between this justice as the epitome of virtue – which is later called universal justice (*iustitia universalis*) – and justice as an individual virtue or a partial instance of virtue (*iustitia particularis*). What is looked at as just – as δίκαιον – is now no longer set up by the law, but beyond that by a further principle: through fairness (τὸ ἴσον). Fairness belongs to justice in the sense of *iustitia particularis*. An offence against the law and an offence against fairness relate to each other as the whole to the part: 'for all that is unfair (ἄνισον) is unlawful (παράνομον), but not all that is unlawful (παράνομον) is unfair (ἄνισον)' (ibid., 1130b 12f. with 9ff.). Within *iustitia particularis* Aristotle differentiates two further kinds of what is *just* (δίκαιον), seen as *fairness* (ἴσον). These are, on the one hand, distributive justice (δίκαιον διανεμητικόν) – later to be called *iustitia distributiva* and, on the other hand, corrective justice (δίκαιον διορθωτικόν or

(δίκαιον) 'as a "right" person . . . is' fairness (ἴσον). 'It must be considered unjust when one person 'has more' at the cost of another . . . Equality, which is the issue here, is seen in two ways; first, material and non-material goods must be distributed equally to the members of the society – that means considering the tasks and obligations of each person . . .'[20] That is, equality as an analogous geometrical proportion (distributive justice, *iustitia distributiva*). 'Matters are simpler when we come to "*compensatory*" justice (*iustitia commutativa*), which is to be observed

---

ἐπανορθωτικόν), later known as *iustitia directiva*. This latter kind aims at legal restitution – *iustitia correctiva* for *obligationes ex delicto* – as well as contractual justice – *iustitia commutativa* for *obligationes e contractu* (cf. F. Dirlmeier, *Kommentar zu: Aristoteles, Nikomachische Ethik* E, 1130b 30 – 1131a 1, *Werke in deutscher Übersetzung*, ed. E. Grumach, vol. 6, 1967, 404). Corrective justice provides for legal and contractual relations between individuals to be in order. 'Here there must be introduced the balance between performance and payment either against (punishment) or according to (payment) the will of the perpetrator' (A. Dihle, 'Gerechtigkeit', 261). Aristotle is thinking in his second case of voluntary relations, such as buying and selling, money lending, rent, etc. while in his first case he is thinking of involuntary relations such as theft, assassination, false witness, assault, kidnapping, manslaughter, slander. Justice in all these cases of contractual relations is the same in the sense of an arithmetic absolute proportion:

$$10 - 4 = 2 + 4$$
$$6 = 6$$

The just judge takes the surplus away from the unjust gain (e.g. of the thief) and so makes things even (in the case of the murderer, by taking away his life). Even with distributive justice what is just (δίκαιον) is equality (ἴσον). Except that in these cases equality (e.g. the distribution of wartime booty or public honours, etc.) is reckoned not by arithmetic, but by geometric proportion:

$$10 : 5 = 8 : 4$$
$$2 : 1 = 2 : 1$$

For the one who has invested more, for example in a war, will also deserve more booty. Similarly, but inversely, for punishments.

In both forms of *iustitia particularis* justice consists in the proportional equality of a four-part proportion (A : B = C : D), which in the case of corrective justice must be read as arithmetical, in the case of distributive justice as geometrical (Aristotle, *Nicomachean Ethics*, E, 1131a 9 – 1132b 1). Nevertheless, for both forms it holds that justice is a virtue which gives to each what is due on the principle of equality and in obedience to the law.

[20] A. Dihle, 'Gerechtigkeit', 260f.

above all in criminal justice and in economic exchange.'[21] Equality is required here as an absolute arithmetical proportion.[22]

The Aristotelian definition of justice finds its judicial analogy in a definition by Ulpian (*c.* AD 200), which has become authoritative: 'Justice is the constant and perpetual wish to render every one his due.'[23]

If we take this meaning for justice as our basis when we come to think about how the Bible speaks of God's righteousness or justice, we find that it calls God's being *just*, in so far as he gives to each what is due – according to the law. As far as justice relates to others, God would be *just* in his dealings with human beings if he rewarded them (in the sense of distributive justice) according to their virtuous deeds, and punished them in accordance with their evil deeds. And, since for humans justice seen in this way is the highest of the virtues, so that one who acts virtuously deserves to be called just, God would be just in his dealings with us if he rewarded just people and punished the unjust. In view of Romans 3:9f., which says that 'all . . . are under the power of sin', so that 'there is no one who is righteous, not even one', this understanding of justice, by which God himself is righteous, necessarily means for human beings that they experience the *just* God as a *punishing, wrathful* God.

However, Paul's central statements about the righteousness of God are not to be taken simply in that way. It is vital for a correct understanding that the Pauline concept 'never means penal righteousness'.[24] It is, of course, true that in the traditions which Paul used, both Jewish and early Christian, *the righteousness of God* also meant that righteousness of God by which God himself *is* righteous. However, the very fact of God's being

---

[21] Ibid., 261.
[22] Cf. Aristotle, *Nicomachean Ethics* (E, 1131a 31 – b 24, 1132b 18f.), 379.
[23] Domitius Ulpianus, quoted in *The Institutes of Justinian*, with an English introduction, translation and notes by T. C. Sandars, London: Longmans Green, 1869, 77 = *Iustiniani digestorum seu pandectarum* I, I, 10: 'Iustitia est constans et perpetua voluntas ius suum cuique tribuendi.'
[24] E. Käsemann, *Romans*, 25.

righteous is given a *new* understanding by Paul; no longer does it have the sense of distributive justice.

II. The Christian concept of the righteousness of God

The fact that Jesus Christ died for our sins and was raised from the dead for our justification (Rom. 4:25) gives the Christian concept of the righteousness of God its distinctive meaning. Since Paul's letters are crucial to the understanding of the concept, we shall pay special attention to them in what follows.

1. The righteousness of God as a relational concept

When the New Testament speaks of the righteousness of God, it links in with the Old Testament understanding of the righteousness of Yahweh, which is a relational concept, and to that extent resembles *justice* in Aristotle. It is 'the relationship which Jahweh had offered to Israel'.[25] Or, to be more precise, that covenant faithfulness which God provides and without which neither individuals nor the people as a whole can *live*. At the same time as being a covenant faithfulness, the righteousness of Yahweh is a power that creates and maintains life. Human beings can only live in the community which Yahweh provides: we can only live as people *whom God acknowledges*. However, it is a condition of such acknowledgement that we behave as a community and so fulfil the righteousness of God – a righteousness that always obligingly anticipates us. So righteousness in human beings is *the fact of our being acknowledged by God*. And 'a man lives from this acknowledgement – "he is righteousness, he will live" (Ezek. 18:9)'.[26]

Paul also presupposes this understanding of the righteousness of God. Since at first he does not formulate anything of his own apart from the Old Testament and Jewish tradition, our

---

[25] von Rad, *Theology of the Old Testament*, vol. 1, 372. [Von Rad's German term 'Gemeinschaftsverhältnis' conveys more than does Stalker's translation 'relationship'. We may think of a relationship of companionship in community (Tr).]

[26] Ibid., 379 [altered (Tr)].

hermeneutical procedure compels us to look at the *additions* which we can find in Paul, in order to gain a better understanding of the *Pauline* meaning of the concept. For Paul, the concept of the righteousness of God evidently needed amplification. Thus the correct hermeneutical approach is to give attention to the additions that Paul makes to the concept. The *Formula of Concord* called these additions the *particulae exclusivae*.[27] Paul's usage of the *righteousness of God* which defines his concept will emerge from such additions. This usage is what makes the concept's structure, taken over from the Old Testament, fruitful for the preaching of the gospel and in the Christian sense gives it clarity.

2. The Pauline use of the expression

The crucial additions which mark the Pauline use of the expression 'God's righteousness' are: the phrases 'through faith' (διὰ πίστεως) and 'apart from the law' (χωρὶς νομόυ). However, their meaning must first be examined. It is obvious that the phrase 'apart from the law' is used to express negatively what is said positively by 'through faith'. 'Apart from the law' is the antithesis of 'righteousness through the law'. The phrase 'through the law' (διὰ νόμου), and its equivalents, is often found when the expression 'righteousness' occurs without the genitive 'God's' (cf. Gal. 2:21). From this it follows that God and the law are mutually exclusive in the matter of righteousness. This is confirmed by the opposition between the 'righteousness which comes from God' and the 'righteousness which comes through the law' in Philippians 3:9 (cf. Gal. 3:21): 'God' and 'the law' compete with each other in bringing about righteousness.

---

[27] Cf. *The Formula of Concord, Solid Declaration,* Article III: 'And this is St Paul's intention when in this article he so earnestly and diligently stresses such exclusive terms [that is, terms that exclude works from the article of justification by faith] as "without works", "without the law", "freely", "not of works" . . .' (*BC,* 545): 'Atque ea ipsa de causa Paulus particulas exclusivas (videlicet sine lege, sine operibus, ex gratia, gratis), . . . in hoc articulo tanta diligentia tantoque zelo urget. . . .'

From Philippians 3:9 ('the righteousness which comes from God') it seems reasonable to suppose that the genitive 'God's righteousness' is to be seen as a genitive of the author *(genitivus auctoris)*: the righteousness which God accomplishes. Rudolf Bultmann called for the phrase in Philippians 3:9 to be read as an authentic commentary by Paul on the expression *God's righteousness*.[28] Then *God's* righteousness is at the same time the opposite to *my own* righteousness; this fits in with the contrast in Romans 10:3 between 'God's righteousness' and '(one's) own righteousness'. If my *own* righteousness is both what I have produced *by myself* and also the righteousness *which distinguishes my essence*, then by the same token the righteousness of God must be seen as both the righteousness produced by God *and therefore* that righteousness which distinguishes his divine essence. At the same time it must be noted that this righteousness, as it is produced by God, both *is* his righteousness and *becomes* my (our) righteousness. The difference between *my* (own) righteousness and *God's righteousness* will then consist in the fact that *my* righteousness, *if* it were to be achieved, would still only be my *own* righteousness, while *God's* righteousness takes its uniqueness precisely from the fact that it is a *sharing* righteousness, one which *passes over* from God to human beings.

Accordingly, God's righteousness consists for Paul in the fact that God is not righteous for his own sake, but that he is only righteous himself in so far as he is the one who provides righteousness for human beings. However, it is at this very point that this is *true* righteousness, a righteousness which can never be satisfied with the righteousness of those who are righteous. True righteousness wishes rather to *win through*, to create righteousness, *where ever* unrighteousness holds sway. So the righteousness of God is a 'power' by which God 'brings back the fallen world into the sphere of his legitimate claim'.[29] But

[28] R. Bultmann, 'ΔΙΚΑΙΟΣΥΝΗ ΘΕΟΥ' in idem, *Exegetica. Aufsätze zur Erforschung des Neuen Testaments* , 1967, 470–5.

[29] Käsemann, *Romans*, 29. It would be even more appropriate to say that God's righteousness is a power that penetrates into the fallen world in order to make over anew the world's unrighteous relationships. This gives it a creative

this desire to win through on all fronts is equally valid for human righteousness. So unrighteousness never leaves truly righteous people in peace; righteous people are never satisfied with simply being righteous. Truly righteous people *ensure* that righteousness happens. Truly righteous people never boast of their own righteousness as though it were a merit. That sort of boasting is given a negative label by Paul: it is *a righteousness of one's own.* Thus the apostle makes clear the meaning of God's righteousness, as against *a righteousness of one's own based on works of the law,* when he asks the rhetorical question in Romans 3:27: *Then what becomes of boasting? It is excluded,* 'and then [in Rom. 4:1ff.] refers to Abraham, who, having believed God, had no "boast" '.[30]

If we may put it rather untheologically for the moment: true righteousness is only interested in and insists on *universal* righteousness. The urge to move from particular righteousness and attain global righteousness is an integral part of true righteousness. Thus true righteousness cannot be satisfied with the simple fact that the righteous person *is* righteous. A righteousness which boasted in its own righteousness, which *fixated* on its own righteousness as a personal asset, would cost righteousness its *urge towards universality.* Aristotle emphasized this when he taught that justice seen as *the* epitome of virtue exists not only as an asset of the one who has it (that is, of the one who is just) but always exists for the advantage of others as well. It is 'in relation to others'.[31] In the Pauline context this aspect appears in particular contrast against the background of Old Testament and late Jewish tradition.

However, such 'untheological' phraseology serves at most as a preliminary to Paul's discussion of the righteousness of God. Paul knows *only God* as the one who is truly righteous, who in his own righteousness urges us powerfully towards a universal

---

dimension, 'the dimension of new creation' (P. Stuhlmacher, 'The Apostle Paul's View of Righteousness' in idem, *Reconciliation, Law and Righteousness: Essays in Biblical Theology,* Philadelphia: Fortress Press, 1986, 68–93, 81).

[30] R. Bultmann, *Theology of the New Testament,* vol. 1, trans. K. Grobel, London: SCM Press, 1965 (1952), 242.

[31] Aristotle, *Nicomachean Ethics* (E, 1129b 25, 1130b 1), 377.

righteousness, whose righteousness consists in creating global righteousness. In so far as the state, acting as a 'superior authority' does the same, it is a 'power instituted by God' (Rom. 13:1) and is 'God's servant' (Rom. 13:4).

3. Wrath and the righteousness of God

Now, the very power of the state that urges justice shows that, even in describing God's righteousness as a force pressing outwards and *creating universal righteousness*, we have not gone beyond a merely formal description. In this merely formal sense, creating justice is also the very task and characteristic of the state, which approves the one who does good (Rom. 13:3), but which 'bear[s] the sword . . . to execute wrath' (Rom. 13:4) on the one who does wrong. The fact that the 'bearers of power' here are servants of God and his 'representative agent[s] for wrath'[32] makes the contrast with the concept of God's righteousness completely clear. For 'the righteousness of God' and 'the wrath of God' are used in Romans 1:17f. as opposing concepts. This antithesis is clearest in the distinction between law and gospel. For, while the righteousness of God is revealed only *in the gospel* (Rom. 1:17), according to Romans 4:15 it is *the law* that brings wrath. The revelation of the righteousness of God does, of course, point to the revelation of wrath from heaven. However, and this is the crucial issue, *this* way which God has of working against unrighteousness is not the way of *divine righteousness*, even though according to the usual human understanding of righteousness ('to each what is due!'), God's wrath as judge coming down against universal unrighteousness should be seen as a manifestation of the righteousness of God. Rather, for Paul the *wrath* of God falling on unrighteousness is the opposite concept to the *righteousness* of God. Wrath belongs to the category of the law, not to the gospel. The law imprisons the lawbreaker within his transgressions and their consequences. That is precisely how its wrath works.

---

[32] According to Käsemann, *Romans*, 355–6.

Wrath (seen as eschatological judgement) is revealed directly against unrighteous humankind: God has delivered the unrighteous, 'who by their wickedness suppress the truth' (Rom. 1:18), over to their unrighteousness (Rom. 1:24, 26, 28); that is to say, he has handed them over to the 'curse of evil deeds, that they will never cease to breed and bring forth evil'.[33] The revelation of the wrath of God consists in God not stopping people in their wrongdoing; the perverseness that wrongfully suppresses truth is allowed to grow to its full potential. The revelation of the eschatological wrath of God is basically the world, as run by human beings, taken to its logical conclusion: 'the world's history is the world's judgement doom'.[34] This has been revealed *now, from heaven*, with eschatological inevitability.[35]

This *now*, to which the words 'is revealed' in Romans 1:18 refer, was made clear in the previous verse and will also be expressed in Romans 3:21: it is the time of the gospel and of the righteousness of God to be revealed in the gospel, so that only through the revelation of God's righteousness is God's wrath revealed. 'Prior to the gospel man does not really know what sin is even though he lives in it. Similarly he does not know about the wrath to which he has fallen victim'.[36] It is not a case of 'two different revelations', but of 'one and the same act of revelation',[37] which is however accomplished in two antithetical means of revelation. Of these two, the revelation of the righteousness of God which is accomplished in the gospel is primary. When looked at stylistically in Paul's writing, it brackets the revelation of the wrath of God (Rom. 1:18 – 3:20) between

---

[33] F. Schiller, *The Piccolomini*, in *Friedrich Schiller: The Robbers/Wallenstein*, trans. F. J. Lamport, Harmondsworth, Penguin, 1979, 310.

[34] Idem, 'Resignation', in *The Poems and Ballads of Schiller*, trans. E. Bulwer Lytton, London and New York: Frederick Warne, 1887, 304.

[35] Cf. Enoch 91:7. 'A great chastisement shall come from heaven upon all these.' Paul sees the punishment as being in the vices and their results.

[36] Käsemann, *Romans*, 35.

[37] Ibid. Cf. G. Bornkamm, 'Die Offenbarung des Zornes Gottes', in idem, *Das Ende des Gesetzes. Paulusstudien, Gesammelte Aufsätze*, vol. 1 (*BEvTh* 16) 2nd edn, 1958, 9–33, 10 and 30–3.

the two similar sentences of Romans 1:17 and 3:21. That is to say: the revelation of the righteousness of God in the gospel presupposes the wrath of God and at the same time limits it. We have now reached the decisive point for understanding the righteousness of God in Paul.

4. The gospel: the place where righteousness is revealed

Paul knows that he has been chosen as the apostle for the gospel of God by God himself (Rom. 1:1). He will and must preach the gospel, in Rome, as everywhere else (Rom. 1:15). He will in no way be ashamed of the gospel (the word *ashamed* is meant politically rather than psychologically). He bases this on the fact that in the gospel God's righteousness is revealed: the gospel is 'the power of God for salvation to everyone who has faith . . . for in it the righteousness of God is revealed through faith for faith' (Rom. 1:16–17). So, to express it formally, the gospel is the *place* where God's righteousness is revealed. Expressed materially, the gospel is the 'message about the cross' (1 Cor. 1:18) which shows us the resurrected Christ as *the one crucified for us*. It is the message which brings to us the *effect* of Jesus' *death*. It has *its own timing*. Its *content* is bound up with the time of Jesus, or more precisely with his death. And *publicly*, since the resurrection of Jesus from the dead, it is *timely*. We summarize both ideas together when we say: the gospel is the eschatological Time-Word of God. It says something new, which makes other things new: for it is the power of God for salvation, which, in the light of the revelation of God's wrath described in Romans 1:18 – 3:20 can only mean it is a power that fundamentally renews everything.[38]

So the gospel is not only information, it is an address to me that gives me information: it speaks to me directly. But it is not only this, it is above all a creative address, an eschatological announcement: the announcement of the new age that has broken in. The gospel addresses me – and not only me! – with a

---

[38] Cf. 2 Corinthians 5:17: 'everything old [that is, what is described in Rom. 1:18ff.] has passed away; see, everything has become new'.

new possibility I could not have dreamt up; and it grants that possibility to me as a reality. This is where the distinction between the revelation of the righteousness of God and the revelation of God's wrath has its real point. While the revelation of God's righteousness in the gospel introduces a new age, the revelation of God's wrath falling unmistakably from heaven discloses the nature of the old world age, which is now totally obsolete. The eschatological revelation of God's righteousness in the gospel presupposes the revelation of God's wrath from heaven in such a way that the *new present, made new* by God, exposes the *old present,* in which humankind lived and still lives, as being the result of our own past and thus as imprisoned by the past. We now see 'the nature of the world before Christ and outside him'[39] as 'so much garbage' (Phil. 3:8 [NEB]: πάντα . . . σκύβαλα). The gospel sheds such light on the world that, starting from heaven and spreading across the whole earth, it is clear to what extent God had handed the world, warped by humankind, over to its own twistedness. He did this by leaving it to its own bent towards the past. This is what is meant by the wrath of God. Certainly this *wrath* of God marks the 'cosmic breadth and depth'[40] of the *saving* message of God's righteousness. But it is the exact opposite of his divine righteousness. What, then, is meant by the *righteousness of God?*

This much is clear: the *righteousness of God* is a salvific concept when it is revealed in the gospel. We must insist rigorously that God's righteousness is revealed in the gospel and only in the gospel, if the real meaning of the expression in Paul is to be shown. Looking back over the beginnings of the Reformation, Martin Luther claimed that this was the real discovery made by the Reformation: it is the gospel, as the place of God's revelation, which decides on the meaning of the righteousness of God. Thus we shall repeat, from a Reformation perspective, the exegetical insights which were made.

[39] Käsemann, *Romans,* 35.
[40] Ibid.

5. Martin Luther's discovery at the Reformation

Luther writes:

> I had indeed been captivated with an extraordinary ardour for under-
> standing Paul in the Epistle to the Romans. But . . . a single word in
> Chapter 1 [v. 17], 'In it the righteousness of God is revealed', . . . had
> stood in my way. For I hated that word 'righteousness of God', which,
> according to the use and custom of all the teachers, I had been taught
> to understand philosophically regarding the formal or active right-
> eousness, as they called it, with which God is righteous and punishes
> the unrighteous sinner.
>
> . . . I did not love, yes, I hated the righteous God who punishes
> sinners, and secretly, if not blasphemously, certainly murmuring greatly,
> I was angry with God, and said, 'As if, indeed, it is not enough, that
> miserable sinners, eternally lost through original sin, are crushed by
> every kind of calamity by the law of the decalogue, without having God
> add pain to pain by the gospel and also by the gospel threatening us
> with his righteousness and wrath!' Thus I raged with a fierce and
> troubled conscience. Nevertheless, I beat importunately upon Paul at
> that place, most ardently desiring to know what St Paul wanted.
>
> At last, by the mercy of God, meditating day and night, I gave heed
> to the context of the words, namely, 'in it the righteousness of God is
> revealed, as it is written, "He who through faith is righteous shall live"'.
> There I began to understand that the righteousness of God is that by
> which the righteous lives by a gift of God, namely by faith. And this is
> the meaning: the righteousness of God is revealed by the gospel,
> namely, the passive righteousness with which merciful God justifies us
> by faith, as it is written, 'He who through faith is righteous shall live.'
> Here I felt that I was altogether born again and had entered paradise
> itself through open gates. There a totally other face of the entire
> Scripture showed itself to me. Thereupon I ran through the Scriptures
> from memory. I also found in other terms an analogy, as the work of
> God, that is, what God does in us, the power of God, with which he
> makes us strong, the wisdom of God, with which he makes us wise, the
> strength of God, the salvation of God, the glory of God.
>
> And I extolled my sweetest word with a love as great as the hatred
> with which I had before hated the word "righteousness of God". Thus
> that place in Paul was for me truly the gate to paradise.'[41]

---

[41] M. Luther, 'Preface to the Complete Edition of Luther's Latin Writings' (1545),
in LW 34, 323–38. The quote is from 336–7. The Latin is in WA 54, 185, 14–86,
16: 'Miro certe ardore captus fueram cognoscendi Pauli in epistola ad Rom., sed
obstiterat . . . unicum vocabulum, quod est Cap. 1: Iustitia Dei revelatur in illo.

In old age, Luther looks back, recalling his original experience at the Reformation, which was nothing more nor less than an exegetical discovery about the meaning of the Pauline text in Romans 1:17. More precisely, the discovery was about the

---

Oderam enim vocabulum istud "Iustitia Dei", quod usu et consuetudine omnium doctorum doctus eram philosophice intelligere de iustitia (ut vocant) formali seu activa, qua Deus est iustus, et peccatores iniustosque punit.

Ego autem . . . non amabam, imo odiebam iustum et punientem peccatores Deum, tacitaque si non blasphemia, certe ingenti murmuratione indignabar Deo, dicens: quasi vero non satis sit, miseros peccatores et aeternaliter perditos peccato originali omni genere calamitatis oppressos esse per legem decalogi, nisi Deus per euangelium dolorem dolori adderet, et etiam per euangelium nobis iustitiam et iram suam intentaret. Furebam ita saeva et perturbata conscientia, pulsabam tamen importunus eo loco Paulum, ardentissime sitiens scire, quid S. Paulus vellet.

Donec miserente Deo meditabundus dies et noctes connexionem verborum attenderem, nempe: Iustitia Dei revelatur in illo, sicut scriptum est: Iustus ex fide vivit, ibi iustitiam Dei coepi intelligere eam, qua iustus dono Dei vivit, nempe ex fide, et esse hanc sententiam, revelari per euangelium iustitiam Dei, scilicet passivam, qua nos Deus misericors iustificat per fidem, sicut scriptum est: Iustus ex fide vivit. Hic me prorsus renatum esse sensi, et apertis portis in ipsam paradisum intrasse. Ibi continuo alia mihi facies totius scripturae apparuit. Discurrebam deinde per scripturas, ut habebat memoria, et colligebam etiam in aliis vocabulis analogiam, ut opus Dei, id est, quod operatur in nobis Deus, virtus Dei, qua nos potentes facit, sapientia Dei, qua nos sapientes facit, fortitudo Dei, salus Dei, gloria Dei.

Iam quanto odio vocabulum "iustitia Dei" oderam ante, tanto amore dulcissimum mihi vocabulum extollebam, ita mihi iste locus Pauli fuit vere porta paradisi.'

Emanuel Hirsch, in his *Hilfsbuch zum Studium der Dogmatik*, offered some grammatical explanations for this piece of self-interpretation by Luther: 'In the terminology which Luther received and used, the active meaning of the genitive is called *gen. sub [iectivus]* and *poss[essivus]*. The passive meaning is called the *gen. obi[ectivus]* and *auctoris*. The classification of *iustitia dei* under this terminology . . . presupposes a peculiar observation about the Hebrew construct state which expands the terminology. Compare the following from *The Bondage of the Will* (On Rom. 3:23: "they lack the glory of God" = Lat. *egent gloria dei*). One could take "gloria dei" here in two ways: active and passive. This comes from the fact that Paul frequently uses hebraisms. The glory with which he is glorified in us is active (*qua ipse in nobis gloriatur*). The glory (*Ruhm*) with which we are glorified in him is passive (*qua nos in deo gloriamur*). [Perhaps we do better to translate it differently from Hirsch: *Gloria dei* is active – the glory (*Herrlichkeit*) with which God glorifies himself in us. The glory with which we are glorified in God is passive.] However, it seems to me that it should be taken as a passive here. Just

meaning of the words *the righteousness of God*. Luther had originally come to understand the concept in the manner of the philosophers and lawyers, as active justice, *iustitia activa* (*distributiva*), by which God himself is just and distributes to each according to what he or she deserves (*qua deus ipse iustus est suum cuique tribuens*), as *the law* commands. This would mean, as we have shown, that salvation and life is granted by a just God to those people who do good; but to those who do evil, disaster and death. But since all are sinners (Rom. 3:9f.), *the righteousness of God* would then mean, in a concrete sense, that God is *just* in condemning everyone. So the righteousness of God would in reality be identical with the wrath of God (Rom. 1:18).

However, the context of Romans 1:17 tells against this interpretation of *the righteousness of God*. The context shows that God's righteousness 'is revealed through faith for faith' and that life comes from faith, for 'the one who is righteous shall live by faith'. The phrase 'by faith' is obviously an essential addition for the understanding of *the righteousness of God*. But *where* does faith come from? From the preaching of the gospel

---

as *fides Christi* in Latin is "the faith, which Christ has", but is understood by the Hebrews as "the faith which is had in Christ", so also *iustitia dei* is that righteousness which God has, but which is understood by the Hebrews to be that faith which is had from God and before God' (E. Hirsch, *Hilfsbuch zum Studium der Dogmatik*, 4th edn, 1964, 130. Cf. M. Luther, *The Bondage of the Will, LW* 33, 265: 'You can take "the glory of God" here in two senses, active and passive. This is an example of Paul's habit of using Hebraisms. Actively, the glory of God is that by which God glories in us; passively, it is that by which we glory in God. It seems to me, however, that it ought to be taken passively here – like "the faith of Christ", which suggests in Latin the faith that Christ has, but to the Hebrew mind means the faith we have in Christ. Similarly, "the righteousness of God" in Latin means the righteousness that God possesses, but a Hebrew would understand it as the righteousness that we have from God and in the sight of God'. = *De servo arbitrio*, 1525, WA 18, 768, 36–769, 2: 'Gloriam Dei hic possis bifariam accipere, active et passive. Hoc facit Paulus suis Ebraismis, quibus crebro utitur. Active gloria Dei est, qua ipse in nobis gloriatur, passive, quo nos in Deo gloriamur. Mihi tamen passive accipi debere nunc videtur, ut fides Christi latine sonat, quam Christus habet, sed Ebraeis fides Christi intelligitur, quae in Christum habetur. Sic iustitia Dei latine dicitur, quam Deus habet, sed Ebraeis intelligitur, quae ex Deo et coram Deo habetur.')

(Rom. 10:17). So in order to understand the righteousness of God in Paul it is vital that it be revealed in the gospel which brings about faith, according to Romans 1:17, and not in the law. Luther's discovery was that the concept of *righteousness*, as seen in its context in Romans 1:17, gains a new meaning over against the philosophical and legal meaning. How a word is used is what determines its meaning. And the New Testament use of language concepts is, according to Luther's insight, basically determined by the fact that they refer to Jesus Christ. It is not only the creation that Christ renews (2 Cor. 5:17), but he also gives vocabulary a new meaning.[42] In the case of the righteousness of God the new meaning of the expression is seen in the additions which Paul makes to it: 'apart from law' (Rom. 3:21), 'by faith apart from works prescribed by the law' (Rom. 3:28), 'through faith' (Rom. 3:22), 'by faith' (Rom. 1:17).

Luther's original experience at the Reformation therefore consisted in the discovery that God's righteousness is *not* legal righteousness, according to which God gives to each what is due, but is the righteousness that gains a new meaning from the relation between gospel and faith. If the gospel is the word that God speaks *in favour of* human beings, if the gospel is thus not only an informative address, but *creative words of encouragement*, then the righteousness of God which is revealed in the *gospel*, as opposed to *legal* righteousness which gives each what he deserves, must mean that unrighteous human beings *are pronounced righteous* by God. The *righteousness of God* will then be that righteousness by which God makes righteous people out of the ungodly. That, then, is Luther's rediscovery of Paul's gospel of the justification of the ungodly.

So far, so good. However, the conclusion has been made from this understanding of the righteousness of God, by which God makes righteous people out of the ungodly, that the righteousness of God is meant exclusively as a gift, which then characterizes the giver in his essence as compassionate and kind,

---

[42] Cf. M. Luther, *Disputatio de divinitate et humanitate Christi*, 1540, WA 39/II, 94, 17f.: 'omnia vocabula in Christo novam significationem accipere'.

but not as *righteous*. The righteousness of God as a *gift* of God is then played off against God's own *being* righteous. A more modern way of putting it is to say that the argument is whether God's righteousness is only God's gift or only God's power or both of these.[43] But the expressions 'gift' and 'power' are not appropriate. When we talk of righteousness we are always talking of a relational concept, a fact which both expressions easily overlook. To that extent the older ways of framing the question 'God's being righteous' or 'being declared righteous by God' or 'being made righteous by God' are more appropriate. But the *simple opposition* of terms used by such language also misses the Pauline sense of the expression 'righteousness of God'.

Luther's 'pre-Reformation' conception of God's righteousness as distributive or formal or active justice (*iustitia formalis seu activa*) was, of course, mistaken. But setting up the *justifying* sense of righteousness in an absolute way *over against* God's being righteous (however that may be understood) threatens equally to miss Paul's usage of the term. Luther himself knew this. Augustine and later Melanchthon were the ones who took this one-sided view of the question, no doubt causing Luther in his autobiographical retrospect to make the *critical* assessment that Augustine had expressed himself imperfectly and had not given a clear explanation of justification.[44]

Augustine had explicitly taken the idea of God *making* or *declaring* the sinner righteous as the opposite to God's *being* righteous. On a number of occasions he observes that 'the righteousness of God' is to be understood not as 'that by which God is righteous', but as 'that wherewith he clothes man, when he justifies the ungodly';[45] 'the righteousness of God' is then 'not that by which he is righteous but that by which we are

---

[43] Cf. Käsemann, *Romans*, 28: 'Paul himself permits us to reconcile the apparent contradiction, for power and gift are not true antitheses in his eyes.'

[44] Cf. Luther, *Vorrede zu Band 1 der Opera Latina*, 1545, WA 54, 186, 18f.

[45] *Augustine: Later Works* (Library of Christian Classics, vol. 8), trans. and intro. by J. Burnaby, London: SCM Press, 1955, 205 = A. Augustinus, *De Spiritu et Littera*, c.9, *PL* 44, 209: 'Justitia Dei, non qua Deus justus est, sed qua induit hominem.'

made so by him';[46] 'the righteousness of God' is then 'not . . .
that whereby the Lord is righteous, but whereby He justifieth
those whom of ungodly He maketh righteous'.[47] This does get
to the point of Paul's teaching on the righteousness of God.
However, one of the relative weaknesses in this basically accurate
exposition is that it makes a separation between God's *action* in
making righteous and the fact that he *is* righteous. The doctrine
of justification would then have no meaning for the concept of
God; it would be hermeneutically irrelevant to the understanding of the being of God. On the other hand, Karl Holl was
correct in issuing the challenge that we pursue 'God's action in
justification to the very depths of the thought of God'.[48]

6. God is righteous because of the fact that he makes us righteous

We shall be doing precisely that if we firmly hold to the fact
that God's righteousness is not simply his own *preserve*, but his
own righteousness, and *as* his own righteousness it *reaches others*.
Over against the 'legal' understanding of this urge towards
universal justice we have now achieved a *gospel* understanding
of the righteousness of God which allows us to state the
proposition: 'God *is* righteous because of the fact that he *declares*
or *makes* [unrighteous people] righteous.'[49] In Romans 3:24–
26, Paul makes it clear that God's justifying act also implies that
God is righteous. Here Paul accepts the traditional view of the
righteousness of God in the sense of a subjective genitive. He

---

[46] *Augustine: Later Works*, 219 = A. Augustinus, *De Spiritu et Littera*, c.18, *PL* 44, 220:
'Justitia Dei, non qua ipse justus est, sed qua nos ab eo [iusti] facti.'

[47] *Sermons on Selected Lessons of the New Testament by S. Augustine*, vol. 2, Oxford: J. H.
Parker, 1845, p. 591 = A. Augustinus, *Sermo* 131, c.9, *PL* 38, 733: 'Justitia Dei, non
qua justus est Dominus, sed qua iustificat eos quos ex impiis iustos facit.'

[48] K. Holl, 'Die iustitia dei in der vorlutherischen Bibelauslegung des Abendlandes',
in idem, *Gesammelte Aufsätze zur Kirchengeschichte*, vol. 3: *Der Westen*, 1928, 171–88,
187.

[49] Cf. E. Jüngel, *Paulus und Jesus. Eine Untersuchung zur Präzisierung der Frage nach
dem Ursprung der Christologie* (*HUTh* 2), 6th edn, 1986, 44–7; H. Conzelmann,
'Die Rechtfertigungslehre des Paulus: Theologie als Anthropologie?' in idem,
Theologie als Schriftauslegung. Aufsätze zum Neuen Testament (*BEvTh* 65), 1974, 191–
206, 198.

says that God has shown his righteousness now – at a time marked by the death of Jesus – 'to prove . . . that he himself is righteous and that he justifies the one who has faith in Jesus'. The word *and* 'has almost an explicative sense'.[50] God's own being righteous shows itself in the fact that he makes (the one who believes on Jesus) righteous. What Paul means by the expression 'God's righteousness' cannot be demonstrated more clearly than in this double statement.

It is now clear that the righteousness of God is to be taken as a *genitivus auctoris* in such a way that the *genitivus subiectivus*, which is always presupposed, is maintained intact as a deeper dimension of the *genitivus auctoris* and is reinterpreted. The *Gospel* understanding of the righteousness of God in the sense of a *genitivus auctoris* gives a new meaning to what Paul found and consciously used – that the phrase means God's being righteous (the *genitivus subiectivus*). This new meaning is in turn indispensable for the deeper dimension of the *genitivus auctoris*. And the new meaning is that God is *just*, but not in the sense of distributive justice, which gives to each what he or she deserves. No, God is *just* because he practises *grace*. Grace and justice are for God not so separate that *grace* should be enacted *before right*. Rather, God accomplishes his justice in the very fact of practising grace. As a *gracious* God, who also remains *a faithful covenant partner* to ungodly human beings, God *acts in keeping with himself*, is faithful to himself, is *just* in himself and behaves rightly towards the ones he has created. So that very faith in God's grace 'refer[s] consistently to God's righteousness'.[51] For 'God . . . in His grace is in the *right*'.[52] Such is the sense of the unity of being righteous and making the sinner righteous to be found in the concept 'God's righteousness'. It is the task of

[50] Käsemann, *Romans*, 101.

[51] Barth, *CD* II/1, 384. Here, with the Reformers, Barth has taken the view that the righteousness of God is a refinement of the discussion of God's compassion and grace. However, it is unfortunate that he has then also tried to re-emphasize the factor of *iustitia distributiva*, so that God's pardoning righteousness is seen additionally as a judging and punishing justice (*CD* II/1, 390–406). In Barth's doctrine of reconciliation he argues differently.

[52] *CD* IV/1, 530.

systematic interpretation to make this clear, to give *significance* to the words 'God *is* righteous because of the fact that he *calls* us righteous'.

7. God's righteousness and our righteousness

It is worth mentioning that we are picking up a formulation used by *Luther*. He proposed that God's *being* righteous should be viewed in a new way because of the *newly* discovered sense of 'God's righteousness' as a righteousness by which God *makes* us righteous. In his *Operationes in Psalmos*, expounding Psalm 5:8 ('Lead me, O Lord, in your righteousness because of my enemies') Luther explains: 'We must become accustomed to seeing "God's righteousness" . . . according to the true canonical meaning: not as that through which God himself is righteous and condemns the ungodly, as it is normally taken to be, but – as St Augustine says in *De spiritu et littera* – as that with which he clothes man, when he makes him righteous [or: justifies him (Tr)] – that means, as compassion or justifying grace itself, through which we are declared righteous before God . . . However, it is called *God's and our* righteousness because it is given to us through his grace . . . Although it is not to be rejected in every respect that "God's righteousness" is also, in the [new] expression already mentioned, that righteousness by which God himself is righteous, so that through *one and the same* righteousness God and we may be righteous – just as God through *one and the same* word creates and we are what he himself is, so that we may be in him and his being may be our being'. Of course, Luther then adds: 'But those are higher things than the verse [Ps. 5:8] can now bear, and it is meant in a different sense from that of the scholastics. And although these are useful and necessary things, they are nevertheless to be said at another time.'[53] But for our part we cannot continue to postpone our

---

[53] M. Luther, *Operationes in Psalmos*, 1519–21, WA 5, 144, 1–23. '"Iustitia dei" . . . Oportet, ut assuescamus vere canonica significatione intelligere, non eam, qua deus iustus est ipse, qua et impios damnat, ut vulgatissime accipitur. Sed, ut B. Augustinus de spiritu et litera dicit, qua induit hominem, dum eum iustificat: Ipsam scilicet misericordiam seu gratiam iustificantem, qua apud deum iusti

exegesis of this matter any longer. We need to take the plunge now.

III. The righteousness of God is shown in the person of Jesus Christ

1. *The righteousness of God in his humanity*

Our reflection on the way Paul speaks of the righteousness of God has made it clear that such righteousness does not exist unless it also communicates itself to people and that it simultaneously characterizes God as righteous. Thus it is true to say that God is faithful to himself, that he acts in keeping with himself when he justifies the ungodly, the sinner, the unrighteous. God *forfeits* nothing by *forgiving* us.

It follows, then, that the doctrine of justification sees God *as being utterly consistent with himself* and therefore *righteous*, when it conceives of him as the *justifying* God who *justifies* not the righteous, but the unrighteous, not the pious, but the ungodly. What appears at first to be a contradiction must be seen as absolutely free of contradiction on the basis of God's being God. This is only possible if we decide on what a righteous God is like, *not* on the basis of the normal use of the concepts, but only on the basis of his justifying the ungodly. As we have said, 'God's righteousness' is the title of an *event*, something that happens. And in this very event God is totally *consistent* with himself. He is consistent when he *gives himself* to the other and fundamentally affirms that other's otherness.

When God justifies, this means that God is righteous in his contact with the sinner. That is to say, he is faithful to himself in his grace; he affirms himself in his identifying with one who

---

reputamur . . . Vocatur autem iustitia dei et nostra, quod illius gratia nobis donata sit . . . quanquam non sit penitus reiiciendum, iustitiam dei etiam tropo iam dicto esse iustitiam, qua deus iustus est, ut eadem iustitia Deus et nos iusti simus, sicut eodem verbo deus facit et nos sumus, quod ipse est, ut in ipso simus, et suum esse nostrum esse sit. Sed haec sublimiora quam locus nunc patiatur, et alio sensu dicta quam illi sentiunt. Etsi utilia et necessaria, pro alio tamen tempore dicenda.'

was accursed for the unrighteousness of all people (Gal. 3:13); so he is the divine God in his very humanity, which is manifested in the crucified man Jesus. The event of God's justifying the ungodly teaches us to recognize his divinity in the act of selfless self-commitment by God. The New Testament calls this selfless commitment by God *love* – and in particular – love directed towards *people*. In this selfless commitment, that is, in his *love* to people, God is righteous, he is 'OK', he is consistent with himself. God's humanity is the clearest *expression* of his divinity, not a *contradiction* of it (otherwise, talking of God's humanity would be a paradox). God does not contradict himself when he is human. Rather, he is consistent with himself when he justifies the ungodly. So, when all is said and done, the subject of the doctrine of justification is the human God.

2. *The being of Jesus Christ is where God's self-consistency is shown*

However, we could never have spoken of the *concrete event* of God's righteousness if we did not *clearly name* the facts we have described. This is the righteousness of God: that God is the eternal and almighty *Father* and is *at the same time* the *Son* who came as a man in poverty into the world, perishing in and by the world, that is, *Jesus Christ*, crucified in weakness (2 Cor. 13:4). God is righteous in the lack of internal contradiction in this extreme tension between the almighty Father – the origin of all life and being – and the Son who suffered death. This is where the *foundations* lie for the fact that the ungodly are justified. Justification is inconceivable without God taking on himself the results of human ungodliness and in that very way remaining God. Only in his identification with the *crucified Christ, made ungodly* in his accursed death, is God's righteousness so evident that human beings, though they make themselves ungodly, can become righteous (that is, people *suitable for* God). So these two things are true in Jesus Christ: in him God *is* righteous and in him we *become* righteous. In Jesus Christ crucified, God is *consistent with, in concord with himself* by the fact that he himself brings people who are in con*flict* with him into being in con*cord* with him. In Jesus Christ, God's being and our becoming coincide.

So, again drawing on tradition, Paul also called Jesus Christ the one who 'became for us wisdom from God, and *righteousness* and sanctification and redemption' (1 Cor. 1:30). In 2 Corinthians 5:21 the statement about Jesus is even clearer: 'For our sake he made him to be sin who knew no sin, so that in him we might become the righteousness of God.' Only in Jesus – the true God and true Man, who suffered the final consequence of our sins and ungodliness – does the righteousness of God become an *event* to such a degree that, as Luther said, 'through one and the same righteousness both God and we are righteous: *ut eadem iustitia Deus et nos iusti simus*'.[54] Joined with God by one and the same righteousness! If we become 'the righteousness of God' in Christ, then we can expect the most heightened form of fellowship. The ultimate, the real meaning of the justification event is to create this fellowship. In justification, God so appears before the ungodly world that the world can appear *before God* and allow itself to be seen by God. This means that ungodly human beings can exist and stand before God.

Thus the biblical expression 'God's righteousness' speaks of an event on the basis of which ungodly humanity can live together with God. This presupposes God's *coming*, with his righteousness, *into* the context, the *real life* context, of human beings – in Jesus Christ. The justifying God is the God who is equally God the Father in heaven and God the Son on earth. God's righteousness brings him down from heaven to the side of ungodly people: the God from the hereafter appears in the midst of this world. But he appears here in such a way that the real life context of the world is redefined in the power of God the Holy Spirit.

This occurs by God's righteousness fundamentally interrupting the real life context of the world by the cross of Jesus, and by its continuing to interrupt it over and over by 'the

---

[54] Cf. above, note 53.

message about the cross'. The interruption is at so fundamental a level that the ungodliness of the world is condemned to and caused to die. The justification of the ungodly is anything but the justification of what exists, and certainly not the justification of existing ungodliness. Rather, it means the removal of all that. It is the most far-reaching attack imaginable on the real life context of an ungodly world. We have not understood our justification until we see it as a fundamental interruption of our own life context and see Jesus Christ as being this fundamental interruption. We must see this interruption as having the goal of making ungodly people into those in *concord* with God.

In this context we need to return to the truth claim of the gospel. Justification is the truth of life, an interruption for the sake of a concord which comes out of that justification. Truth in the context of our reality and life always first appears at a crisis, an interruption, a judgement. For truth, when it occurs, does so in a context of lies, in a context determined by a sham existence. In the justification event, the issue is truth, which shows God as *true*[55] and everyone a liar: 'although everyone is a liar, let God be proved true'. However, justification consists in the fact that 'through my falsehood God's truthfulness abounds to his glory' (Rom. 3:4, 7). And this can only happen by the sham existence, the lying life context, being interrupted and so destroyed. Truth, in the context of the doctrine of justification and the Christology which bears it, is an eschatological interruption of unmatched proportions. Yet in this it brings healing. It interrupts in order to heal. And it heals by making possible and introducing an unbreakable fellowship with God: 'therefore, since we are justified . . . we have peace with God' (Rom. 5:1).

---

[55] Reformation theology, too, stresses that the issue in the relationship to God is *truth*: 'The very highest worship of God is this, that we ascribe to him truthfulness, righteousness, and whatever else should be ascribed to one who is trusted' (Luther, *The Freedom of a Christian*, *LW* 31, 350). But to ascribe truth to God has the immediate corollary that we are affirming him as the God who makes us true.

3. The justification event in the being of the triune God

We have called God's righteousness an event and given this event a name: Jesus Christ. This person joins heaven and earth, the Godhead and humanity. But he joins humanity with the Godhead in such a way that we must make some basic distinctions: within the humanness of humanity, the distinction between sinner and righteous; within the Godhood of God the quite differently based distinction between Father, Son and Holy Spirit. This trinitarian differentiation of God's Godness is in a manner of speaking the theological (one could also say: the ontological) backbone of the justification event. And it 'cannot be strongly enough emphasized that without the early church's doctrine of the Trinity and Christology, the whole Reformation teaching of justification and atonement is left up in the air and loses all meaning'.[56] Thus we cannot avoid following the challenge of Karl Holl, mentioned above, that we pursue 'God's action in justification to the very depths of the thought of God'.[57] This is best done, in the ecumenical respect as well, by giving an account of the meaning of the trinitarian self-differentiation of God as Father, Son and Holy Spirit in the context of discussing God's righteousness.

We have already explained that righteousness advances life's relational riches. If we say of God himself that he is righteous, this has the meaning for Christian faith that God affirms and favours the relational riches of life, not primarily in relation to his creation, but in his relation to himself. However, according to the confession of the Christian faith, God exists in relation to himself in such a way that he exists as Father, Son and Holy Spirit. He so relates to himself in this threefold personal existence that Father, Son and Holy Spirit mutually affirm each other in their respective *otherness*. When we talk of God's righteousness this is the decisive point of view: that God is not a

---

[56] F. Lieb, 'Orthodoxie und Protestantismus', in idem, *Sophia und Historie. Aufsätze zur östlichen und westlichen Geistes- und Theologiegeschichte*, M. Rohrkrämer, ed., 1962, 41–54, 47.

[57] Cf. above, note 48.

lone being, but that in God himself, *otherness* has been and is being affirmed: not the otherness of three different beings, but the otherness of distinct ways of being or persons of one and the same being. In this sense a very early confession (the so-called *Fides Damasi*)[58] explains that God is not a single being in himself, not *solitary (solitarium)*. Rather, he exists *in one person* as the Father, *in another person* as the Son and *in another person* as the Holy Spirit: *alius, alius, alius*[59] – and yet he is never a different *thing*, an *aliud*.

The Father, the Son and the Spirit affirm each other in their mutual personal otherness and so form the most intimate fellowship; the trinitarian fellowship of mutual otherness. Consider the following: The heavenly Father is the Other to the Son who became man, in that he, the eternal Source and Creator of life, sends the Son into the world of sinners and there, in the depths marked by transitoriness and death, affirms him as his beloved Son (Mark 1:11). And as far as the Father is concerned, the Son is the Other, as he obediently resigns himself to this mission and thus affirms the Father: he is obedient to the point of death on the cross (Phil. 2:8). The personal otherness of Father and Son implies nothing less than the contrast between life and death. It is scarcely possible to imagine a mutual otherness which is more extreme. And yet instead of a destructive result with one annihilating or being conformed to the other – which would be to pervert the *alius, alius, alius* into an *aliud, aliud, aliud* – they are creatively linked by the power of the Holy Spirit into a fellowship of mutual otherness. Thus God is in agreement with himself, not excluding the otherness from himself but affirming it in himself. Thus is he righteous. This is, as we have demonstrated, the centre or heart of God's righteousness: that God is in agreement with himself, that God is 'just in himself', that in the midst of such an enormous difference between Father, Son and Holy Spirit, God is in utmost *concord* with himself. 'This harmony with Himself is the

---

[58] *The Fides Damasi, ND*, 10 = *DH*, 71f.
[59] Cf. Gregory of Nazianzus, *Letter to Cledonius* I, 20f., *PG* 37, 180 AB.

right of God.' And this right of God, grounded in the being of God, 'is the backbone of the event of justification. . . He is just in Himself'.[60] He is in *concord* with himself even where we can only detect *discord*. And it is a part of believing in the triune God, despite the contradictions which attack human beings, or rather in the midst of them, to praise God as the one who does not contradict, but is consistent with himself. To confess the triune God *in excelsis* includes believing that the same God is also present *in profundis*.

Only on this basis can we understand the crucial declaration of the good news of justification: that God pronounces and makes the sinner righteous by grace alone. The good news does not say that God enacts grace before right.[61] Nowhere does the Bible, in speaking of God's grace or compassion, mention such a thing. If God is already *righteous* because he affirms *otherness* within himself, and thus is in harmony and concord with himself, then he is also and even more *righteous* by *affirming* in addition the creature, which is, in contrast to him, *completely other*. Of course, God cannot be forced to affirm his creatures. He does so *out of grace*. However, he remains totally consistent with himself even *when he affirms the otherness of his creatures* and is thus *gracious* to his creatures. And in being gracious he is thoroughly *righteous*.

In this, then, God is the gracious God. This is his grace: That he does not wish to be there merely for himself, but also externalizes that fellowship of mutual otherness which, as the triune God, he *is*. He does this by creating an opposite number for himself and steadfastly remaining faithful to this, his creation. This very act of bringing into being such a creation demonstrates his grace as God. His choosing of Israel, and with Israel the choosing of 'all people' as his covenant partner is an even greater act of the grace by which God effects his righteousness. God's righteousness, by giving to the other his due and so leading to a fellowship of mutual otherness, shows

---

[60] Barth, *CD* IV/1, 530–1.
[61] See above, p. 76.

something of love, so that the ancient Roman motto: 'let justice reign, though the world perish' is completely impossible as a motto for the Christian faith.

So there can be no question of God's being righteous on the one hand when he *judges* sinners, but on the other hand of making some downward adjustments to his justice and righteousness when he graciously *justifies* the sinner by allowing mercy and enacting grace before justice. It is exactly the opposite. 'God does not need to yield His righteousness a single inch when He is merciful. As He is merciful, He is *righteous*.'[62] When he is being gracious, God is being just.

4. God's judgement as an act of grace

The judgement by which God accomplishes his righteousness is then also an act of grace. The church and theology have wrongly grown used to seeing judgement and grace as alternatives. We need to learn that in the very act of judging God shows himself to be gracious. Only an ungracious God would allow injustice to run its course. God would not be gracious if he were not the judge as well, for then world history would have the last word. Murderers would finally triumph over their victims. If there is justification for sinners, then it must come about through the grace of his judging, not by bypassing it.

This aspect is of considerable importance because it leads to the centre of the gospel of the justification of sinners. At its centre, the gospel is the message about the cross (1 Cor. 1:18). And the cross is a gallows. It speaks of death and destruction. If the gospel of the grace of God is identical with the message about the cross, then that means that God's righteousness makes no compromises with the unrighteousness of this world, but in the person of Jesus Christ has condemned it to destruction. For that very reason his death is the death of sinners. Together with him, who knew no sin (2 Cor. 5:21), we have been crucified

---

[62] Barth, *CD* II/1, 383.

(Gal. 2:20; Rom. 6:6) and have died (Rom. 6:8). That is one side of the New Testament claim that Christ died the death of the sinner for us, in our place. God's righteousness does not simply pass over the sin of the world; it wins through against unrighteousness. In the death of Jesus Christ, God's righteousness condemns the world to destruction. The Crucified One guarantees that unrighteousness will be banished from the world. Judgement is passed on the world at the cross. That is grace.

Yet – and this is the other side of the New Testament claim – this negative outcome of human injustice and guilt is positively oriented towards a new beginning. The righteousness of God is the epitome of a well-ordered system of relationships which God does not reserve for his own benefit in some fit of divine selfishness; no, he gives his people a part in it by making them partners in the covenant. The non-biblical concept of justice has as its main task the guarantee of equality among equals.[63] God's righteousness, on the other hand, communicates itself to those who are anything but God's equals. God's righteousness is no divine attribute reserved for God alone. It is one which he shares with others: God is righteous in that he makes others righteous.

The negative contrast to this is what the Bible calls *sin*: the urge to pursue one's own right at the expense of others and thus to make oneself into one's own neighbour. Justice regulates the rich network of relationships of persons existing with each other in their mutual otherness in such a way that all persons who are included in that network come into their rights without having to *take* them by force. The distinguishing mark of sinners on the other hand – those who are *unrighteous* before God – is

---

[63] This also applies to the modern theories of justice which take complete cognizance of the inequality of societal relationships between individuals, although with the proviso that there does exist an equality of citizens in regard to the fundamental freedoms. So, for example, John Rawls formulates as one of his two basic principles of justice: 'social and economic inequalities are to be arranged so that they are both (*a*) reasonably expected to be to everyone's advantage, and (*b*) attached to positions and offices open to all'. J. Rawls, *A Theory of Justice*, Oxford: Clarendon Press, 1972, 60.

that they think they must and can *take* their *rights*.[64] In doing so, they break out of the well-ordered system of relationships in which God has included them. And that is precisely how sinners destroy the good order of life and life itself. The sinful urge towards lack of relationships comes to an end in death. Sinners harvest what they have sown: the curse of reckless self-involvement, which is doomed to bring about more and more breakdowns in relationships and in the end to destroy the relationship of persons to themselves. Those who recklessly aim to be their own neighbour will not *find* themselves, but will *lose* out. Those who recklessly aim to *fulfil* themselves will *forfeit* themselves (Mark 8:35). This is the sinner's curse.

But the deepest secret of God's righteousness is that God has taken our curse upon himself. In the person of the crucified

---

[64] The diagnosis given by 'communitarian' social critics of the basic position of people in western liberal societies is not dissimilar. Against a liberal understanding of society they offer the objection that the members of liberal societies no longer believe in anything except perhaps in justice in the sense that they have certain rights on which they can insist at any time and anywhere. This situation is the result of a liberal conception of society which abandons a communal idea of the common good and limits the social convictions of the members of a society to a few basic freedoms. Thus, the 'communitarians' assert, the community spirit of the whole society dissipates and in a liberal society there is no growth of partial communities. In fact, connections between people and adherence to traditions and values deteriorate completely (cf. for example M. Sandel, *Liberalism and the Limits of Justice*, Cambridge: Cambridge University Press, 1982). Against this liberal view, communitarian social theorists propose an understanding which pre-supposes the individual as existing in relationships, institutions and social groupings. They also propose a view of social community which sees it as the premise and property of social dealings (cf. M. Walzer, *Spheres of Justice: A Defense of Pluralism and Equality*, New York: Basic Books (HarperCollins), 1983, 65: 'The signers [of the social contract] owe one another . . . mutual provision of all those things for the sake of which they have separated themselves from mankind as a whole and joined forces in a particular community. *Amour social* is one of those things . . . So the common life is simultaneously the prerequisite of provision and one of its products.') Justice consists here in the sense of a 'complex equality', whereby the life opportunities of the members of the society are distributed in the various spheres of social dealings via rules which have been worked out in common (cf. ibid., 3–30). Thus political participation and social commitment of the citizens in the various areas of distribution of goods and opportunities form a decisive precondition which blocks any dominance by one area of social power.

Christ he has exposed himself in our place to the fatal curse of relationlessness, and where life ends because of sin, has made a new beginning through his love. For love alone, God alone, who himself is love, can create new relationships and new life where everything was relationless and relationships were forever torn asunder. That is exactly what happened when God in Jesus Christ took our relationlessness, the deadly curse of sin, onto himself (affirming the otherness in himself) to accomplish his righteousness, the relational riches of his own life in us, so that new relationships, new ways of living, might emerge in us and we might become justified sinners. That is why 'for our sake [God] made him to be sin who knew no sin, so that in him we might become the righteousness of God' (2 Cor. 5:21).

Luther called this event a 'joyous exchange'. The expression is appropriate, but we must not forget that it is describing a change from death to life. The new beginning which becomes a reality in Jesus Christ is a beginning that can only be compared to a new birth or a resurrection from the dead. In him there is a genuine being born again, in him the new life, resurrected from the dead, really begins: 'The love of Christ compels us to decide that one has died for all; so all have died. And he died for all, that those who live might no longer live with no relationships, for themselves, but in relationship to him who died and was raised for them' (2 Cor. 5:14f. [altered by the author for emphasis (Tr)]).

4

THE UNTRUTH OF SIN

The gospel is the good news of salvation. The gospel in which God's righteousness is revealed is described by Paul as 'the power of God for salvation for everyone who has faith' (Rom. 1:16), so salvation is the goal and purpose, the *terminus ad quem* of the gospel. But the gospel also has a *terminus a quo*. It means salvation for the ungodly, the sinner. But if we are to speak of justification of sinners, we must explain what it is that the gospel saves *from*, when it promises and brings salvation. What is the sinners' sin? What makes human beings into sinners, into ungodly human beings? We must answer these questions if we are to understand the meaning of the article about justification of sinners.

First, we must ask how sin is recognized. Where and how can we get a bearing on human sin so that we can recognize it as sin? Then we will need to explain how everything that deserves to be called evil is present in a heightened form in the sin of human beings. From that it will emerge that simply to talk about evil in a moralizing way totally misses what it is all about. There is a close link here with this question: To what extent is sin the deeds that people do and to what extent is it a force that rules them? In all of that, the gospel is central, since the gospel is the word that *makes* people *true*, people who are tangled up in a sham existence. And because it does this, we will need to clarify what exactly is meant by saying that our sin is *untruth*, showing itself as *unbelief*.

I. Recognizing sin

In discussing the salvation of human beings and our world, it is scarcely possible to say too much about Good. It can hardly be praised enough: 'the whole world rejoices. The heavenly forces and the angelic powers join in too in the praise of your glory without end, saying: *Holy, holy, holy*'.[1] The *Praefatio paschalis*, like many other texts of the church, expresses the fact that there is nothing greater, better, more desirable in heaven or on earth than the salvation that God brings. There is no worldly or earthly existence that can be compared with salvation. 'Salvation is more than being. Salvation is fulfilment, the supreme, sufficient, definitive and indestructible fulfilment of being. Salvation is the perfect being which is not proper to created being as such but is still future. Created being as such needs salvation, but does not have it: it can only look forward to it. To that extent salvation is its *eschaton*.'[2]

Salvation (σωτηρία), as it is understood by Christians, means not only 'more than existence', not only surpassing earthly existence. If we were to be satisfied with seeing salvation as surpassing earthly existence, even 'eschatologically' surpassing it, we would only have touched the surface of what should be called salvation in the strict theological sense. Thomas Aquinas' famous assertion that 'Grace (does not cancel, but) perfects nature'[3] is right, but with qualifications. But if we are speaking of grace and salvation in the strict sense of the words, then we should not only think of the relationship between grace and nature, and not only of the relationship between salvation (*Heil*) and its opposite (*Unheil*). We should also – at the same time – be thinking about the relationship between grace and what is against nature (*Unnatur*), about the relationship between salvation and its opposite and about the relationship between

---

[1] A. Dold, *Sursum Corda. Hochgebete aus alten lateinischen Liturgien* (Wort und Antwort 9), 1954, No. 41, 104: 'totus in orbe terrarum mundus exsultat. Sed et supernae virtutes atque angelicae Potestates hymnum gloriae tuae concinunt sine fine dicentes: *Sanctus, sanctus, sanctus*'.

[2] Barth, *CD* IV/1, 8.

[3] Cf. Thomas Aquinas, *Summa Theologica (STh)*, II^a II^ae, q. 26 a. 9 (ET, vol. 2, p. 1301) with I, q. 1 a. 8 ad 2; cf. I, q. 62 a. 5 corpus and III, q. 69 a. 8: 'gratia (non tollit, sed) perficit naturam'. ET found in St Thomas Aquinas, *Summa Theologica*, literal trans. by Fathers of the English Dominican Province, 3 vols, New York: Benziger Brothers, 1947.

salvation and the corruption of existence. For to be saved is to be rescued. We are talking about the rescue of human nature from its perverted tendency towards what is against nature, the rescue of existence from its corruption, the rescue of existence from the threat of non-existence. Thus when we think of salvation we always need to think of the dramatic movement that frees us from a disastrous situation (*Unheil*) and moves us into a different realm of existence. In the Wisdom of Solomon we read 'there were some who . . . while living among sinners were taken up' (Wisd. 4:10ff.). And the apostle Paul can say that it is the goal of Christ's saving work 'to set us free from the present evil age, according to the will of our God and Father' (Gal. 1:4). The desperate question: 'Wretched man that I am! Who will rescue me from this body of death?' (Rom. 7:24) also fits in here, as does the final cry to God in the Lord's Prayer: 'Rescue us from the evil one [or: from evil]' (Matt. 6:13b).

Salvation is a rescuing from existence which can only be described in dramatic terms. It is a rescue from an existence which is obviously so completely incapable of and unfit for rescuing itself that it can only be rescued, be pulled out by another. Again, the extent of the misery of those who must be dragged to safety is so great, the threat from non-existence so powerful, that there is only one who can be the rescuer – the One who calls existence into being from nothing: God. In that sense, salvation is an event of the utmost dramatic significance which is accomplished by God: it is the rescue of our existence in the face of non-existence and catastrophe (*Unheil*). For that reason we cannot speak too highly of salvation, for in the idea of salvation are included the depths of that disaster that has been overcome.

But the expression *catastrophe* is too formal to adequately describe the depths from which we are rescued in salvation. We need more precise terms, more tangible definitions to sound the fathomless, bottomless depths of that conquered *catastrophe* that is included in the idea of salvation. The necessity of such precise terms will be immediately apparent when we relate the concept of salvation back to the Saviour, and thus reflect σωτηρία in the person of the σωτήρ. 'There is salvation in no one else' (Acts 4:12) than in the person of Jesus Christ. But salvation is in this person *only* because he has conquered *Unheil* by *dying* for us and for our world, by dying the death of a *cursed* person (Gal. 3:13). That is, he has taken the curse of being separated from God onto himself and has overcome it. Separation from God is to be seen as enmity with God. 'While we were enemies, we were reconciled to God through the death of his Son' (Rom. 5:10). The depths of catastrophe (*Unheil*) included in the concept of salvation (*Heil*) take their aspect of enmity with God from the person of the Saviour Jesus Christ, and this aspect has an *aggressive* character.

Theologians see the depths of this concept of *catastrophe*, this aggressive enmity between us and God which was conquered in the person of Jesus Christ, as *evil*. And when they speak of *sin*, theologians are thinking of this evil to which we have fallen prey with heart, mind and soul, with every part of our being. Sin and evil are thus concepts that must fundamentally be defined as *theological*. That means that they are concepts that emerge from our *relationship with God*.

This is true of both concepts: sin and evil. When we speak of our *catastrophe* we are referring to a *bipolar* context. On the one hand, it is the *activity* of humans as enemies of God – a *human behaviour* which is to be seen as evil, *sinful* behaviour. On the other hand, it is *evil*, both the evil which we *do* by our actions and behaviour, and the evil in whose *power* we *suffer*, powerless in the grip of a strange fainting fit. When we encounter salvation through the gospel, we are rescued from both of these, from *doing evil* and from *being in evil*, from *sin as deed* and *sin as power*. So we must discuss both of these: active sinning and the inactive being delivered into the power of sin, that is, the compulsion to sin. For this we shall need the two expressions *sin* and *evil*, without explaining their relationship to each other. Any explanation that is possible will emerge from the discussion.

To attempt to define evil and sin is a difficult undertaking. Even the question of how we can recognize evil and sin has this difficulty. Not everything that is experienced, judged and condemned as evil and bad is necessarily sin, or in the theological sense evil. Nevertheless, the theological concept of evil has to do with everything which really is evil and bad. But what *really* is evil and bad? The correct definition of how sin is to be approached and known (*ratio cognoscendi*) is vital for rightly deciding and relating between what are our negative experiences and what is sin. What, then, is the approach to the phenomena connected with the concept of evil and the concept of sin? Where and how does evil reveal itself as evil? Where and how does sin reveal itself as sin? What is the sinful aspect of sin? What makes evil into evil? Where and how do sin and evil become *identifiable* and *recognizable*?

1. The relationship to God as the basis for defining evil and sin

As sin and evil are emerging as themes within the doctrine of justification, the first thing which has been decided is that we must define the nature of sin and evil from the point of view of *relationship* to God.

Sin has its real place in the relationship to God. But sin tries to make even this place unrecognizable. Sin desires to be *something in itself, independent,* although, as will become clear, it *is* nothing less than this. Therefore sin tries to be *everywhere and nowhere* (and by doing that to caricature *God* in his *omnipresence,* which is, of course, not to be seen in that way at all). So sin tries to be placeless (ἄτοπος) and in so being to be *unidentifiable.* For that very reason we must *locate* sin, we must give it its true place. This place is the *relationship to God.* All theologians worthy of the name are agreed on this. As a representative of this 'cloud of witnesses' we may quote, along with Melanchthon and Augustine, the great Schleiermacher: 'If, then, it is our primary object to ascertain the characteristic element in the consciousness of sinfulness, we ought not, within the sphere of Christian piety, to look for it except in relationship to the God-consciousness, and accordingly the only course open to us is to

reckon everything as sin that has arrested the free development of the God-consciousness.'[4] Or, to use the language of
the Reformers on the same subject: Sin is the lack of fear of
God, of trust in God and is desire ranged against God.[5] Or, as
Augustine put it: Sin is a turning away from God, a *motus
aversionis a deo*.[6] The concept of sin and the corresponding
concept of evil are only considered by theology as relational
concepts, and more precisely as relational concepts which
express a negative relationship to God or the partial or total
negation of a relationship to God. Sin and evil are, so to speak,
the negation of a relationship between creature and Creator.
Sin and evil affect the creature's relationship to God in the
form of an aversion to relationships.

2. The identification of the sinner

As we have pinpointed sin as a theme within justification, we
have expressed, *secondly*, that sin and evil are primarily identified
for what they are in *God's Word*, and are primarily recognized *by
faith* as sin and evil. This is to make the negative claim that they
are not recognizable by themselves. In fact, they prefer to prevent
themselves being identified and recognized, so that they can
go on wreaking havoc, unidentified and unrecognized. According to Romans 7:11, but also in Genesis 3:1ff., sin dissimulates.
It seduces us by happening, even to a person, as if there were no
such thing as sin. And that is precisely why we must not only
locate, but also *identify* sin and evil. It is the Word of God that
identifies sin and evil for the very first time, by addressing the
sinner as sinner, and thereby addressing evil as evil: Adam, where
are you? This question says everything: the sinner is not in his
place; he has tried, in following sin, to make himself placeless
by hiding himself. But the Word of God *identifies* him in his

---

[4] Schleiermacher, *The Christian Faith*, 271.
[5] Cf. *CA* II, *BSLK* 53, 4–6: 'cum peccato, hoc est, sine metu Dei, sine fiducia erga
Deum et cum concupiscentia': 'That is to say, [they are] without fear of God, are
without trust in God, and are concupiscent' (*Book of Concord*, 29).
[6] Cf. Augustine, *De libero arbitrio* I, 16, 35. II, 20, 54, *CChr.SL* 29, 235.272f.

failed attempt to be placeless. The Word of God identifies sinner and sin.

There is wide agreement among theologians even about this. 'It is the nature of sin not to wish to be sin' was how Luther put it.[7] For that reason Luther says it is part of the task of true theology to magnify sin. 'Magnificare peccatum' is the sum and the goal of Paul's letter to the Romans.[8] For 'by faith alone we must believe that we are sinners'.[9] Although there are places where he can differ, Søren Kierkegaard agrees with Luther on this point: 'no man of himself and by himself can declare what sin is, precisely because he is in sin'. For Kierkegaard the claim that 'there must be a revelation from God to teach man what sin is'[10] is typical of Christian theology. For only God can discern the difference between human nature and its corruption. In the same sense Karl Barth explained: 'Access to the knowledge that he is a sinner is lacking to man because he is a sinner. We are presupposing agreement on this point. All serious theology has tried to win its knowledge of sin from the Word of God and to base it on that Word.'[11] The way in which the problem of evil and sin is handled by the doctrine of justification clearly expresses the fact that the Word of Truth is essential for the untruth of sin and evil to be exposed. What Heracleitus once said approvingly of nature (φύσις), is true of evil and sin, but true in a very evil sense: 'Nature likes to hide: κρύπτεσθαι φιλεῖ.'[12] It loves anonymity, even pseudonymity. For that reason

---

[7] M. Luther, *Die Promotionsdisputation von Theodor Fabricius und Stanislaus Rapagelanus*. 1544, *WA* 39/II, 276, 18: 'Natura peccati est non velle esse peccatum.'

[8] Idem, *Romans*, 1515/16, *LW* 25, 135.

[9] Ibid., 215: 'sola fide credendum est nos esse peccatores'. The *Formula of Concord* explains similarly that sin is such a deep injury to human nature that it 'may not be recognized by a rational process, but only from God's Word' (*BC*, 466).

[10] S. Kierkegaard, *The Sickness Unto Death: A Christian Psychological Exposition for Upbuilding and Awakening*, ed. and trans. H. V. Hong and E. H. Hong, Princeton: Princeton University Press, 1980, 95–6.

[11] Barth, *CD* IV/1, 360–1.

[12] Heracleitus, #23, in K. Freeman, *Ancilla*, 33.

we must have the Word of Truth in order to be able to name it by its true name and so identify it.

3. The gospel as a way of recognizing sin: on the correct distinction between law and gospel

In pinpointing sin as a theme within justification, there is a third factor to take into consideration. It is a factor, however, which does not enjoy a theological consensus: evil and sin *are not recognizable without the gospel.* This contradicts the impression that sin and evil are both identifiable and recognizable through a law – a law which makes the claim of being itself *independent of the gospel.* A law which does not differentiate between law and gospel confuses our understanding of sin and evil. Such a law too easily usurps the promise of the gospel and thus misses both the essence of being set free from sin and the essence of sin itself. For to those who follow such an understanding of the law it promises freedom from sin and a restoration of fellowship with God which was made problematic by sin. But in doing so, it risks a fairly crass distortion of the concepts of the true God and true fellowship. As one of these promises runs: 'The harsh shackles of the Law bind nought but the slave mentality which scorns them. With man's resistance disappears the god's majesty as well.'[13]

The opinion which is being negated here usually makes an adequate job of defining sin as a contradiction and resistance against the law. What appears plausible about this idea is that it identifies and tries to make recognizable sin (and with it, evil) through the very authority which sin and evil contradict and violate. It is clear that sin is recognizable from what it is pitting

---

[13] F. Schiller, 'Das Ideal und das Leben' in idem, *Sämtliche Werke*, vol. 1, 201–5, 204. [I have rendered Schiller in a prose translation to capture the sense appropriate to Jüngel's argument. An English version in verse was made by E. Bulwer Lytton under the title 'The Ideal and the Actual Life': 'Scorn not the Law – permit its iron band / The sense (it cannot chain the soul) to thrall. / Let man no more the will of Jove withstand, / And Jove the bolt lets fall!' in *The Poems and Ballads of Schiller*, London and New York: F. Warne, 1887, 256 (Tr).]

itself against. Sin does not appear as sin or evil as evil in itself, but only in the other, in the other who is attacked and wounded by it. If sin is to be recognized through the law, it is because it is defined as a violation of the law. The converse is also true: if sin is to be defined as a violation of the law, that is because it is claimed to be recognizable through the law. There is something plausible about the structure of this relationship between the definition of sin and the *ratio cognoscendi* of sin. We shall need to emphasize this structure, but this will need to be with the not unimportant clarification that sin is recognized much more distinctly by what is aligned against it than by what it is aiming at. And what is aligned against it condemns it effectively to destruction: the gospel and the gracious God who speaks and communicates himself through the gospel. It is the grace of God that enables us to identify and recognize sin as sin, and of course, evil as evil. It is God's overcoming grace which seizes and holds sin and evil in their anonymity and pseudonymity, in their restless evil (cf. the human tongue in James 3:8). This grace which is able to imprison sin finds its life-setting in the gospel. That is why it is only possible to identify sin – or rather to recognize sin in such a way that a clear definition is possible – through the gospel, that is, in the tension between law and gospel.

So we are not claiming that the definition of sin as a violation of the law is simply wrong. We are only making the claim that it does not go far enough and for that reason is dangerously abstract, despite its apparent concreteness. The fact that to define sin as a violation of the law is not simply wrong is shown by the biblical statement that 'everyone who commits sin is guilty of lawlessness; sin is lawlessness' (1 John 3:4). And the fact that the law has something to do with the recognition of sin is shown by Paul's claim (as long as it correctly interpreted) that 'through the law comes the knowledge of sin' (Rom. 3:20).

The Bible makes these and other statements about the con- nection – admittedly very dialectical – between law and sin. Linked with these statements, the definition of sin as a violation of the law (which is recognized through the law) and thus a turning away from or separation from God has won the day. There are two extremely important definitions by Augustine which recur over and over again in many variations, even sometimes with their significance totally played down. In his work *Contra Faustum*, Augustine gives this definition: 'Sin, then, is any transgression in deed, or word, or desire, of the eternal law.'[14] Together with this definition of sin is frequently found a second Augustinian definition which we have already mentioned. According to this definition, sin is a *motus aversionis a deo*, a movement away from God, and at the same time a *motus conversionis ad creaturas*, a movement of conversion towards the creatures. This double movement is then seen as being defective in itself, as a *motus defectivus*, or as a deprivation of the good, a *privatio boni*.[15] There is a place for calling evil a *privatio boni*. It is appropriate when *privatio boni* means not only the logical (partial) negation of good, but when it is ontologically and aggressively injured and dispossessed. Sin has the sense of *privatio boni* when it comes too close to the good and desires its non-existence, desires to harm it. In that sense to turn away from God has the simultaneous meaning of aggression against the Good, of an act of robbery.

[14] A. Augustinus, *Reply to Faustus the Manichaean, Early Church Fathers: Nicene and Post-Nicene Series 1*, ed. P. Schaff, Peabody: Hendrickson, 1995 (reprint), vol. 4, 283 = *Contra Faustum Manichaeum* XXII, 27, *PL* 42, 418: 'peccatum est, factum vel dictum vel concupitum aliquid contra aeternam legem'. But what is the 'eternal law'? The law, in so far as its understanding is not based on the gospel, can have many different names and aspects. It can be identified with God, to the extent that God is law. It can be seen as the epitome of the good order of all eternal and thus of all temporal truths. It can be understood as the embodiment of reason, as the embodiment of the rationality and necessity of all being. For if something has the character of law, then it is reasonable. However, it can also be seen as the embodiment of the demanding and commanding will of God, so that the eternal law says what must be. If, however, what exists is reasonable as such, if created nature as such has the character of law, then the eternal law can be seen as a natural law, as a natural right. It will tell human beings what is good and what reason requires of them, even if on occasion it requires the cancellation of the demanding and commanding will of God. What is 'the eternal law'?

[15] Cf. idem, *De libero arbitrio* I, 16, 35; II, 19, 53; II, 20, 54, *CChr.SL* 29, 235.272f.; idem, *Enchiridion ad Laurentium de fide et spe et caritate* III, 11, *CChr.SL* 46, 53, 34f.; idem, *Contra adversarium legis et prophetarum* I, 5, *CChr.SL* 49, 40, 150; idem, *De civitate Dei* XI, 22, *CChr.SL* 48, 341, 22f.

The definition of sin as 'a deed or word or desire against the eternal law' is deficient in not understanding and defining the eternal law itself from the standpoint of the gospel. When it fails to do this, when the concept of the eternal law is seen as self-evident or as interpreting itself, this definition remains ambiguous. The law only becomes unambiguous through the gospel. For the gospel excludes all demands. It is God's giving Word, his bestowing Word, his liberating Word. It is a Word which forms the *indicative* of a new being. Therefore it relegates the law to the category of *imperative*, of *demand*. Of course, the law, as God's Word, does not only make new demands, but it highlights the most universal demand in such a way that it simultaneously identifies us existentially *as those on whom a demand, a claim has been made*. It speaks in the imperative mood and thus always serves to *identify* those who are addressed.[16] The law can only convict us for violation of the law because it identifies us *as those on whom a demand, a claim has been made*. Not only does the law require, however, that we fulfil its demands, but also that we enjoy doing so. Only those who are happy to keep the law are really keeping it.[17] But in order to do that we must already be righteous, and if we are no longer

---

[16] This is why Kant also formulated the law of practical reason as a *categorical imperative*, which identifies me as the one of whom a demand is made: 'act in such and such a way! . . .'. Now, against this, we have a situation where the law's function (of identifying me as the one of whom a demand is made) is on the wane, but we have a society which, while overflowing with legal statutes, has fewer and fewer citizens who are aware of the law's requirements. So they feel able to demand even more.

[17] Luther says that the law desires 'to be kept with a happy, free, cheerful will' (M. Luther, *Adventspostille*, Evangelium am 3. Adventssonntag, 1522, WA 10/I, 2, 156, 27f.). Kant saw that Christianity had 'something about it which is *worthy of love* [his emphasis] . . . Christianity has the intention of furthering love out of concern for the observance of duty in general' ('The End of All Things' in *Religion and Rational Theology* (The Cambridge Edition of the Works of Immanuel Kant, vol. 6), trans. and ed. by A. W. Wood and G. di Giovanni, Cambridge: Cambridge University Press, 1996, 229–30. In addition to the great sense of duty which is evoked by the divine laws as preached by Christianity, comes 'love, as a free assumption of the will of another into one's maxims', which 'is an indispensable complement to the imperfection of human nature . . . For what one does not do with liking he does in such a niggardly fashion' (ibid., 230).

to be sinners, then we must already have been touched by the gospel.[18] But if sinners fulfil the law at all, they do so gnashing their teeth or because they see advantages in it for themselves.[19]

Thus the definition of sin as violation of the law is totally inadequate. It is, as has been said, not completely wrong. It has a *particula veri*, in fact more than just a *particula veri* on its side. But it is inadequate. This inadequacy is not of the kind that can be remedied by simply filling in a gap. A complete change of direction is needed, one which takes its point of departure firmly from the gospel that overcomes sin and evil, from the Word of God that graciously covers and at the same time reveals sin. It then must make good the *particula veri* that sin is a violation of the law. No one can dispute the fact that sin is taken captive when it is forgiven, or that evil is identified and recognized when it is overcome. Here we find ourselves on a solid foundation. This is the foundation that is laid by the gospel as the Word of Truth bringing salvation.[20] It is the Spirit of

---

[18] Even Kant says that human beings by nature can never completely manage to love the law: 'The highest goal of moral perfection of finite creatures, never completely attainable by human beings, is, however, the love of the Law' (Kant, *Religion Within the Boundaries of Mere Reason*, in ibid., 170).

[19] Cf. Luther, *Romans*, LW 25, 59, n. 10 ['but he who does not have this is active unwillingly and almost in fear or in a desire for his own convenience'].

[20] Lately there has been an objection raised to the theological decision to move forward from the firm foundation of the definition of sin. For example, C. Gestrich, in his careful but rather ponderous work, indicates that sin is also experienced without any encounter with the gospel, indeed that 'a person can *understand* sin' without '*recogniz*[*ing*] his own sin in particular' (*The Return of Splendor in the World*, trans. D. W. Bloesch, Grand Rapids: Eerdmans, 1997, 168). We may agree with this to the extent that the experiential dimension of sin is highlighted and the writer means that in this world we will always encounter evil, even evil which is clearly our own fault. More importantly, the evil which is only recognizable as sin when in relationship to God is never clearly distinguished from worldly wrong (cf. G. Ebeling, *Dogmatik des christlichen Glaubens*, vo. 3, 1993 (3rd edn), 203). The human ego normally encounters evil in its relationship with the world and with itself. However, it is not possible to recognize from such experiences that what is evil about evil is sin, and what it means in the theological sense to sin. Then there remains Gestrich's claim: 'How sin happens must be made comprehensible not only to believers' (loc. cit. [translation altered]), which is a completely ambiguous sentence. It is made powerless

Truth, in harmony with this Word, who, according to John 16:8f., convinces the world of its sin.

The identification and recognition of sin is possible where the Word of Truth makes sinners true and thereby convicts them as liars. It is my sin which is forgiven: my very own sin, which no other sinner can take from me, which I cannot delegate to any other sinner, even though that is exactly what all sinners hope to do – delegate their sin. What the apostle says applies to all people. All have sinned (Rom. 3:23). There is no one who is righteous, not even one (Rom. 3:10). Here the individual factor coincides with the universal. For this reason, too, no one can remove sin from another. I must be *condemned* as a sinner and be *destroyed* if my sin is to cease to be *my* sin. The gospel says that this is precisely what happened when he who knew no sin, for our sakes was made sin by God (2 Cor. 5:21). The one who witnessed to the truth witnessed to him as the Lamb of God who bears the sin of the world (John 1:29). In him, what sin is becomes recognizable. The gospel leads us to recognize sin as enmity against a gracious God, enmity which can only be conquered by God himself.

However, the gospel uses the law in order to identify the sinner – the law, which addresses and accuses the sinner as a sinner. While performing its *opus proprium* and setting sinners free from their sin, yet at the same time exposing sin as sin, the gospel hands sinners over to its *opus alienum*: the law, which identifies sinners as sinners. That is, it identifies me as the enemy of God's grace, an enemy who can only be conquered by that same grace. While the gospel, by conquering sin, at the same time makes possible its recognition, it is the function of the law – whether the written or the unwritten law (Rom. 2:15ff.) – to identify in person the sinner in such a way that each must confess: *mea culpa, mea maxima culpa*. But the law

---

because of its utter correctness. To put it in Gestrich's own terms, borrowed from Barth: 'sin is *initially* an ambiguous experience. However, *forgiveness* is immediately an unambiguous experience. It is an experience that interprets itself' (op. cit., 68).

can only do this to the extent that the gospel is doing its job. Without the gospel the law is powerless (Rom. 8:3–8). The gospel gives the law its ability to function properly, albeit in a limited fashion.

II. Sin: the epitome of evil

The reality of human beings and their world is plagued by evils, and no one would doubt this. It is fairly easy to reach agreement about this. The myth of Pandora's box is a classical expression of this agreement which has always existed about the evil nature of reality. A similar purpose is served by the myths of a lost golden age, or a lost paradise. Within this framework of broad agreement it is possible to argue whether this evil reality is totally brim full of evil or only more or less evil. Pessimism and optimism form only a relative contrast in this overall picture of agreement. The boundaries between these two attitudes of pessimism and optimism are somewhat fluid; in fact, one shades across into the other. We celebrate enthusiastically or are plunged into the depths of gloom. That seems to sum us up.

Theology is well-advised not to opt for either of these alternatives. It is only with great reservations that it can describe our reality as an *evil* one. On the one hand theologians are aware of the *auspicious origin* of creation by the will of a Creator who wishes good and only good for it. They know that God took pleasure in his handiwork, because it was good: 'God saw everything that he had made, and indeed, it was very good' (Gen. 1:31). On the other hand, they are aware of the fall of this creation and realize that it was an evil event which went beyond all other evil and which was the origin of all the evils of the actual world. Not that reality is *evil*, either more or less evil or totally evil, but the reality which was *good* when made by God is *evil*, has become evil and always proves itself to be so. That is the problem which confronts theology. To put it very plainly: the fact of evil, the fact that good became evil is the real object of theological hamartology.

1. The nature of evil

The first question theology has to deal with here is the *nature* of evil. What is there that is evil about evil?

(a) If the *ratio cognoscendi* of evil is the gospel, then the basis of the answer is that God has broken the power of evil. He has done this by precisely the divine act that evil so opposed and will continue to oppose as long as it can. This divine act is the love of God that brings about reconciliation, that promises and delivers salvation. It is an act of grace which expresses the good that God wishes and does. It also expresses the opposite: all that deserves to be called evil. Evil in the theological sense is simply that which contradicts the good that God wishes and does. But this good is simply what God in his gracious act sets in place, highlights or creates anew.

If, on our quest for an answer, we start with the theological concept of *good*, it becomes immediately clear that good and evil are decided by God's love and grace. These are the things that set good in place by overcoming evil. But to be more precise, what is it that is set in place and what does evil prove to be as it is being overcome?

(b) In God's loving act of grace there is set in place our existence as *people in covenant with God*, or, better, as people with whom God has joined himself in a covenant. For this implies the resurrection of Jesus Christ from the dead that is proclaimed in the gospel: God has for ever allied himself to us and has joined us to himself. That is what defines our creaturely existence: being joined in a covenant with God. What is being put in place then is our fellowship with God. Obviously, this is a good thing; we are not left to our own devices, but are intended to be with another, that is, with God. And that is especially good: the God with whom we are intended to be is there for us. He has made himself responsible for us.

This is the first, decisive point about good and evil: Good means *existence together*. Evidently, the Creator grants the same goodness and quality of communal existence to his creation

which characterizes his own existence. For, as has been shown,
God is no lone being existing in splendid isolation; he exists as
the triune God in the fellowship of mutual otherness. God's
existence is as Father, Son and Holy Spirit. God is good; the
divine existence is the epitome of good. The divine existence is
for ever and ever an existence together, a fellowship existence,
one which relates to others. That is why it is good. This is true
by analogy for the creation. Created existence is also togetherness, a fellowship existence, one which relates to others. And
that is the very reason that it is good. To that extent, and to that
extent only, can we claim with the scholastic theologians: 'every
being as such is good: *omne ens, inquantum ens, est bonum*'.[21] Of
course, this is with the proviso that existence in an ontological
sense has always had the original meaning of togetherness. This
is even more true of *living* existence. Life is only possible as life
together: both in the microbiological sphere and the personal.
So any assault on life together becomes deadly.

(c) However, even though we have defined existence as
togetherness, we have still not defined what is decisive, what is
good about Good in a sufficiently tangible manner. 'Together'
can be perverted. Togetherness also exists as pack hunting, as
the taking of an oath by one group against another. One type
of togetherness can set itself against another type, and by so
doing set itself against existence. Creature can exist together
with creature without God and even against God. Togetherness can take the form of Korah's gang which placed itself
above Yahweh's community (Num. 16:3) and 'gathered together
against the Lord' (Num. 16:11). Togetherness can have the
features of the ungodly pack who are set against God and his
people (Ps. 119:61). Obviously the important thing is with whom
we have our togetherness.

So now, from the biblical consensus, there is no doubt whatsoever that existence in an ontological sense always had the
original meaning of togetherness with God. That is, of course,

---

[21] Thomas Aquinas, *STh* I, q. 5 a. 3 corpus (ET, vol. 1, p. 25).

a good thing. And that is why God is the epitome of goodness: he affirms togetherness in the trinitarian fellowship of mutual otherness. In addition, as Creator, Reconciler and Redeemer, he wills, affirms, makes possible and brings about togetherness with the ones who are completely opposite to and different from him.

We can express this theological fact most concisely when we trace back all of the following to *the fundamental act of mutual affirmation*: (*a*) God's togetherness with God in the trinitarian fellowship of mutual otherness, and (*b*) the togetherness of the triune God with the creation which is completely opposite to and different from him and which was called into being by him at the very beginning, and (*c*) the togetherness of the creation with its Creator, leading to (*d*) the togetherness of the creation with the creation. God the Father, Son and Holy Spirit are the three divine persons of one divine being, who mutually affirm each other in their mutual otherness. The creation is affirmed by God as what is other than himself and is therefore called upon to affirm him as God and also to affirm all other creation. This affirmation is the act which constitutes existence as togetherness. 'Yes' is the first divine word of existence. 'In the beginning was the Yes. And the Yes was with God. And God was the Yes. This was with God in the beginning. All things came into being through it and nothing which came into being did so without it' (John 1:1–3).[22]

(d) From here on it is of the utmost importance to state that all non-divine existence owes its origin to this divine Yes alone. *God's Yes alone* is a creative Yes in a totally unrestricted sense. It is a Word which calls into existence out of non-existence. This is also true in a restricted sense for the *human* Yes, which is in its human fashion also a creative Word. However, it creates nothing from Nothingness. It calls nothing into existence *ex nihilo*. Thus the human Yes always affirms existence which has already been affirmed by God. It has connections

---

[22] The suggestion for this paraphrase was provided by my own teacher Ernst Fuchs.

and preconditions. Its fundamental precondition is God's own unrestrictedly creative Yes.

What this means for our life together with God is that our human affirmation of God can never under any circumstance have or obtain a function which is creative in regard to divine existence. Even in our Yes to God, we remain reliant upon God. Such dependence on God does not exclude human independence and freedom. Quite the contrary. Reliance on God and human independence and freedom grow comparably, but not reciprocally.[23] If we remain in our free and dependent Yes to God, but reliant on God, this view which the mystics had (but not only the mystics) is blasphemous: 'God cannot live a moment without me; if I am destroyed, He must needs give up the ghost.'[24]

If *what is good* is founded in God's Yes (in the Yes which the triune God from all eternity has been saying to himself in the fellowship of mutual otherness, which he however says to that which is other than himself, to the creation which originates in this Yes), it follows that existence as togetherness is *good*, because it owes itself to God's Yes and is in accord with it. *Evil* then begins with *the false Yes* which we say to God and thus to ourselves. The *false* Yes declares itself free from God's creative Yes by claiming to be creative in opposition to God, instead of affirming God in free thankfulness.

It must be noted that evil starts not with an *abstract No* to God, but with *a false Yes* to God. The real trouble in our relationship with God starts when, instead of being glad that

---

[23] Cf. K. Rahner, *Foundations of Christian Faith: An Introduction to the Idea of Christianity*, trans. W. V. Dych, London: Darton, Longman & Todd, 1978, 78–9.

[24] 'daß ohne mich Gott nicht ein Nun kan leben / Werd' ich zu nicht Er muß von Noth den Geist aufgeben' (Angelus Silesius [Johannes Scheffler], *Cherubinischer Wandersmann*, critical edition ed. by L. Gnädinger, 1984, 28 [I, 8. 'Gott lebt nicht ohne mich']). Luther's famous or infamous statement, that *fides* is the *creatrix divinitatis*, should not be confused with these witty lines. Luther says that faith is 'the creator of the Deity, not in the substance of God but in us': *fides est creatrix divinitatis, non in persona, sed in nobis* (M. Luther, *Lectures on Galatians*, 1531, *LW* 26, 227 = *WA* 40/I, 360.5f.). Faith brings God onto the scene with us by affirming that we have already been affirmed by God!

we are takers and receivers in regard to God, we claim to be *givers* in our own right. Those who give usually think they can make claims. So our giving to God turns into demanding. Cain's offering was the exact opposite of a thank-offering. It was a *gift* to God which was then asserted as a *claim*. This led to a breach in the relationship with God and with his brother Abel (cf. Gen. 4:3–10).[25] The *false Yes* gives birth to the *destructive No*.

(e) This false Yes, concealing a destructive No, starts to be seen as the origin of evil when we accuse it of *lying*. Then the *false* Yes has destructive power because it is an affirmation which is *contrary to the truth*. It also holds in itself a *destructive No* because it is *lying* as it says *Yes*. It is a *lie* to want to be a creator in comparison with God. It is a *lie* to want to appear as a giver in comparison with the Giver of all good and perfect gifts. The No to God starts with the lying Yes to God. So does sin. And so does the realization of evil. God's Yes is true, dependable in itself and the embodiment of what is true. Because it is a lying Yes, sin is a direct attack on truth.

In recognizing this, we have moved on into the central part of what must be noted in regard to evil and sin. We have recognized the nature, the vile nature, of sin and also what is evil about evil. As Gerhard Ebeling put it, echoing the best theological tradition: 'What is evil about evil is sin.'[26] We may put it more concretely: What is evil about evil is the untruth of sin. In its form as a lie, sin is the embodiment of evil. We need to explain this insight.

(f) Sin in its original form of a lie is the evil counterpart to the truth, which shows itself to be dependable. In its substance and nature sin is untruth. Because of this it really has no substance, nature or centre. It is in itself lacking any foundation or basis.[27] It should be seen as *what is simply unreliable,* in contrast to what is true, which is marked by its dependability. In its original form as untruth, as a lie, sin is that on which we may

[25] See above, pp. 8–11.
[26] G. Ebeling, *Dogmatik des christlichen Glaubens*, vol. 1, 3rd edn 1987, 294.
[27] Cf. Barth, *CD* III/3, 289–368; *CD* IV/3, 368–478.

never depend. It even lies when it quotes the truth (cf. Gen. 3:1; 3:4f.).

However, sin is not, so to speak, in and of itself that which is simply unreliable. As a lie, it is never something that exists for itself. It is never just there in and for itself. Because it is a lie, it falsifies what is true. Because it is a lie, it is never simply unreliable in itself. No, it is out *to make unreliable* what is dependable. By *being* untrue, it is *spreading* untruth. Lying, the untruth of sin, is above all aggressive. In contrast to faith, it does not say, *Yes, yes,* or *No, no* (Matt. 5:37; James 5:12), but *lyingly* says Yes and at the same time says an *evil* No. In doing that, it *spreads* untruth, makes reality unreliable and has the effect of being the great underminer. Its goal is not to *undermine beneficially*, which is occasionally very useful, but to *undermine detrimentally*. 'Did God say . . . ?' (Gen. 3:1) – it uses tactics like this to begin its attack on what is dependable and true.

There can be no community life, no being together in fellowship – and when all is said and done, no existence at all – when nothing is *dependable*. The truth is the basis and condition for any possible life as community. Any attack on truth is also an attack on life in fellowship and on what is good. The untruth of sin directs itself against God, his Spirit of Truth, and his Word of Truth. By doing that, it reveals itself as the most serious of problems not only for our fellowship with God, but also for any other form of life together, and finally for existence itself. For if God can no longer be depended on – and that is precisely what sin is whispering to us as it lurks at the door (Gen. 4:7) – what *can* be depended on? The attack on the God who is faithful and dependable in his truth carries over into fratricide and is shown again in this context as a lie. When God asks him where his murdered brother is, Cain the murderer replies: 'I don't know.' And to avoid receiving short shrift for the boldness of this lie, he adds cheekily: 'Am I my brother's keeper?' (Gen. 4:9). The untruth of sin undermines truth as well as the embodiment of truth: life together with God, with others, in fact the whole quality of existence as life in community. Even the sinful person can no longer agree with himself. As the untruth of sin takes hold of the sinner, that person is a self divided. The liar is by definition a person split to the roots.

In this sense we can start to use the definition of evil as a negation, a *privatio*, a στέρησις, even though this definition is often used in way which understates its force. Sin is fundamentally a negation of what is true, a *privatio veri*. It is an act of aggression against God's truth and dependability, and thus an attack on everything true and dependable. It approaches truth too closely, in order to destabilize it. It is thus a negation of the Good, a *privatio boni*, because, in its attack on the dependable, it acts against fellowship with God and every kind of dependable fellowship. *Because* it is a *privatio veri*, sin is *also* a *privatio boni*. It also approaches what is good too closely, in order to destabilize it. As it attacks and undermines, the untruth of sin is the enemy of God's creative, loving Yes, which forms the basis of all existence. By saying Yes in such an underhanded and unloving way, the untruth of sin is not creative, although it is admittedly quite inventive and productive in the art of *destruction*. By saying Yes deceitfully, the untruth of sin – the lie – is the primal act of destabilizing, destructive negation: the epitome of evil.

There is some sense, then, in personified evil's appearance in literature in the form of the Devil, as the primal act of negation personified. 'I am the Spirit that denies! / And rightly too; for all that doth begin / Should rightly to destruction run; / 'Twere better then that nothing were begun. / Thus everything that you call Sin, / Destruction – in a word, as Evil represent – / That is my own, real element.'[28] Is this mephistophelian self-irony? It is quite possible that Goethe meant it like that. Anyway, his words hit the nail on the head.

In the Gospel of John, which rightly does not allow the devil to appear as a fascinating figure into which the poet has slipped his Mephistopheles, the *diabolos* is called a murderer and liar from the beginning: 'and does not stand in the truth, because there is no truth in him' (John 8:44). From this text, then, it is

---

[28] J. W. von Goethe, *Faust* (Great Books of the Western World), trans. G. M. Priest, Chicago: Encyclopaedia Britannica, 1952, 33, lines 1338–44.

a good thing to emphasize the context of murder and untruth. Then the idea that murder is bad, but lying is in contrast rather harmless, becomes unacceptable. The Johannine devil is not a murderer on the one hand and a liar on the other, but he begins his murderous work by lying. In being untruth and in spreading untruth, he splits what should be together, the context of life, the life context of God and people together, of person and person, human beings and the world. And in doing that he splits the life of the one he possesses: the life context which forms a human being's self-relationship. If we put aside the concept of the devil, we can express it thus: the sinner's life becomes a *sham existence*.

2. Sin as a lie

Having established the fundamental piece of knowledge that the epitome of evil is sin in its basic form of the lie, we must briefly outline certain further issues which arise from this. These develop in various directions what is implicit in our knowledge of sin as untruth.

(a) First, untruth is nothing in and by itself. If sin appears as sin, or evil as evil, it becomes necessary to observe what the lie *is directed at*, or what is directed at the lie. Lying is directed first and foremost at the Word of Truth, the Word of God. And this is done by robbing God's Word of its explicitness. Instead of 'take and eat' it says 'first perform, then you eat'. The untruth of sin places the unconditional nature of the gospel under the condition of the law and thus makes the good news into a new morality. It makes God's explicit Word ambivalent and thereby prevents this Word from discovering *faith*. In all of this, sin makes God himself into a liar. For 'those who do not believe in God have made him a liar' (1 John 5:10). In its aggressive negation of what is true and good in every part, sin is only an antithesis, an evil antithesis. Like every lie, it lives off the truth it denies.

We shall take as being characteristic of this parasitic nature of sin the early church definition of evil as an 'existing thing' which is totally dependent.[29] (Here 'existing thing' is a term used with certain reservations.) When he denied that evil has existence among things, in a way Aristotle was also teaching that evil has no being of itself, that it is fundamentally an ἀνυπόστατον.[30] Evil takes its place where something else should have been: 'Evil takes its place where Good should and could have been.'[31] This discussion of the parasitic nature of evil and sin expresses vividly the fact that there are no ontologically definable modes of being peculiar to the untruth of sin. As we have said, it is in itself unreliable and therefore has no substance, essence, foundation or basis. For that reason it has no mode of being; it only has a borrowed or rather, a stolen existence. In itself the untruth of sin is simply nothingness.[32]

But what do we mean by *simply nothingness*? We shall need to take up the thought of *creatio ex nihilo* in order to understand how something can be *simply nothingness*.

Part of the presence of creaturely being is its existence between God as its Creator and the void, the Nothing, from which it was created. This ontological nearness of the creature to non-being helps us understand that there can occur an in-breaking of nothingness into God's good creation. We are following Thomas Aquinas, who ascribes darkness to the creature because it came from nothing.[33] Thus Aquinas' understanding of the

---

[29] Cf. The documents in W. Kern, in *Mysterium Salutis: Grundriß heilsgeschichtlicher Dogmatik*, J. Feiner and M. Löhrer, eds, vol. III/2, 1969, 561, n. 64.

[30] Cf. Aristotle, *Metaphysics IX*, 1051 a 17–19, in *Aristotle, Metaphysics I–IX* (Loeb Classics), trans. H. Tredennick, London: Heinemann, 1968 (1933).

[31] W. Mostert, 'Gott und das Böse. Bemerkungen zu einer vielschichtigen Frage', *ZThK* 77 (1980), 453–78, 465; this article contains further remarks useful for the present discussion.

[32] Cf. R. Bultmann, *The Gospel of John: A Commentary*, trans. G. R. Beasley-Murray, Oxford: Blackwell, 1971, 321 (on John 8:44): 'And just as ἀλήθεια . . .' refers 'to God's reality, in particular to God's reality as it unveils and reveals itself to man and so brings him to his authenticity, so too ψεῦδος here . . . refers to the will which is opposed to God, which indeed creates its deceitful reality only by such opposition; that is to say, it refers to nothingness, which in its revolt claims to be something and whose only being lies in this revolt.' In its nothingness the sin is in the fact that it wants to be something, by lying and deceit.

[33] Cf. Thomas Aquinas, *Quaestiones disputatae*, vol. I, *De Veritate*, q. 18 a. 2 ad 5: 'creatura est tenebra in quantum est ex nihilo'.

openness of our human will to evil is that it does not stem from the creation of the will *by God*, but from its creation *out of the void*: 'and yet the ability of the will to be directed to evil does not come from the fact of its being from God but from that of its being made out of nothing'.[34]

We shall take up this thought, but interpret the facts which it points to according to the knowledge we have gained so far. Thus the void, the Nothing, from which God created the world is not considered evil or even empty. The Nothing is nothing other than nothing. It has no merits and no demerits. It is quite simply meaningless. The void gains meaning only in the context of being. This is what gives the void its character of evil: the Nothing *which is called into being within the framework of creation* and dominates creation. It is the *possibility* of being annihilated which *threatens* existing things *within creation*. Only the void *which is called into being*, only the Nothing which is *called into being* over the created fellowship, only that determines the dreadful aspect of Non-existence. And this is exactly what sin does: it calls that void into being, and that is all.[35] That is what makes up all of its wretchedness as well as its perilous depths.

(b) The void, the emptiness of sin is made tangible in the form of a *disruption and destruction of the relationships* in which all togetherness takes place and without which existing things

---

[34] Ibid., q. 22 a. 6 ad 3; cf. Q. 24 a. 8 ad 4: 'quod voluntas sit flexibilis ad malum, non habet secundum quod est a Deo, sed secundum quod est de nihilo'.

[35] Thus we must at all costs avoid imitating Paul Tillich by defining existence as a self-alienation of creation, simply because it is seen as 'stand[ing] out of nothingness' (P. Tillich, *Systematic Theology*, vol. 2, Welwyn, Herts: James Nisbet, 1964 [1957], 22). Nor should we imitate Tillich's further assertion: 'There is a point in which creation and the Fall coincide' (ibid., 50). There is no way in which creation and the Fall coincide. Nor is there anything evil about existence standing out from nothingness (*ex nihilo*), since in itself the Nothing is not evil. Only the false, lying Yes to God as the origin of being, the untruth of sin, makes the Nothing evil and sin vain. It is vain and empty in the sense that it is nothing for itself and desires to annihilate the other on whom it exists as a parasite. It aims in its insecurity to make everything insecure. In its lack of substance it attacks the substance of the creation. In its emptiness it seeks to annihilate what has being. Since it is empty in itself, it must steal being from somewhere else in order to have any place in creation. And this sort of *privatio* is what is aimed at in the annihilation of beings that have been robbed.

cannot exist. It disrupts and destroys the fellowship between God and people, among people, between people and the world, and it splits the ego. As we have already noted, *to be* means to be in relationship. It is in relationships that God is what he is: Father, Son and Holy Spirit and also Creator, Reconciler and Redeemer. The creation is what it is in a complex network of relationships. Human beings are what they are in relationships: they exist in relationship to God, to the world and to themselves. The untruth of sin calls into question the dependability of all these relationships without which there can be neither existence nor co-existence. At the same time it calls good order into question, or to put it more accurately, it calls peace into question, the *shalom* of fellowship. We can define sin more exactly as a breaking away from the relational riches of existence, of *peace-full* existence. It is the urge towards relationlessness and dissociation. Having no relationships itself, and thus having no limits, sin pushes everything towards relationlessness. Thus, in the context of existence, it calls non-existence into existence over existence. For non-existence is the very expression of relationlessness. The urge towards relationlessness must end in death.

(c) Sin – untruth and lying – is the imitation, the mimic of what is true, dependable and good. This has already been highlighted when we called sin the lying Yes which after a fashion reproduces the creative Yes of God. Sin has no liking for and will not tolerate God's creative Yes. Sin wants to be creative itself. It does not want to receive the good that God gives. It wants to be the giver. Therein lies its arrogance, its *hubris*, its *superbia*. And in order to lend itself the appearance of being the creator and source of good, it imitates the Creator and Giver of all good and perfect gifts. By imitating it strives to be like God. Other fundamental attributes of sin are linked with this, such as its pseudonymity, its multiform nature and its ugliness.

This urge to imitate which characterizes lying determines its tendency towards pseudonymity. Sin appears mostly under

assumed names, the best of assumed names. This befits its parasitic existence. Of course, it endeavours to conceal its emptiness
by imitation and pseudonymity. This is the only way that the lie
can hide its own hollowness. It is the evil nature of the lie to
give itself the appearance of being true. It is the nature of evil
to give itself the appearance of being good, of being the source
of all good. That is why sin never appears under the name of
sin. That is why it hides itself behind the best addresses.

And it will use any means to achieve this. It shrinks at nothing,
as far as imitation goes. It is a many-faced scourge. Because its
fundamental shape is a lie, that is, it has no shape, it keeps
reappearing in new shapes. Aristotle was right here too when
he called evil a multiform evil, a κακὸν πολύμορφον.[36]

Together with this characteristic – of hiding its own shape-
lessness behind the multiform nature of the untruth of sin –
goes the fact that sin itself is the epitome of ugliness. Every shape
that sin assumes is only a façade behind which the scourge of
sin can hide as *privatio veri* and *privatio boni*. Even as it assumes
the form of truth and goodness it robs them of their form. Sin
disfigures what is true. Evil disfigures what is good. The evil of
sin disfigures human beings, made in the image of God. Sin is
the thing that is really ugly, because it has a disfiguring effect
in its lying, because its nature is the ill-nature of disfigurement.
By giving the appearance of walking uprightly, it contorts us
into people twisted around into ourselves, so that we each
become a *homo incurvatus in se ipsum*. By lending itself the appearance of religion and piety, it distorts God into an idol. By
distorting itself, it distorts everything. This is what makes it into
the epitome of ugliness.

Nevertheless, sin has boundaries, so that it cannot complete
its disfiguring task. This is only because God has not dodged
this disfigurement, but has exposed himself to it. God, in the
disfigured form of the Crucified One, has exposed sin in its un-
truthfulness, and, suffering this disfigurement, has overcome

---

[36] Cf. Aristotle, *Eudemian Ethics*, H, 1239 b 12. [See *Aristotle*, vol. 20, Loeb Classics,
pp. 396–7.]

it. Thus, if we are to correctly understand the beauty of God, we must say that he has suffered this disfigurement. The ugliness of the cross is an integral part of the correct understanding of the beauty of his love.

III. Human beings: perpetrators and slaves of sin

1. Sin as deed and power

Sin occurs where people are sinning. 'Sin came into the world by sinning.'[37] Sin's existence is a deed, a doing, or more precisely, a wrongdoing. Both deeds and misdeeds have perpetrators. The act of sinning has a subject who is responsible for the deed. The subject of the sinning, the perpetrator of sin is the human being.

This has been a presupposition up to this point, but has never been specifically emphasized. What has been dominant until now has been the understanding of sin as a power to which human beings are subjugated and enslaved. This is not an incorrect understanding of sin. It is indispensable. It highlights a major insight into human beings as sinners. To see sin as a power which wreaks evil emphasizes that sinners are dominated by, are slaves to sin.

However, we must be more precise: a sinner is dominated by and a slave to his or her own sin. Unless we narrow the matter down like this, our discussion of sin would run the risk of losing its anthropological and theological seriousness and thus its whole point. It would risk degenerating into a sin-myth or a speculation about sin. To all sound observers, it would risk turning into a discussion of sin which simply missed what is theologically true. But the gospel, as a *ratio cognoscendi* of sin, makes it clear that the theologically decisive and vital thing about sin is the sinner. To speak in a theologically responsible way of sin is to aim at the truth that all talk of sin is about my

---

[37] R. Bultmann, *Theology of the New Testament*, vol. 1, trans. K. Grobel, London: SCM Press, 1965 (1952), 251.

sin, about me as a sinner. So a theologically responsible discussion of sin aims at confession of sin.

At the same time we must not lose sight of the fact that, although it is my deed, sin is also a power which defines my being. This brings with it implications which are extraordinarily important and far-reaching, but also extraordinarily difficult. In theological tradition they are expressed as a series of distinctions, of which the most important are those between being a sinner and committing sin, between sin as power and sin as deed, and between original sin and actual sin. The relationship between these two groupings has been subject to much dispute among theologians. While for the scholastics the real sin in the life of the Christian is the individual actual sin (*peccatum actuale*), on the other hand Luther stresses that actual sin, even in the life of the Christian, is original sin. Luther customarily denotes this sin by a whole range of further concepts, such as *peccatum radicale* (radical sin), *peccatum capitale* or *principale* (major sin), *peccatum personale et naturale* (personal sin, which also marks human nature), *peccatum substantiale* (the essential sin which underlies all actual sin) and *peccatum mortale* (the sin which brings about spiritual and eternal death). Some of these concepts are interpreted in quite a different, even in a contrary way, by the scholastics.[38] This controversy between the Reformers and the scholastics remains today – so far as it is noticed at all. In fact, it has recently become more relevant, just when the whole question of original sin seemed to have become totally irrelevant or even lost to people of the so-called modern world. The corresponding heritage of Augustine and the Reformers appears to have totally ceased to have any application. Ernst Troeltsch tried to note such a loss when he made this diagnosis about the culture of the modern world: 'With it falls the doctrine of the absolute corruption of mankind through original

---

[38] Cf. G. Ebeling, 'Der Mensch als Sünder. Die Erbsünde in Luthers Menschenbild', in idem, *Lutherstudien*, vol. 3: *Begriffsuntersuchungen – Textinterpretationen – Wirkungsgeschichtliches*, 1985, 74–107.

sin'.[39] In the modern world and as far as the feelings of modern people are concerned, the 'myth of the Fall and the curse upon the world has practically ceased to have any influence . . .'.[40] At least as regards *peccatum originale*, people of today appear to really live *etsi peccatum non daretur*. Therefore even more weight falls on our evil deeds. What was understood by the theological tradition as actual sin (*peccatum actuale*), is still very up-to-date. It seems as though even people today cannot live without there being perpetrators of wrongdoing, of atrocities. But we must immediately ask whether actual sin is seen as sin at all without that reference to original sin. Does not the moralizing aspect of the concept of sin consist in seeing sin as just a human deed, and no longer as a power which defines human *being*? And does not such moralizing of the concept of sin mean a radical detheologizing of it?

2. Biblical testimony to the bipolarity of sin

To clarify these matters we need to reflect on the bipolarity of sin which is plainly a characteristic of the biblical treatment of the subject. According to biblical understanding, sin is in its very nature two things. It is not this, then the other; it is both the human act of sinning and the power which governs human existence. This piece of information opens up the gospel to us as the *ratio cognoscendi* of sin. For the gospel sets sinners free from their sin and at the same time challenges them to sin no more (John 8:11; cf. John 5:14; 1 Cor. 15:34; Eph. 4:25; 1 John 2:1; 3:6; 5:18). The gospel leaves no doubt that it expects those set free from their sin to sin no more, and this makes it clear that sin is our deeds, our doing – and wrongdoing. On the other side of the coin, it is quite clear that when we are set free from our sin by the gospel, we are set free from a power under whose sway we had been living. When the Bible says of our

[39] E. Troeltsch, *Protestantism and Progress: The Significance of Protestantism for the Rise of the Modern World*, Philadelphia: Fortress Press, 1986 (1912), 26.
[40] Ibid., 49.

existence under sin 'I am of the flesh, sold into slavery under sin' (Rom. 7:14); 'the scripture has imprisoned all things under the power of sin' (Gal. 3:22; cf. Rom. 3:9; 11:32), it makes it perfectly clear that sin is a ruling power whose claim to hold sway over us has been made a nonsense once and for all by the good news of the death and resurrection of Jesus. So now we may, we *must* conclude: 'sin must no longer reign in your mortal body' (Rom. 6:12 NEB). Above all, we are made aware of the extent of this power by the fact that he who knew no sin (2 Cor. 5:21) bears the sin of the world as the Lamb of God (John 1:29). It had to come to this: that God in the Person of the Son of God placed himself under the power of sin in order to break that power (Gal. 4:4f.; Rom. 8:3).

Obviously, the power which the Bible attributes to sin highlights the dreadful seriousness of the situation in which sinners find themselves. Perhaps one single sinful deed is forgotten over time. Even a whole series of individual sinful deeds can be overlooked. No doubt time heals many wounds. Why not these as well? It is no coincidence, there is a sense in the fact that an individual crime is subject to a statute of limitations in many countries. Perhaps *peccatum actuale* could also be considered in this way. But original sin can never be so. By definition it can never lapse, because it is always present. We can only be *rescued* from it, snatched out of its clutches. In Romans 7:24 the one who is under the sway of sin, under the law of sin and death (Rom. 8:2), cries out in despair: 'Wretched man that I am! Who will rescue me from this body of death?' Sin is just like our own inherited nature; it is always there. We cannot be rid of it unless we are rescued.*

3. Original sin – an inappropriate concept?

How then can sinners be made to give an account of their sin? How can an inherited sin be passed off as *my fault*? If sin is

---

* The argument in these last two sentences depends on the normal German word for original sin, *Erbsünde*, which would translate as inherited sin (*peccatum haereditarium*) (Tr).

inherited, how can sinners be pronounced guilty? If such an inheritance is to be binding in law, must we not at least have accepted and recognized it? Goethe's words, although composed with a quite different purpose, may be relevant here: 'All that you have, bequeathed you by your father, / Earn it in order to possess it.'[41] If there is such a thing as original sin (*peccatum originale*), should we not first have to specifically acquire it through individual actual sins (*peccata actualia*), in order to possess it as an inheritance?

(a) A glance back through history

The Humanists of the Renaissance, together with the Socinians[42] and Arminians[43] who continued their educational tradition, laid the groundwork for the theology and philosophy of the Enlightenment, and it was this philosophy which protested against the *expression* 'original sin' as well as against what the term represented. Their protest was so strong that both the expression and the concept have become totally obsolete to people of today. We need to distinguish between the *expression* 'original sin', which, as has already been said, can be interpreted or even perhaps replaced by a whole range of other expressions, and the *theological fact* which is meant by this expression. However, the philosophers of the Enlightenment intended to criticize both the term and its content. They believed that both were impossible. For example, Hermann Samuel Reimarus[44]

---

[41] J. W. von Goethe, *Faust*, 18 (lines 682–3).

[42] Named after Lelio Sozzini and in particular his nephew Fausto Sozzini (d. 1604), who gained recognition for their antitrinitarian movement which spread out from Italy through Switzerland to Poland and the Siebengebirge from about 1600 and lasted several decades. This movement, which criticized existing doctrine, had a noticeable effect on later theology.

[43] Named after the Protestant theologian from Leiden, Jacob Arminius (d. 1609), who questioned the central Reformed doctrine of predestination. The Remonstrants or Arminians based their beliefs on the teaching of Arminius. They found their scholarly champion in Hugo Grotius (d. 1645), who called for historico-grammatical exegesis.

[44] H. S. Reimarus, *Apologie oder Schutzschrift für die vernünftigen Verehrer Gottes*, published by Lessing after 1774 in a series of 'fragments' (*Fragmente eines Ungenannten*). Now available as *Apologie oder Schutzschrift für die vernünftigen Verehrer*

reduced the doctrine of original sin *ad absurdum* by analogy
with a theoretically constructed original murder – which was in
itself absurd. Reimarus says that the language of original sin
mirrors the baseness of our nature. However, he says, to have
to see this baseness as guilt is an impossible demand. He declares
that it is not possible to love a God who 'imputed the baseness
of our nature as our sin-guilt'.[45] For, as he continues, 'sin and
righteousness are something personal and particular to the
individual. It is as difficult for my private sin to become the sin
of another, or for the private righteousness of another to
become mine, as for one person to be exchanged for another'.[46]

Reimarus understood the language of original sin in a legal
manner and criticized it for that reason, because the legal concept of guilt as indebtedness presupposes responsibility for the
debt. But even when we take the concept in a medical sense –
and in this sense the Reformers describe original sin as a
sickness, a *morbus*,[47] and human nature fallen prey to original
sin as 'poisoned'[48] – there are problems from the Enlightenment
point of view. Thus, for example, Kant declared the description
of original sin as a sickness (*morbus*) to be incongruous, because
sickness is the domain of the medical faculty, which 'would
represent the inherited evil somewhat as it represents the
tapeworm, concerning which certain natural scientists are
actually of the opinion that, since it is not otherwise found in
an element outside us nor . . . in any other animal, it must
already have been present in our first parents'.[49] Even if we

---

Gottes, edited under the auspices of the Joachim-Jungius-Gesellschaft der
Wissenschaften Hamburg by G. Alexander, vol. 2, 1972, 469–71.

[45] Ibid., 467.

[46] Ibid., 490. Alexander's edition reads 'privative' instead of 'private'.

[47] [Jüngel provides both the German and the Latin versions. Since they differ
slightly, the *Book of Concord* supplies translations for both: German: 'Moreover,
this inborn sickness and hereditary sin {Erbsünde} is truly sin'; Latin: ('quodque
hic morbus seu vitium originis vere sit peccatum'): 'And this disease or vice of
origin is truly sin', *The Augsburg Confession, BC*, 29 (Tr).]

[48] *The Heidelberg Catechism with Commentary*, Philadelphia and Boston: United Church
Press, 1963, Qu. 7, p. 26.

[49] Kant, *Religion Within the Boundaries of Mere Reason*, 86 n.

disregard Kant's doctrine of radical evil, which is obviously aiming in a totally different direction, the supreme irony which he uses when he comments on the doctrine of original sin lets us see more clearly than any argument that the world of the Enlightenment simply no longer knew what to do with such a doctrine. No argument could be more fatal for the doctrine of original sin than Kant's ironic comparison with a tapeworm. Hegel's comment on the subject also stands out above the others in the milieu of the Enlightenment: 'The Christian doctrine that man is by nature evil is superior to the other according to which he is good ... When he exists in an immediate and uncivilized condition, he is therefore in a situation in which he ought not to be, and from which he must liberate himself. This is the meaning of the doctrine of original sin, without which Christianity would not be the religion of freedom.'[50]

However, as has been said, Hegel is a major exception. In order to make a sound judgement about the aversion and complete misunderstanding shown by people today regarding the doctrine of original sin, we need to remember that even the theology of the pre-Reformation period could not manage to form an adequately serious idea of it, at least as far as the lives of baptized people were concerned. In fact, the reigning dogma in the whole of the church was 'since the fall of Adam all men who are born according to the course of nature are conceived and born in sin'.[51] But it was the Reformers, using Augustinian theologumena, who were the first to clearly emphasize that this is the really deadly sin which defines us from our very birth. Original sin is what gives real meaning to the individual sins of commission. Scholastic theology is mainly directed at these sinful deeds. It gives its attention in particular to the lives of those who have been baptized, who have been so freed by baptism from the tyranny of original sin that there is now only a leftover, a tendency towards sin. Of course, the Scholastics

---

[50] G. W. F. Hegel, *Elements of the Philosophy of Right*, ed. A. W. Wood, trans. H. B. Nisbet, Cambridge: Cambridge University Press, 1991 (§18, Addition H), 51.
[51] *The Augsburg Confession, BC*, 29.

taught that before baptism the fundamental sin, the *peccatum substantiale*, is original sin, which brings with it spiritual death. But after baptism only sinful deeds matter, and become relevant in the sacrament of confession. This is true whether they take the form of venial or new mortal sins of commission.[52]

On the other hand, speaking of original sin, Luther claims: 'This sin is not committed, as are all other sins; rather, it *is*. It lives and commits all sins and is the real essential sin which does not sin for an hour or for a while; rather no matter where or how long a person lives, this sin is there too.'[53] The difference is clear. Luther sees sin as something which determines our being, from which sinful deeds grow like rotten fruit. Thus it is not that sin takes its concrete shape from sinful acts, but that the concrete shape of sin is the sinner in person.[54] The Scholastics, on the contrary, see tangible sin in the individual sinful deed and understand the person of the sinner as being made up of his or her deeds. In this sense, being a person means no more than being a *doer*. From such a premise, original sin in

---

[52] Behind this stands the belief that at the Fall we lost the image of God, the *imago dei*, in which we were created. This is only true in a limited way for the Scholastics. When discussing the image of God, they distinguish between *imago* and *similitudo*. The latter is defined as original righteousness – *iustitia originalis*, which is what constitutes the reference to God in *imago dei*. It is this *iustitia originalis* which is lost in the sinner. Original sin, the Fall itself, consists then of the *carentia iustitiae originalis*, the loss of original righteousness. What remains of the *imago dei* are the natural powers. This includes a remainder of free will. This is admittedly just a leftover, as it lacks the orientation towards God, it is damaged and in some disarray. But this disarray is not so strong as to prevent anything being added to it. The Reformers say the opposite. The *imago dei* is totally lost in the Fall. There are even some who say that it has been perverted into the *imago diaboli*. Thus, according to the Reformers' teaching, the fact that original sin remains after baptism leads logically to saying that the baptized person is both entirely righteous and entirely a sinner – *simul iustus et peccator*. How are we to understand this? Luther puts it this way: 'When I allow myself to respond through the gospel in such a way that at the same time I allow a relationship with the God who justifies sinners, the gospel places me outside myself. It is precisely in that measure that I am entirely righteous. But to the extent that I do not allow the gospel to call me out of myself, I am entirely fixated on myself and thus remain a sinner' (on this, see below, pp. 214–24).

[53] M. Luther, *The Gospel for New Year's Day, Luke 2:21*, 1522, *LW* 52, 149–58, 152.

[54] Cf. Ebeling, 'Der Mensch als Sünder', 82; cf. also 79 and 82–8.

the life of a baptized person loses theological significance in comparison with sinful deeds.

How much more must this be the case in our present enlightened age which has human beings as agents, as *doers*, in every respect? To be human means to be *the* actor on the world stage: in the domain of theoretical reasoning we create whole worlds and prescribe laws for everything; in the domain of practical reasoning we build a moral world and transform the natural environment into an artificial one. We lack any sense of sabbath rest, in which we are persons, and nothing but persons. Not only are we always busy doing *something*, but in our activity we make even ourselves into what we are. We *gain* our recognition by our *doing*, and by our *wrong-doing* we *lose* it: *opus facit personam* – this becomes true both in a positive and negative sense. By this process only what people do can be considered as sin. There is no place for anything like original sin in the plan when people are identical with their deeds.

But does theology *have* to give up the concept of original sin? *Can* it? We shall begin answering this question by using the words 'inherited sin' and so bring our attention back to the theological fact which is expressed or at least meant by those words.[55]

(b) The expression 'inherited sin' – peccatum haereditarium

The expression 'inherited sin' does not occur in the Bible. It probably came from a combination of Romans 5:12 and Psalm 51:5. The latter says: 'I was born guilty, a sinner when my mother conceived me', while Paul says: 'just as sin came into the world through one man, and death came through sin, and so death spread to *all* because (or: in that – ἐφ᾿ ᾧ) *all* have sinned'. There is no longer any debate about the exact exegetical meaning of the two verses. However, the combined sense of the two verses has been completely misunderstood. The link between the sin

---

[55] G. Freund's penetrating and profound study will be found particularly instructive on this matter: *Sünde im Erbe. Erfahrungsinhalt und Sinn der Erbsündenlehre*, Stuttgart: Kolhammer, 1979.

of *one* man, Adam, and the sin of *all* people has been interpreted as being based on reproduction (*propagatio*) and so the sexual act of begetting human life has been taken to be the sinful means by which Adam's sin must for ever more bring forth sin. Nor should we misinterpret in this sense the psalmist's confession that he was born and conceived in sin. The expression 'inherited sin' (*peccatum haereditarium*) *does not need to be* an indispensable part of the Christian doctrine of sin. And in one particular interpretation, which links inheritance of sin to the act of procreation and even denounces sexual passion, the expression *must not be* indispensable. Now, whether the expression 'inherited sin' retains any meaningful use for the teaching about sin should be decided by seeing whether the theological content that it is intended to have is able to exist without those misunderstandings which appear to predominate. The heart of the matter is expressed far more clearly by the other two expressions which have also been in use: *peccatum originale* and *peccatum radicale*. Both of these expressions complete each other; only when they are used together do they highlight appropriately the theological fact which was intended.

(c) Original sin – peccatum originale

From the time of Augustine on, the expression *peccatum originale* – 'original sin'— became common in both church and theological use. It denotes the sin which, because of Adam's fall, came to hold sway over all people from the *origin* of human history. Of course, the expression itself is no more biblical than is 'inherited sin'. However, there is no doubt at all that a passage such as Romans 5:12 has precisely this in mind: sin has reigned – and with or through sin, death – ever since human beings have existed. It has reigned uninterrupted since Adam. The first potent interruption to its reign was in the person of the new Adam, who shattered its overweening power: Christ, who suffered while guiltless of sin. Sin can no longer reign wherever he is King and his reign meets with faith. But those who shirk his reign remain still under the sway of Adam's sin, the *peccatum originis* or *originale* – the sin from the beginning, the original sin.

Augustine's theory, that this sin which dominates all humanity is inherited through the act of procreation and may thus be termed 'inherited sin' – *peccatum haereditarium*,[56] is only good as far as it expresses the idea that we are sinners not only because of our acts, but because we are sinners through and through. Discussion of *peccatum originale* and its rule over all, together with a careful use of the term *peccatum haereditarium*, show that not only our individual deeds but our whole being is sinful and has always been so.

(d) Sinners from the roots upward – peccatum radicale

The all-pervading nature of sin is highlighted even more by Luther when he speaks of *peccatum radicale*. This expression de-emphasizes the main idea in *peccatum originale*, that sin as it now reigns can be traced back to *Adam's* sin, and instead underlines the fact that we are *sinners ex radice*, from the roots upward. There are, however, historical distinctions to be made.

(a) The Scholastics speak of a sin which is the *causa*, the *radix* and the *initium* of all sins, although, according to Ebeling,[57] they nowhere mention the expression *peccatum radicale*. In connection with this root cause of sin, *superbia* and *cupiditas* (*avaritia*) are mentioned, referring to Sirach 10:13 ('the beginning of pride is sin' – *superbia*)[58] and 1 Timothy 6:10 ('the love of money is the root of all evils' [RSV] – φιλαργυρία; Luther translates this as *Geiz*; the Latins as *avaritia* or *cupiditas*). That is to say, the Scholastics speak of specific vices (*vitia*), which in turn are *peccata specialia*, special sins.[59] The same is true of the

[56] Saint Augustine, *The Retractions*, trans. M. I. Bogan, Washington: The Catholic University of America Press, 1968, 54.

[57] G. Ebeling, 'Der Mensch als Sünder', 78.

[58] Cf. Luther's translation. Sirach 10:13 according to the LXX has ὅτι ἀρχὴ ὑπερηφανίας ἁμαρτία. [Cf. Also the ET in R. H. Charles, *The Apocrypha and Pseudepigrapha of the Old Testament*, vol. 1, Oxford: Clarendon Press, 1968 (1913), 'for sin is the rallying-place of insolence' (Tr).]

[59] Cf. Thomas Aquinas *STh* Iᵃ IIᵃᵉ, q. 84 a. 1 corpus: 'dicendum est quod cupiditas, secundum quod est speciale peccatum, dicitur radix omnium peccatorum' – 'we must say that covetousness, as denoting a special sin, is called the root of all sins' [ET vol. 1, 962]; a. 2 corpus: 'dicendum est quod superbia, etiam secundum

concept of the seven cardinal sins or capital vices (*vitia capitalia*), which is used in conjunction with this. These are said to be not only the basis (*principium*) but the guiding power of all other sins: 'Whereas a capital vice is not only the principle of others, but is also their director and, in a way, their leader.'[60] Even these capital vices, considered to be compulsorily notifiable at confession, are *peccata specialia*, sins which may be specifically named: *superbia* (vainglory or pride), *acedia* or *tristitia* (extreme sadness), *luxuria* (seeking pleasure), *ira* (anger), *gula* (gluttony), *invidia* (envy) and *avaritia* (covetousness).[61] The scholastic models aim to emphasize that every sin is the cause of another: 'quod unum peccatum est causa alterius'.[62] However, the sin from which other sins stem is again understood as a sinful deed.

(b) For Luther on the other hand the *peccatum radicale* is inherited sin, which lies at the root of all sinful deeds and produces both them and their fruits: 'So-called original sin (*Erbsünde*), *peccatum originale*, is itself the real sin, the *peccatum radicale*.'[63] The stress here is on the radical sinfulness of the person, so that it is possible to speak of an existential interpretation of the doctrine of original sin. Emphasis on primal history as the fixed point (in the sense of *terminus a quo*) of world history retreats in favour of an interest in the root of human depravity in the being of the sinful person.

(c) It was Karl Barth who brought about a logical further development of the Reformers' interest in that depravity which reaches to the roots of all humanity. He managed at the same time to do justice to modern awareness of the problem as he

---

quod est speciale peccatum, est initium omnis peccati' – 'for we must take note that pride, even as denoting a special sin, is the beginning of every sin' [ET vol. 1, 963].

[60] Ibid., p. 964; in Latin: q. 84 a. 3 corpus: 'vitium capitale non solum est principium aliorum, sed etiam est directivum et quodammodo ductivum aliorum [peccatorum]'.

[61] Cf. ibid., q. 84 a. 4.

[62] Ibid., q. 84 intr. [ET vol. 1, 962].

[63] Ebeling, 'Der Mensch als Sünder', 78f.; references at 77, n. 14 and 79f., n. 19.

interpreted Adam's sin and Adam as a sinner as *primus inter pares*. In his work there is an explicit criticism of the doctrine of original sin. Barth sees Adam as the representative of all human beings, the *primus inter pares*,[64] and with him all people as 'those who are represented in his person and deed'.[65] Thus it is impossible that any person *has to* sin because of Adam's sin. Nobody *has to* sin. Barth cannot share Augustine's idea that since Adam's fall there is a necessity to sin, a *non posse non peccare*. He is quite clear on this: 'He was in a trivial form what we all are, a man of sin . . . That does not mean tht he has bequeathed it to us as his heirs so that we have to be as he was. He [!] has not poisoned us or passed on a disease. What we do after him is not done according to an example which irresistibly overthrows us, or in an imitation of his act which is ordained for all his successors [!] No one has to be Adam. We are so freely and on our own responsibility'.[66] This is why Barth says about the old doctrine of *peccatum haereditarium*: 'We cannot avoid a serious critical study of this question. There can be no objection to the Latin expression *peccatum originale* if it is not given this more exact definition. It is indeed quite adequate, telling us that we are dealing with the original and radical and therefore the comprehensive and total act of man, with the imprisonment of his existence in that circle of evil being and evil activity.'[67]

We need to note that Barth sees this 'circle of evil being and evil activity' as being triggered by an 'original and radical and therefore . . . comprehensive and total act of man'. This could be misunderstood in the sense of the scholastic idea of sinful acts as 'real' sin. But Barth expressly dissociates himself from this concept.[68] His discussion of sin, as the original, comprehensive and total act of man, is meant in the sense of a life-act, a deed which marks one's whole life. The charge which identifies man as a sinner means 'himself, and himself in the

[64] Barth, *CD* IV/1, 511.
[65] *CD* IV/1, 510.
[66] *CD* IV/1, 509.
[67] *CD* IV/1, 500.
[68] Cf. *CD* IV/1, 499f.

totality of his existence ... although it does relate specifically to individual acts, it relates primarily to his life as a whole'.[69] For Barth, man is 'the whole man ... in the unity of his activity and being'. 'Man is what he does. And he does what he is.'[70]

There are no doubt critical questions to be asked about such an easy symmetry. It is true that we *do* what we *are*, but according to the gospel it is never true to say that we *are* what we *do*. Still, it is acceptable to say that sin can be considered as an original life-act which makes us totally into sinners. And from that point it is possible to overcome a whole range of conceptual problems in the doctrine of original sin.

(e) Original sin: entanglement in a sham existence

The conclusions reached so far suggest that we may translate discussion of sin as deed into the conceptual framework which we previously established, that sin is an untruth which corrupts God's truth.

(a) If sin in its most primitive form is the *untruth* which corrupts the truth of divine love and does not even allow itself this love, then the deeds we do in life can be called nothing else than a sham existence. Such a sham existence is then more primitive than deeds. In this sham existence, being and deed are inseparably united. Liars lie and deceive themselves in such a sham existence. The one who lies simultaneously becomes the one who is lied to; the subject becomes the object and thus the criminal falls victim to himself: a deceiver deceived. In this sham existence human beings contradict themselves so funda-mentally, so completely, that they can no longer stop lying to themselves. Lied to by themselves about themselves, those who are *lied to* become *liars* again. Evil turns on itself in a vicious circle. And those who are entangling themselves in the untruth of sin can then no longer disentangle themselves from this vicious circle unless they have outside help. They can only be

---

[69] *CD* IV/1, 499.
[70] *CD* IV/1, 492.

pulled out of it and rescued from the outside. They must be *told the truth.*

(b) In this sense we can now take up the definition of sin as *peccatum originale* and *peccatum radicale.* From such a position we can then regain some useful aspects of that much maligned – and often, justifiably, much disputed – concept of original sin. This much is clear, that we can no more speak of sin inherited by procreation than of Adam passing on his sin by the act of procreation. What the Yahwist history has to offer us is something other than a *terminus a quo* of human history understood in a historicist sense. There is no more room for foolish pseudo-theological apologetics in the doctrine of sin than anywhere else in honest evangelical teaching.

However, over against Barth's restricted interpretation of Adam as simply the representative of all sinners, we need to emphasize not only that Adam represents each individual sinner, and *thereby* as it were sums up all sinners. We also need to state that he stands for the *interrelation* between all sinners. He stands for the *interrelation in reality* – made up of *peccatum originale* and *radicale* – not only of one single human life, but of the lives of all people. It is never the case that a sinner deceives him or herself only by lying. Other people are always involved. Lying, especially the lie of the sham existence, is a definite *social* (or antisocial) phenomenon; it is never simply an *individual* one. Since nobody can exist without his or her sham existence, the untruth of sin is a *blinding interrelation* which awaits every single person in a different guise. This is what the concept of original sin is able to make clear in a way that no other concept of sin can do: we are born into a set of constraints. One of these is the disastrous constraint that we do not wish to grant ourselves the good which God has intended for us and has provided for us once and for all in Jesus Christ.

4. Do we have to sin?

So, do we have to sin? Is it true to say: *non possumus non peccare?* The answer given by the gospel as the *ratio cognoscendi* of sin appears at first sight to be extremely dialectical or even para-doxical. For in this one case it says both Yes and No.

(a) To the extent that all of us are laid under the *legal charge* of being guilty before God, the answer can only be *No*. No, we are not *compelled* to sin. If we had to sin, we would *not* be *responsible* for our sin, we would be *not guilty*. We can only be charged and found guilty in relation to what can be imputed to us. Kant emphasized this clearly in a way that is of great use-fulness not only for our modern self-understanding.[71] And only what someone has done in complete freedom can be attributed to that person. We have this freedom only so far as we receive it from God, by relating to God afresh every moment, by living on his love and thus seeing ourselves as coming from God. Con-ceiving ourselves as being from God, living on his love, seeing ourselves as coming from God – all this means nothing other than believing. In believing we resign ourselves to God, we resign from ourselves in order to resign ourselves to God; we live away from our own little centres. This is the freedom for which God created us: free for God and thus free of ourselves. This is what we are when we believe. Created for faith, we are free from the compulsion to sin. No, we do not need to sin. *Possumus non peccare.*

(b) However, we must now simultaneously state the exact opposite and answer *Yes* to the question whether we have to sin: Yes, we are under a compulsion to sin. We cannot not sin: *non possumus non peccare.* Such an affirmation of the compulsion to sin is only dialectical or even paradoxical in relation to our denial of the necessity to sin as long as we are relating both statements *in the abstract* to human beings. When we claimed that human beings do not have to sin, we did our best to avoid such an abstraction. What we said was that human beings are not under a compulsion to sin to the extent that they have faith. In just such a way the contrary response, that human beings are

---

[71] Cf. I. Kant, *The Metaphysics of Morals*, trans. and ed. M. Gregor, Cambridge: Cambridge University Press, 1996, 15–16; ibid., *Religion Within the Boundaries of Mere Reason*, 73–4.

compelled to sin, is only meaningful in a concrete sense. It is those who do not receive themselves from God, do not live from God, do not see themselves as coming from God, but rather are self-actualizing, recklessly self-involved, presume to do good and reduce God to being the recipient of all human goods – it is these people who place themselves under a compulsion. They place themselves under a compulsion to repeat their sins. We give this fundamental sin its real name when we define it as the exact opposite of belief. The *peccatum originale et radicale* which allows itself to be forced to be repeated and thus ensures that evil will ever turn in a circle is *unbelief.* 'Did God say . . . ?' All unbelief begins with this distrust of God. It fears that God will withhold what is really good. So it grasps after what it thinks is good, the presumed good. It covets being like God, being like what it thinks is God. Unbelief, in its craving to be like God – which is the real meaning of *concupiscentia*! – turns away from God, and exists in estrangement from God. 'Therefore the root and source of sin is unbelief and turning away from God.'[72] The real sham existence is unbelief. Those who do not believe God deceive themselves, and not only themselves. Those who do not believe God make God himself into a liar, put him in the wrong and accuse him of untruth. And as they do this, they can do nothing else but continue in the same pattern. Those who do not believe God place themselves under the compulsion of not being allowed to and of being unable to believe God.

We may now pick up our earlier definition of sin as a compulsion to relationlessness and dissociation. For *concupiscentia*, the evil desire to be like God and to achieve a reckless self-actualization, is in reality nothing other than the urge to subjugate all other relationships to one's relationship with oneself. This urge sacrifices us to a relationlessness in which everything is dissociated. Every lie makes us more or less relationless and dissociated. The lie that profanes God forces the compulsion towards relationlessness into a frightful

---

[72] Luther, *Lectures on Genesis*, *LW* 1, 162: 'Radix igitur et fons peccati est incredulitas et aversio a Deo'; cf. idem, *The Disputation Concerning Justification*, 'Dr Martin Luther's Fourth Disputation: Concerning the passage Rom. 3:28', *LW* 34, 153–7.

obligation to plunge ever more deeply into dissociation, until the state of total relationlessness – death itself – makes an end of the whole devilish mess. Death is really the final balance line of unbelief; it is the wages of sin (Rom. 6:23). The compulsion to relationlessness that is generated by each person anew and encountered by each person as well – this is our so-called original sin. 'And deeper, deeper still I fell, / My life became a living hell, / For sin enslaved me wholly.'[73] Thus we are prisoners of our own sinful deeds, prisoners of sin. This is precisely the correlation of damnation which Adam represents in the language of the Bible. Adam stands for the disastrous correlation of committing sin and being a sinner, which the sinner accomplishes *volens nolens* – willy-nilly.

(c) If we consider both the answers we deemed necessary to the question whether human beings have to sin, the Bible's treatment of Adam as the one person in whom all people must recognize themselves becomes completely clear. Adam, the representative of the dawning of human history which determined the situation of all humanity and every human being, highlights the dual, the dialectic origin of human existence. On the one hand, Adam highlights the fact that each person is determined by the origin of humanity which was set into motion by God. Thus each person remains answerable for the fact that his or her sin is in no wise necessary, but that it is his or her own *reckless* deed and fault, for which they must yet give a *reckoning*. It is his or her *wilful* urge – though it is not a *compulsory* one – to a relationlessness and dissociation which perverts all relationship to God, the world and oneself. Human beings, deceiving themselves, surge ahead away from their own freedom, for which God has created them. We thrust forward freely from freedom into that unfreedom, which makes us slaves of sin. Just as truth makes us free (John 8:32), so untruth makes us unfree.

So on the other hand Adam underscores the fact that every person is defined from the beginning by the situation of

[73] *Lutheran Hymnal*, Adelaide: Lutheran Publishing House, 1973, 322.2.

humanity which is marked by sin and at the same time is defined by his or her own sin. Adam also emphasizes that every person is thus answerable for the fact that his or her whole being – not just the relationship to self – stands under a compulsion. This is a constantly self-produced yet pre-existing compulsion to follow one's own wilful urge towards relationlessness and to maximize the perversion of one's relationships to God, others and self. In Adam the disastrous correlation that sinners wreak is graphically highlighted: *nolens volens, volens nolens.*

5. The consequence of sin

Volens nolens! This is the real paradox, the real *self-contradiction* about sin. Sinners want to contradict God. But they don't want what goes with this: self-contradiction. Sinners want to live like God. But they don't want what goes with this: dying. Sinners want to lift themselves up. But they don't want what goes with this: being brought low. Sinners do not want to admit *quanti ponderis sit peccatum,* how grave a matter sin is. Having to do all these things that they don't want to do because they want what they don't need to want and should not want – all this is what constitutes the self-contradiction of sinners.

The Bible sees this self-induced contradiction as the *punishment* which God's wrath brings upon sinners. It has become customary for theologians to avoid the concept of divine punishment as too painful. However, when it is understood correctly it is indispensable. Of course, it is not a punishment which is especially linked to sin. It is simply the logical consequence of our sin which we would only too gladly escape, but God has handed us over to it (Rom. 1:24, 26, 28).[74] This is what Paul means when he says that God or the Scripture has *imprisoned* everyone under sin or under disobedience (Rom. 11:32; Gal. 3:22). None will be allowed to escape their own sin. None will be able to imagine they can slip out of the self-induced vicious circle of being a sinner, sinning and being a sinner. For if

[74] See above, p. 67.

sinners were able to manage this, sin would be complete. A sin which escaped its own evil consequences would be the perfect sin. Its thrall would be chaos and its slaves *irredeemable.*

But God has *imprisoned* all under sin and disobedience so that he might be merciful to all (Rom. 11:32). God's mercy, available for all, makes no precondition of sin or even that *all people have* to be sinners. Yet sin as it exists must be taken seriously in its consequences; all sinners must suffer the punishment of being handed over to the curse of the evil of their sin. This is God's wrath, rightly understood: that sinners be delivered up to the consequences of their sin. Yet this very wrath of God is in the service of divine love. For it is only when sin, as it infects and seduces all people, is unable to escape its own consequences, only when all sinners are handed over to the results of their sin, that sinners are able to be identified and judged and their sin forgiven and overcome. The very punishment of being delivered up to the consequences of one's sin proves to be in itself an act of God's grace. But this grace really becomes an unparalleled event when sinners do not have to suffer the final real effect of their sin, the cursed death of being absolutely abandoned by God, because Jesus has suffered it in our place. So even this final real – you could almost say, spiritual – consequence of sin is suffered, not by us, but by him, by Jesus. God takes sin as seriously as that, right down to its final effect. And in this act of taking sin so seriously, God condemns it to destruction. It can never be complete. If you reflect on this grace of God, you have rightly understood how grave a matter sin is. Sin is condemned by the grace of God to be the great incompletion.

We have now delineated the field of study which is implied by the fact which the gospel provides, that we are all sinners. The clear basic shape or misshape of sin has appeared: it is unbelief. Unbelief is the enemy of the Word of Truth. In addition, we must name the two other basic forms of sin which appear beside that of unbelief. Just as unbelief is the enemy of the Word of Truth, so also sin in the form of lovelessness is the enemy of the Word of love. Similarly, the enemy of the Word of hope and consolation is sin in the form of hopelessness and inconsolability. These two other basic forms of sin are treated in ecclesiology and eschatology. In the context of the article of justification we need now to make a closer examination of sin as unbelief.

IV. Sin as unbelief

Everything which is called and deserves to be called sin proceeds from unbelief. We must now develop this biblical proposition.

The fundamental statements concerning sin have already been made: sin lies, and the essence of sin is untruth. Sin lies by contradicting the truth: the truth which is God himself and the truth of God's Word. Thus it is always in blatant contradiction of the truth of faith, which emerges from the Word of Truth. Sin, as a human act, is the *actus contrarius* of faith. This means that the untruth of sin takes on a concrete form in unbelief. So, with Luther, we understand unbelief as the primary form of sin. Luther is right when he describes unbelief as the 'root and source of all sin'.[75]

1. The unbelief of Christians increases the power of sin

Labelling the basic shape of sin as unbelief, contradiction of the truth of the gospel, appears to make sin out to be a 'pre-Christian' or 'non-Christian' phenomenon. However, appearances are deceptive. What this label does is to highlight the fact that there is no difference between the sin of non-Christians and that of Christians. Unbelief and superstition by no means only appear as evidence of non-Christian living. Rather, unbelief and superstition reach their worst excesses in Christian living. They strive to assert themselves with regard not only to the possibility, but also to the reality of faith. It ought not to be, it must not be, that Christians, though free from the power of sin, sin and become Adam again. However, it is a fact. Christians are *de facto* the old

---

[75] M. Luther, *Preface to the Epistle of St Paul to the Romans*, LW 35, 369. Cf. idem, *Psalm 118*, LW 14, 47ff.

Adam and Eve. They are simultaneously justified and sinners. *De facto* we reinstate original sin. Thus we have the specifically Christian form of unbelief and superstition. Its chief characteristic is that it claims not to contradict the truth of God's Word but to match it. In the Christian form of unbelief and superstition, sin makes its most blatant contradiction of the truth of the gospel by embracing and even kissing the truth, as Judas did with his Lord. Christians betray the truth of the faith when they domesticate and make it harmless by embracing it.[76] This is the unbelief of the Grand Inquisitor and all the petty inquisitors. Just as importantly, it is the unbelief of those who simply *hand down* the faith, but can no longer believe. It is the superstition of those who confuse spirit and letter, replacing the knowledge of living truth with a counterfeit recital of dead verities, and directly identify the Word of God with the human word of the Holy Scripture, of confessions and of dogmatic tradition. This Christian superstition simply bristles with 'truth'. It is the superstition in which heresy assumes the form of sterile orthodoxy and denies the insight that recognition of truth must always begin at the beginning.

We will not at present continue to name the Christian forms of unbelief and superstition. For the sake of clarification, mention may only be made of this, that Christians are *de facto* not less, but more sinful than non-Christian sinners. Their sin is not less, but more potentially sinful than the sin of non-Christians. In both cases their basic form is the contradiction of the truth of the gospel and the truth of the faith which emerges from it. The outline we are making of this contradiction is just a general one, listing a number of traits which are peculiar to the sin of unbelief.

2. Unbelief: theft of God's divinity

Describing the untruth of sin as unbelief brings out another point which our considerations up till now have highlighted,

---

[76] Cf. Barth, *CD* IV/3, 436ff.

but perhaps not clearly enough. Untruth and lying are by no means just theoretical concepts; sin is not simply an inhibition or confusion of the consciousness. No, unbelief, like faith, is an act which affects the whole person and destroys the wholeness of the whole person. Just as faith makes us in the best sense of the word ek-centric, so also unbelief makes us self-involved, in the worst sense of the word. Just as faith gives God his due only in so far as it takes from God and allows itself by grace and only by grace to receive of the fulness of God's kingdom revealed in Jesus Christ (cf. John 1:16), so also unbelief robs God of his due. Unbelief strives to rob God of his divinity by not allowing itself to receive from God, but instead wants to take from him what it lusts after. Unbelief is a theft of God's divinity.[77] Seen in this light, the definition of sin as untruth resists the misunderstanding that it is simply an inhibition or confusion of the consciousness, just a theoretical concept. In its form as unbelief, *privatio veri*, as we called sin, is nothing other than *privatio dei*, *theft from God.*

3. The vicious circle of unbelief

We may define the sin of unbelief more precisely by saying it is the vicious circle of lust and distrust: the lust to be like God and distrust of God. It is debatable whether the lust to be like God gives birth to distrust or distrust of God brings forth the lust to be like God. It is more important that each always brings the other in its train, so that here too we have a vicious circle as we noted in the relationship between doing sin and being a sinner. In all its forms, evil always turns in a circle.

The sad fact of the biblical story of the Fall can be made still clearer. It is a story based on contrasts. The first of these is that between God's unambiguous command and the ambiguous interpretation given to it by the serpent. God's *command* not to

---

[77] Cf. Luther, *Exposition of Psalm 147*, *LW* 14, 107–35: 133–4. Cf. idem, *Treatise on Good Works*, *LW* 44, 15–114: 42–3; idem, *The Bondage of the Will*, *LW* 33, 3–295: 226; idem, *Enarratio des 51. Psalms*, *LW* 12, 327–31 = *WA* 40/II, 325, 21–31.

eat from one single tree, the tree of the knowledge of good and evil, is only the reverse side of his *permission* to eat from all other trees. That is, the *command* only marks the *boundary* of a *generous bounty* towards human beings and is thus another expression of *divine provision* for human lives ('for in the day that you eat of it, you shall die' – Gen. 2:17). But the serpent interprets this command as an expression of God's *selfishness* in wishing to prevent the human beings from knowing good from evil and thus becoming like God (Gen. 3:5). Note well that it is the insinuation that God is *selfish* which makes the human being *distrust* God and thus *selfishly, covetously* demand to be like God. The human being who has been made distrustful covets what an apparently selfish God seems to be withholding from him: '*If* there were gods, how could I endure not to be a God?'[78] Both in the act of mistrusting God and in the act of the covetous desire to be like God, unbelief has the character of unbelief towards the *goodness* of God as the *giver* of all good and perfect gifts. Unbelief mistrusts God's goodness by insinuating that God does not really give to human beings everything which is good for them. This is why their distrust of God is at the same time a lust for what is apparently being withheld. And that is not God's divinity; it is what sinners imagine it to be.

By craving for divinity, human beings miss out on their highest good, that is, *being together in fellowship* with God. Anyone who wants to be God, that is to replace God, *can* by definition no longer be *with* God. Such a person replaces the goodness of being with God by the horror of the *lonely* existence of a *selfish being*. In his delusion he thinks this to be the divine existence of the divine being, while the true God *is* from all eternity and has been putting into effect for our benefit the fellowship of mutual otherness as Father, Son and Holy Spirit. In our distrust of God and our craving to be like God, we deceive ourselves about God's true existence and the truth of the divine being. We also deceive ourselves about our own existence as, in desiring to be like God, we fundamentally distrust the goodness of our own

---

[78] See above, p. 45, n. 106.

human existence. Unbelief is always a distrust of what is good: of God's goodness and, with that, of the goodness of our own being. From this distrust there necessarily grows the craving to be different, to be better, to be like God. Sin is the desire for self-improvement, raised to the nth degree.

Without any doubt, the biblical story of the Fall considers unbelief to be what is later identified in the Torah as *breaking the first commandment.* Human beings, wishing to be like God, quite obviously want to have other gods beside the one who is God alone (though he is by no means solitary). Those who want to be like God become the fount of all idolatry. Perhaps they do not discover other gods, but they set themselves and their desires up as idols beside God. Luther said of human nature: 'it is its own first and greatest idol'.[79] Unbelief is the origin of every form of idolatry.

4. Unbelief's desire to discern between good and evil

Sin's vicious circle may also be represented by defining the content of unbelief: human beings desire by themselves *to discern between good and evil.* In doing this they also crave to be like God. For in a fundamental sense it is God's role to decide between good and evil. Sinners usurp this divine role. We want to decide what is good and what is evil. We have scarcely begun to do so, to decide between good and evil – as we understand the difference, when we are already of necessity mistrusting both the God who calls us and ourselves. Instead of doing the only sensible thing, which is trusting, as sinners, in the God who calls us, we are afraid of God and hide from him. We transfer our guilt to others by inventing a genealogy of guilt (Gen. 3:9–13). Immediately our eyes are so opened about ourselves that we start to distrust our own nakedness. We are ashamed of our natural state. We distrust ourselves.

Distrust is the fruit which grows from that discernment between good and evil which we had craved. When we have the

---

[79] Luther, *Romans*, *LW* 25, 346.

knowledge of good and evil, we do not live in a guiltless state. We have to live with this knowledge as transgressors of God's commandment, as those who have become guilty. Thus it follows that whenever we decide between good and evil, we have to identify ourselves as evil. But we cannot do that. It would kill us. Any self-knowledge which penetrated so deeply as to lead to us recognizing our own evil nature would be fatal. So we use our knowledge of good and evil to divert attention from our own evil nature by identifying others as evil. We become both accuser and judge. The judge's task is to decide between good and evil. Wanting to be like God means wanting to judge like God. Craving to be like God means presuming that we can judge *like God* – even though sinners can never do such a thing. We *can* judge and forever *must* judge only *as sinful human beings!*

By starting to judge, we place ourselves under a compulsion which we can never escape. It is no longer a case of *being able* to decide between good and evil. Now we are *forced* to do so. Similarly, we are forced to be judges. We can never cease judging as long as the world goes on. But held in the grip of this compulsion to judge, we become distrustful of everything. What else, basically, are the courts of this world – together with all its prosecutors and lawyers – than the necessary institutions which have come from original distrust? In our compulsion to judge we constantly destroy the fundamental trust which was directly linked to trust in God.

5. *The vicious circle of pride and the fall into stupidity*

Finally, the sin of unbelief shows itself in the vicious circle of pride and fall.[80] That craving, to discern between good and evil as God does, is the *pride* which brings us to our *fall.* In our lust, fed by distrust, we raise ourselves above God's relationship to us. In that relationship, God is gracious and comes down to us. We also put ourselves above all our relationships and live so far above them that we fall. We press forward towards a lack of

---

[80] Barth, *CD* IV/1, 358–513.

relationship and in doing so *fall prey* to that urge. By starting to live without connectedness, we instantly find ourselves living in opposition to any connectedness. From the Bible's point of view, this is what our unrighteousness consists of: hatred of relationship. One connection after another dies in favour of our reckless quest for a connection to ourselves.

We can give a more precise label to what happens when we fall prey to compulsive relationlessness; we can call it the fall into stupidity. Craving the knowledge of good and evil makes us stupid. As long as we are only serving our own interests by this craving to be like God, as long as this craving places self-love (*amor sui*) in the place of love of truth, we are forced to restrict our ability to perceive. And so stupidity sets in. We are no longer able to discern what is truly good and what is bad for us. We can no longer see that God, instead of selfishly holding out on us, not only offers us what is good for us, but offers us himself. Sinners live with a particular narrowing of the ability to perceive. Selective perception is the mark of a *limited* intelligence. This limiting of intelligence is the *stupidity* to which sinners fall prey. Note that we are not talking here of that dim-witted stupidity which belongs beyond good and evil. It is our own stupidity, the stupidity of a mind which has grown relationless, the stupidity by which intelligence itself lies and deceives. In our arrogant positioning of ourselves above all relationships, we fall prey to this stupidity of a limited intelligence. Then sin reveals itself for what it is: stupidity without limits and deceit most profound.

6. Unbelief as guilt: human ingratitude *

It is *their own fault* that sinners fall prey to stupidity. The Christian doctrine of sin must never suppress the truth about sin's *guilt nature*. Wherever the relationship to God is harmed, human beings take on themselves the *blame* of seeking to rob God of

---

* In this section, the reader should bear in mind that the German root 'Schuld' forms the basis for such diverse English translations as 'debt', 'guilt', 'fault', 'blame', 'owe' and 'due' (Tr).

his divinity. That is why unbelief is by definition guilt. We shall clarify this guilt nature of sin with some explanations.

(a) First, we need to underline the fact that the sin of unbelief is *guilty of ingratitude* to God. You cannot be grateful to someone you distrust. You cannot be grateful to someone whom you are envying and craving to be. By distrusting God and lusting after an existence like his, you cannot help becoming *ungrateful*, someone who denies the gratitude due to God. And by remaining ungrateful to God you become *indebted* to God, a *guilty* person.

Scripture has always labelled as ingratitude that guilt connected with the sin of unbelief. The fact that human beings who have known God have not honoured him as God is proven, according to Romans 1:21, by their not having given him thanks. Ingratitude is clearly the most blatant form of dishonouring God, the *privatio divinitatis maxima*. The Bible says that refusing to give thanks is the inescapable consequence of craving to be like God and of that distrust of God which comes with it. For when we crave to be like God, we are not happy with God's goodness and with the goodness of our own humanity. In fact, we distrust this goodness as though it were an evil. The full fruit of this distrust and covetousness is the ingratitude of unbelief. This sin of ingratitude is the most blatant form of guilt debt because not only does God *not* owe us anything, he grants us the greatest of all things, fellowship with himself. Nothing can excuse the sin of ingratitude.

(b) It is most important for linking sin as unbelief with sin's other perverted shapes – lovelessness, inconsolability and hopelessness – that sin's ungrateful character (or lack of character) should emerge by itself. For when we are ungrateful to God we are at the same time ungrateful to what God has made. As has been shown, along with our distrust of God's goodness, we distrust the goodness of what he has made. That is why we imagine we can get away with misusing the beings God has created, both ourselves and our fellow creatures. Ingratitude takes away our inhibitions and our scruples. 'Nought rests to hallow – burst the ties / Of life's sublime and reverent awe; / Before the Vice the Virtue flies / And Universal Crime is Law!'[81] Ingratitude towards God is never *only* a sin which affects our relationship to God. Ingratitude to God's work and gifts always shows itself in the way ungrateful human beings insolently misuse God's good gifts. Ingratitude, linked as it is to unbelief, makes it clear that the sin of unbelief, which apparently only affects our relationship to God, is in reality a sin that draws the whole of creation along in sympathy. This is at least hinted at in Romans 8. Ingratitude towards God always affects our relationship with the world and with ourselves. While sinners refuse to repay their debt of gratitude to God, they are also in debt to their fellow creatures and even to themselves. Ingratitude towards the Creator has an immediate effect on our relationship with creation.

Instead of realizing our task to subdue the earth (*dominium terrae*) in gratitude to God, so that it will be respected, revered and protected as God's good creation, we twist this task into one of *imperium terrae*, as a *carte blanche* to exploit ruthlessly what we should safeguard. The highest good is perverted to serve our own purposes, as might and power. We sacrifice to the desire for power everything which stands in the way of our exercise of that power. Along with our unpaid debt of gratitude to God, we owe a debt of responsibility to God's creation.

(c) The same is true for our relationship to those of our fellow creatures who are closest to us: our fellow human beings. We are ungrateful to God and can conceive no debt of gratitude to our fellows. Instead, we only too readily misunderstand them and see them as objects which we can use any way we like. If I can see no reason to thank God for my fellow beings, and can see no reason to thank them myself, that means that I am not someone who can *receive* from my fellows. The sinner says: I owe them nothing. If I apparently owe them nothing, my fellow human beings turn into raw material for my activities, for me to dispose of as I wish. They become human *things*. If I owe

---

[81] F. Schiller, 'The Lay of the Bell' in *The Poems and Ballads of Schiller*, trans. E. Bulwer Lytton, London and New York: F. Warne, 1887, 256.

an unpaid debt of gratitude to God in regard to my fellow human beings, I will also be tempted to despise their value and thus become indebted to them.[82]

(d) Ungrateful people are also in debt to themselves. If they cannot thank God for the gift of their own existence, they fall prey to the delusion of being their own lords and masters. However, this means that they are also their own slaves. Lording it over themselves, they are mercilessly delivered up to themselves. Thus they can treat their own self-worth with contempt. Ungrateful to God, they have no respect for themselves. Here we see self-hatred and self-destruction as the other side of the coin of uninhibited self-love.

It is very easy when ungrateful people have such a disturbed relationship with themselves for it to cast a shadow over their relationship to the world in which they live. Suffering from themselves, they suffer from everything, from the whole world. There is nothing which can give them pleasure. Pleasure has disappeared with gratitude, such that in general those who are ungrateful are unhappy as well. This deep misery of the un-grateful spreads a staleness and emptiness over God's whole creation. The colours of creation now appear as unrelieved grey. Those who are ungrateful finish up being overcome by *acedia* and *tristitia*, disgust with the world and with self, and by incon-solable sadness. By refusing to discharge their debt of gratitude to God, they continue to owe themselves joy and hope.[83]

Thus the ingratitude of unbelief makes it abundantly clear that unbelief as a debt to God brings with it a debt to one's fellow creatures and to oneself. We shall content ourselves with these indications and turn again now to the guilt character of sin.

7. The unbeliever as homo incurvatus in se

What we owe to God is not just something we could supply with a bit of luck. With guilt there is by definition no reparation. By the

---

[82] Here the sin of lovelessness comes from that of ingratitude.
[83] Here the sins of inconsolability and hopelessness come from the sin of ingratitude, in stronger or in weaker forms.

sin of unbelief we owe God not only *something* but nothing less than a *personal debt of guilt*. In our unbelief we have withdrawn from God. We want to be something all by ourselves. That is why we refuse to allow God *to be there for us*. We refuse to be constantly re-conceived by God. We want to exist, to stand out by ourselves. Thus we are fundamentally guilty of a debt to God. And we stay in debt to God by refusing to allow God to make demands on us and by avoiding his claims. Nothing expresses our debt of guilt towards God better than Luther's much quoted concept of the *homo incurvatus in se* – 'man turned in on himself'.[84] When we are turned in on ourselves, we *will not* and *cannot* believe. We are unbelievers.

8. Unbelief – inability to speak, and our cry for deliverance

One of the problems of being sinners turned in on ourselves is that *we lose our ability to speak* our faith. Our guilt makes us dumb. Instead of talking to God, we talk about him. Of course, we can hide our speechlessness behind vapid chattering. The fact remains that we have nothing to say about God. By refusing to utter the one thing we have to say as sinners, our confession of sin, we have nothing at all to say before God or about God. By remaining silent at the wrong time, we are forced to remain completely silent. We can find no words that are true. The sin of unbelief is matched by sinners' inability to speak before God.

Such speechlessness is the passive dimension of that active urge to relationlessness of which we spoke. It comes home to roost when sinners find themselves unable to speak. And with that inability, sinners suffer the whole lack of substance and insecurity of their sin. They suffer it while alive in the form of a shadow constantly cast over them by death. And they suffer it in death because the silencing of sinners in death is final.

Sinners can only be released from this state of speechlessness by the power of a resurrection. They can only be saved by the

---

[84] Cf. Luther, *Romans*, *LW* 25, 345: ['Scripture. . . describes man as so *turned in on himself* that he uses not only physical but spiritual goods for his own purposes and in all things seeks only himself.']

vitalizing Spirit of Truth and the Word of Truth bringing forgiveness from guilt. For the Spirit of Truth testifies and the Word of Truth proclaims the encouraging news of forgiveness and blotting out of sins, so that where sin increases, the grace of God abounds all the more (Rom. 5:20b), so much so that it sets sinners free to confess their sin.

A confession of sin of this sort will, of course, not be satisfied with what Peter said: 'Go away from me, Lord, for I am a sinful man' (Luke 5:8). Sinners could not have a more foolish reaction. The abundance of divine grace towards the excess of our human need and guilt rather suggests that we pray: 'Lord, come in to us, for we are sinners!' Where such a prayer is prayed, in a world full of death and darkness the Christian church emerges, drawing its life from God's compassion and sharing it with others.

Such a prayer is the only way. It is, in fact, the way which has been given to us to participate in the overcoming of sin, to work together with the grace of God as συνεργοὶ θεοῦ.[85] Given this one, this unique way, we cannot be *synergetic* enough. By crying out for forgiveness of sins, for deliverance from evil, for that matchless fellowship with God the Redeemer, sinners are doing the only thing they can to become *justified* sinners. To cry out for forgiveness of sins and deliverance from evil, despite the apparent simplicity of such an action, is the one great thing that human beings can do to contribute to their justification by faith alone.

---

[85] However, when Paul calls believers συνεργοὶ θεοῦ (1 Thess. 3:2; 1 Cor. 3:9) he has another aim. He is thinking of human co-operation in 'evangelization'.

5

THE JUSTIFICATION OF SINNERS: THE MEANING OF THE EXCLUSIVE FORMULA USED BY THE REFORMERS

The doctrine of justification deals equally with God and human beings: with the God who justifies and sinners who are justified. To put it more accurately: it deals with the event of divine justification of unrighteous human beings who are becoming righteous through this event. Up to this point we have been talking about *the God who justifies* by asking the real meaning of the expression '*the righteousness of God*'. Moving backwards from the *activity* of justification, we have also been asking about the *being* of the God who is righteous because he justifies.

The most important summary we can make from all this is to say that *God, in his grace, is in the right*. God does not contradict himself, but is consistent in himself when he pronounces sinners justified. Thus justification is deeply relevant to the doctrine of God. Yet it applies in particular to the justification of *sinful human beings* and is thus equally relevant to anthropology. What we have said so far in this book has made it very clear that the doctrine of justification brings out the importance not only of *the being of God* – the one who speaks in the law and the gospel and acts and suffers in the person of Jesus Christ, but also of *the being of sinful humans* – as they are pardoned, as they are recipients of God's gifts and requirements and as they overreach themselves.

If we are now *deliberately* underlining the status of *justified sinners*, it is because the question of *how human beings* are involved in their justification by God has made the doctrine of justification a subject of dispute among Christians. A vast array of

slogans from the arsenal of theologians have become attached
to this question. We cannot go into them here. However,
Reformation theology provided a list of criteria which serve the
purpose of guarding the purity of the doctrine of justification.
It is imperative that we examine these terms, in particular the
exclusive formulae (*particulae exclusivae*) of Christ alone (*solus
Christus*), by grace alone (*sola gratia*), by the Word alone (*solo
verbo*), by faith alone (*sola fide*). In particular, we need to bring
out the meaning of the word 'alone', which is used four times
in this list. This is best done by highlighting the status of justified
sinners.

There is something more that is left out when we say 'alone'.
What this may be in each respective case must be sought in
the domain of human existence and action. It is human beings
who must from a certain point of view be excluded when it
concerns their own justification. Thus we are again even more
thrown back onto God when we come to speak of human beings.
In all four of the above phrases the real nub of the matter is
the correct understanding of a single one: *solus deus*. Here
the Reformers' terminology picks up a fundamental Old
Testament concept (cf. Isa. 2:17; Zech. 14:9; Ps. 51:6; 71:15f.;
83:18; 86:10).

Humans are indeed to be excluded with the aim of properly
including them in their justification. Just how we are excluded
and included in our justification was the real point of controversy between the Protestant and Roman Catholic doctrines
of justification. We shall limit our discussion to what is for
systematic theology the most important part of the historical
information. In that respect the decisions of the 'doctrinal office
of the church' are the most vital for the Roman Catholic. It
cannot be the task of Protestant theology to make judgements
about how these decisions are to be interpreted, revised or not
revised. Here Protestant theology can only ask questions, express
hopes and issue challenges. To what extent this has an influence
on the current internal processes of clarification in the Catholic
Church is one of the burning questions of today's ecumenical
dialogue. Conversely, linked to this is the question of how far

those Catholic processes have a positive influence on the Protestant understanding of justification.

I. Christ alone (*solus Christus*)

The God who justifies is the triune God who in the person of the Son of God became man, died for us and for our justification was raised from the dead. The Christian church believes in and confesses Jesus Christ as true God and true man. A key issue in the doctrine of justification is the identification of the Son of God with Jesus the man. The death of Jesus can only have any meaning for justifying sinners if *God himself* is also present in the death of this *man*. If Jesus' death on the cross were to be considered *only* as the end (whatever that may mean) of the life of a human being, then the cross of Christ would have no saving effect, no power to justify sinners and no meaning for our salvation. If the death of Jesus meant simply the end of an important man, then this death could in no way be considered a salvific event (*sacramentum*); at the most it would be seen as a moral example (*exemplum*). Then, as Luther so clearly put it, Jesus would not be our Saviour, but would himself need a saviour.[1] It is the identification alone of the Son of God with Jesus the man which makes Jesus Christ the Saviour, the σωτήρ, through whom alone the world is saved and sinners are justified. Since God himself has acted once and for all in this man alone, the *particula exclusiva* of *solus Christus* is both possible and essential.

1. The exclusiveness and the inclusiveness of Jesus

The beginning and end of the Christian faith is to be found in our justification in Jesus Christ alone. This was highlighted when we attempted to understand justification as the truth of life and to identify this truth with the person of Jesus. The definitive text for any such attempt is John 14:6: 'I am the way, and the

---

[1] Cf. M. Luther, *Confession Concerning Christ's Supper*, LW 37, 209–10.

truth, and the life. No one comes to the Father except through me.' Christ alone is the truth of life.

Whenever it talks of Jesus Christ, it is the habit of the New Testament to either emphasize his total uniqueness or to simply assume it. Thus we read in Acts 4:12: 'There is salvation in no one else, for there is no other name under heaven given among mortals by which we must be saved.' Paul expresses the same idea with the Old Testament picture of the cornerstone (cf. Rom. 9:32f.), but above all when he talks of the foundation: 'For no one can lay any foundation other than the one that has been laid; that foundation is Jesus Christ' (1 Cor. 3:11; cf. Eph. 2:20; 1 Pet. 2:4–8). In Hebrews 13:8, the uniqueness of Christ in the temporal sense is brought out: 'Jesus Christ is the same yesterday and today and forever' (cf. Rev. 1:17f.). This is also what all the Christological titles of divinity say: Jesus alone is the Christ, he alone is the Saviour and Lord of all people. If Jesus is confessed as Lord, then it is not simply in order to proclaim him in addition among all other possible lords, which would obviously include the Roman emperor. No, confessing Jesus as Lord means an uncompromising denial of the title *kurios* to all other lords. After all, the Roman emperor did threaten all of these with the death penalty. And finally, faith in Jesus Christ says that we are believing in Jesus as the Christ, the Son of God, which is also another way of saying: in Christ alone. It is not possible to believe in Jesus Christ and at the same time expect another. 'Believing in him means believing in him alone.'[2] The use of 'Christ alone' excludes all other 'saviours'. Faith in Jesus Christ implies that only he can stand and has stood in the place of all people.

[2] Ebeling, *Dogmatik des christlichen Glaubens*, vol. 3, 220. The question that is immediately raised, of the relationship of the Christian faith to other religions, needs a separate treatment. The most urgent task of such a discussion would be to protect the uncompromising confession of Christ alone from being misused to legitimize religious intolerance. If we say 'Christ is our peace' (Eph. 2:14), then, in the spirit of our affirmation of mutual otherness, the exclusive formulae 'Christ alone' must be considered to be quite simply the foundation of religious tolerance. It is after all in the story of his *suffering* that he shows himself to be the Saviour of all.

Only he and he alone! But this one alone takes the place of all others and so represents all others. That is the *inclusiveness*, which is the goal of Jesus' exclusiveness. Both are fundamentally linked to each other in the *concept of substitution*. This concept links the element of Jesus' exclusiveness to that of inclusiveness. It says that this one single person died for all (2 Cor. 5:14f.). Therefore in him all are made alive (1 Cor. 15:22). Thus the aim of confessing the exclusiveness of Christ is to decide the status of all people. In him *alone* all people are included. His *exclusiveness* consists in the *universal inclusion* of all people.

The possibility of such an exclusive inclusiveness consists in Jesus Christ being at the same time true man and true God. This was our point of departure, to which we must now return, in order to examine it more closely. The personal union (*unitio personalis*), by which the eternal Son of God took on our humanity (*natura humana*) and identified himself with our story, makes it possible for this one alone to represent all. In the face of all kinds of ancient and modern Christological errors which menace us here, we must emphasize forcefully that Jesus Christ is the one who, not because of his particular humanity, but only because of the love of God which identified itself with his humanity, was and is able to stand as a representative for all the rest of humanity.[3] To this extent the phrase 'Christ alone' (*solus Christus*) implies one God alone (*solus Deus*). This means it is *only this God* who has identified himself with this man Jesus and in him has identified himself with our reality and our story. He is thus in his very divinity not 'merely divine' but absolutely human.

2. Christ alone, because God alone

This is how the Reformers understood and emphasized Jesus Christ alone as the centre of their theology and preaching.

---

[3] Ebeling's interpretation of inclusive exclusiveness seems to me problematic, because he argues the other way around: that others have 'in him the just man united with God . . . and thus' can find 'in him the true man united with God' (ibid., 220).

Within the circles of the Reformers, Luther even argued (against Zwingli) that *only* the God who is personally united with the man Jesus in his humanity is our salvation and only thus is *Christ alone* our Saviour. In his major polemical tract *Confession Concerning Christ's Supper*, Luther warns his audience about Zwingli's Christology because, in his opinion, at the crucial point it simply does *not* emphasize the personal unity of God and man in the person of Jesus Christ. It restricts the suffering and death to Jesus' human nature, in order to maintain the metaphysical thesis that the divine nature cannot suffer. But in doing this, it reduces the significance of Jesus Christ to that of a holy person. 'For if I believe that only the human nature suffered for me, then Christ would be a poor Saviour for me, in fact, he himself would need a Saviour . . . Indeed, you must say that the person (pointing to Jesus) suffers, and dies. But this person is truly God, and therefore it is correct to say: the Son of God suffers.'[4] Luther expressed himself in a similar vein and went so far as to speak of the death of God. The Lutheran confession *The Formula of Concord*, in the 'Solid Declaration', Article VIII, has these additional words: 'If it is not true that God died for us, but only a man died, we are lost . . . but since God and man are united in one person, it is correct to talk about God's death when that man dies . . .'.[5]

It is obvious that the formula 'Christ alone' is inadequate. If it is not expressly related back to *God* in Christ, it could lead to the misunderstanding that it was a religious devotion to some hero. The man Jesus would be seen as a holy luminary or heroic saint, a charismatic religious leader or revolutionary hero, and rallying around and honouring him would bring justification. 'Christ alone' would then be a motto 'in the bad sense . . . , that people are convinced that by joining themselves to him, by taking up his cause, they are on the right side and are justified by having the right party badge; they are identified as being just'.[6] However, the exclusive formula 'Christ alone' does not

---

[4] Luther, ibid., 210.
[5] *Formula of Concord, BC,* 599.
[6] Ebeling, loc. cit.

mean such an exclusiveness; it 'does not have the character of an elite group gathered around a demanding leader figure'[7] or around the head of a religious school or of a movement for moral renewal. It says that *in Jesus Christ alone*, none other than *God himself* has come into the world and that therefore in this one person *the salvation of all people* is determined.

3. The representative sacrificial death of Christ

God himself came into the world in Jesus Christ and our salvation is decided only by the God who came into the world. This fact is most succinctly expressed by the representative sacrificial death of Jesus.

(a) Problems of understanding

The tradition that Paul inherited and took over as his point of departure is that Jesus Christ died for us. Paul gives focus to this basic tenet of early Christian proclamation by saying that God made him to be sin who knew no sin (2 Cor. 5:21). This is to say that Jesus in dying took our place so that we might live. His death has the effect of bringing life. As Luther interprets it: by his death Jesus put death to death.[8] In his *Lectures on Galatians* Luther described the death of Christ – the death of deaths – as a sacrificial death: '[the Son of God] . . . gave and offered Himself to God as a sacrifice for us miserable sinners, to sanctify us forever'.[9] The sanctification of sinners through Jesus' sacrificial death should obviously be seen as the self-communication of a holy, godly life made possible by his death. This life is communicated to human beings who are completely unholy and who advance the power of death and bring death down on themselves by their unholiness. This understanding of Luther's brings him close to the biblical model of atonement. By

---

[7] Ibid.

[8] Cf. M. Luther, *Randbemerkungen zu Augustinus, De Trinitate* IV, 3 (Ca. 1509), *WA* 9, 18, 27f. 'per mortem suam mortem momordit'.

[9] M. Luther, *Lectures on Galatians*, *LW* 26, 177: 'Sacrificium offert se deo pro nobis miseris peccatoribus, ut nos sanctificaret in aeternum.'

rapprochement with the biblical model, we shall attempt to explain how the death of Jesus Christ is able to atone for the sin of human beings in such a way that the righteousness of God is communicated to sinful humans.

In doing this we must be aware of a hermeneutical problem. In the ancient world the concept of sacrifice, even an atoning sacrifice, was quite taken for granted. The modern context is totally different and the concept has no value for us. While for the ancients, 'religion and everyday existence interpenetrate so completely that every community, every order must be founded through a sacrifice',[10] in the present time we know of the concept of sacrifice only in the moral sense. For example, wealthy countries make a financial sacrifice for the sake of the poor ones. It is obvious that the procedures and concepts of religious sacrifice, as well as the cultic atoning sacrifice have lost any meaning, as have the cultic rites which were the ancient context for sacrifice. So it is difficult for us to comprehend when the New Testament speaks of the death of Jesus Christ as a sacrificial death in the sense of an atoning sacrifice.

Paradoxically, the fact that the ancient ideas of cultic sacrifice have lost their context and common currency goes well together with the New Testament interpretation of Jesus' death as sacrificial. The crucifixion of Jesus was seen as not only one sacrifice among the many repeated cultic sacrifices, but as the one sacrifice, offered and completed once and for all (cf. Heb. 10:12, 14 with v. 10). For that very reason the institution of cultic sacrifice was obsolete. The rites of sacrifice had been a natural thing until this time. But then they were extinguished with the spread of Christianity and its preaching of the death of Jesus as the sacrifice valid once and for all. At the same time the cultic dimension of the category of sacrifice became virtually meaningless. Sacrifice became primarily a moral category, so that now the primary and dominant ethical use of the sacrifice terminology makes it difficult to achieve a correct theological

[10] W. Burkert, *Greek Religion: Archaic and Classical*, trans. J. Raffan, Oxford: Basil Blackwell, 1985, 59.

understanding of the death of Jesus Christ. It has been the historical result of the model of atonement being used in an exclusively Christological sense that has made it so difficult for us today to understand Jesus' death as an atoning sacrifice. Having said this, we wish nevertheless to endeavour to explain in a systematic way what is really meant by sacrifice. What happens when a sacrifice is made?

(b) Sacrifice: confession of sin and admission of lost perfection[11]

To sacrifice means to make an admission. It means admitting that there is a split in one's own existence: one's life has got caught up with itself. It also means admitting the split between one's own life and one's community – whether that be human community, or community with nature or the cosmos. To sacrifice means to admit the loss of the 'immediate presence of whole, undivided . . . Being'.[12] It also means admitting a total incapacity and inability to reconstruct this being. Sacrificing means admitting that one is the opposite of a holy person and is thus unable to meet the holy God. So the sacrifice is made from the best that one has in order through this means to gain contact with the holy. Sacrificing means acknowledging that one is forced to rely on an intermediary. The sacrifice is thus an admission of human guilt. The one making the sacrifice admits: 'I am a sinful person.'

If this were not the case, there would be no need for a sacrifice. If this person were holy, his or her whole life would express and fulfil the immediate presence of the whole, un-divided being. Where this completeness comes about, nothing else needs to replace it; there is no need of a sacrifice. There would be no split which cast a cloud over one's own life and life context. The holy God himself would be present.

---

[11] What follows is a summary of my essay 'The Sacrifice of Jesus Christ as Sacrament and Example' in *Theological Essays II*, ed. J. Webster, trans. A. Neufeldt-Fast and J. Webster, Edinburgh: T&T Clark, 1994, 163–90.

[12] H. Steffens, *Von der falschen Theologie und dem wahren Glauben*, 1831 (2nd edn), 99f. Quoted by Schleiermacher in *The Christian Faith*, 7.

But since God is not present in guilty, divided human exist-ence, since the split in our own being expresses the deepest possible split, the alienation between God and us, we need to make sacrifices. Thus sacrifice is a substitution. It makes sub-stitution for our missing holiness. To be holy means to be complete. The sacrifice makes substitution for the lost unity of the whole, undivided being. The substitution of the sacrifice occurs *pars pro toto* (the part for the whole), in the strict sense of the term. We are guilty because of the damage that exists to our wholeness. And since we owe God the wholeness of our life context, a part, a sacrifice must substitute for the whole that we owe. If the Godhead accepts the sacrifice, the part has been accepted for the whole.

(c) The promise and the problem of sacrifice

Both a *promise* and a *problem* are connected with the fact that in sacrifice a part of the whole, undivided being replaces the whole that is missing. In a less theological vein, we might also call the promise a religious fascination, and the problem could be called suspicion of religious illusionism or magic.

It is a clear part of the *promise* of sacrifice that human beings do not perish from the guilt of having forfeited the unity of existence. As long as they continue to sacrifice, they must not despair through guilt. The possibility of *a part*, of *something* replacing the whole offers a basic *hope of relief* to the guilty. By sacrificing, we are relieved of the impossible task of supplying what is missing: a whole, undivided existence. We hand this over to God who takes the part for the whole. And with this relief we experience *in, with and under the part*, a foreshadowing, a similitude, a promise of that missing presence of whole, undivided existence. For that reason, with sacrifice there usually comes *fellowship* as the most immediate expression of the promised unity and completeness of life.

However, we must not underestimate the *problem* that is without any doubt linked to the institution of sacrifice. The problem consists in the danger of taking the promise for the fulfilment, the sign for what it actually signifies, but *only signifies.*

This 'representative character of cult', which has accurately been described as 'making the intangible accessible to our senses'[13] conceals what we might term a seductive potential for the sacrifice to be turned into a holy work – in the sense of a rite which is efficacious through its very performance (*ex opere operato*). In such rites, human beings give God something which compels God to reciprocate by giving something more (*do ut des*). The sacrifice then becomes 'a kind of theurgy',[14] by which we paradoxically make our own protection from God. 'Instead of a terror-stricken flight to God', the sacrifice 'may become a sinful flight from Him to a sacred work ... [T]he prophets (Amos 5:21f., Isa. 1:10f., Jer. 7:21f.) and many of the Psalms (like 40:7f., 50:13f., 51:18f.) take up their well-known inflexible attitude against it'.[15] If this misuse of the institution of sacrifice is taken to be its real function, then the critical denunciation of the cult of sacrifice suggests itself as 'a kind of serious "theat[re]" that really has nothing at all to do with God'.[16]

Yet normally such modern objections fall far short of the mark: 'The ancients, however, were aware of the inadequacies of cult . . .'[17] And even the high point of Israelite worship, the sprinkling of the – non-existent – *kapporet* on the – long-lost – Ark in the Holy of Holies was a pretence. 'This provisional nature of cult *as if* [the Ark were there] must have been deeply disquieting to Israel . . .'.[18]

The objection which has more far-reaching theological implications takes, by contrast, a positive view of the promise in

---

[13] H. Gese, 'The Atonement' in idem, *Essays on Biblical Theology*, trans. K. Crim, Minneapolis: Augsburg, 1981, 100. In addition, see B. Janowski, *Sühne als Heilsgeschehen. Studien zur Sühnetheologie der Priesterschrift und zur Wurzel KPR im Alten Orient und im Alten Testament* (*WMANT* 55), Neukirchen-Vluyn: Neukirchener Verlag, 1982; O. Hofius, 'Sühne und Versöhnung. Zum paulinischen Verständnis des Kreuzestodes Jesu', in idem, *Paulusstudien* (*WUNT* 51), Tübingen: Mohr Siebeck, 1994 (2nd edn), 33–49.

[14] Gese, 'The Atonement', 100.

[15] Barth, *CD* IV/1, 278.

[16] Gese, 'The Atonement', 100.

[17] Ibid., 100.

[18] Ibid., 115.

the sacrifice and asks whether human beings are really able to make a sacrifice which replaces the missing relationship with God and the lost unity of existence. Can a part really substitute for the whole?

(d) The Old Testament institution of atonement

The problem of substitution has been raised by this question. We shall examine the problem by paying special attention to the idea of atonement. This is presupposed in the New Testament when it speaks of the salvific significance of Jesus' death.[19]

In Israel, the understanding of sacrifice as atonement, that is, of 'atonement as an element of sacrifice, ... is not found before the post-exilic period'.[20] But at this time atonement is recognized 'as the basis of cult. It was recognized that cult is possible only as an act of atonement, and therefore atonement must determine the nature of the cultic realm'.[21] The New Testament's talk of sacrifice, including its Christological concept of sacrifice, emerges from this 'new orientation'[22] of the cult, which says (according to *P*) that 'not only do the sin offerings bring atonement, but all sacrifices do'.[23] When Jesus Christ – and in particular his death – is seen as a sacrifice, the New Testament means an atoning sacrifice. To understand the importance of this we need to look back to the Old Testament.

It must first be remembered that atonement is something different from making reparations. Atonement is for when reparations cannot be made. The idea of atonement presumes that there is a transgression *which cannot be paid out*, a kind of debt that simply cannot be reckoned in ledgers and balanced like other debts. It is not possible for such a transgression, such a debt to be cancelled out *by human debtors*. It remains there. Any extinction of the debt can only come with the extinction of

---

[19] This idea is explicit in the pre-Pauline tradition (Rom. 3:25) and in Hebrews, and implicit in the Pauline doctrine of justification.

[20] Gese, 'The Atonement', 99.

[21] Ibid., 100.

[22] Ibid., 101.

[23] Ibid., 103.

the debtor. It is not *some thing*, no matter how much, but their *lives* that they must give in order to atone for their debt. So 'for those humans, atonement means a readiness to die'.[24] However, so that they might not die, these debtors bring an atoning *sacrifice*, which takes their place. Thus an atoning sacrifice is *another sacrifice* which substitutes for the life of the one who has deserved death. This other substitutes for the guilty debtor as a sacrifice in the cultic sense. The guilty one lays his or her hand on the head of the sacrifice as a sign of individuality, and thus is identified with the sacrifice. So the laying on of the hand means not the symbolic act of placing one's own guilt onto the sacrificial animal, but an action which has far greater ontological repercussions: 'a transference of the subject'.[25] The result is that the one making the sacrifice recognizes himself or herself in the fatal destiny of the sacrifice. 'The act of atonement is not to be thought of as a transfer of sins with the subsequent execution of the one bearing the sins, the sacrificial animal . . . Instead, in cultic atonement the sacrifice of the victim's life is a substitution that includes the one bringing the sacrifice.'[26]

We need to recall further that the sacrifice seen as an atoning substitution does not have the function of merely annihilating the victim. If that were the case, sinners could atone for themselves. In a manner of speaking, they would quench God's wrath by making an end of the sinful life by (*a*) a transference of the subject and (*b*) the killing of the sacrifice with which they had identified. Atonement would then mean: to appease a wrathful God by a blood-offering (or, taking a leaf from Anselm of Canterbury: to give satisfaction to the divine majesty by the offering of a life). However, this idea, which recurs endlessly in church doctrine and preaching, is unbiblical. It is not God who is conciliated, but God who reconciles the world. Sinful human beings do not atone for themselves; the Holy God removes the sin from sinful human beings. He does this by granting his

---

[24] Ibid., 99.
[25] Ibid., 106.
[26] Ibid., 106.

holiness to those who are totally unholy. This giving, this contact of the holy with the unholy is what *kills*. 'Cultic atonement thus is not accomplished merely by the death of the sacrifice, but in the commitment of life to what is holy, in contact with holiness.'[27] And only in so far as the holy God is pleased with the transference of the subject from the sinful human being to the sacrificial animal can the death of that animal validly atone for the one making the sacrifice – an atonement which allows the sinner to 'escape . . . from the guilt that deserved death.'[28] The atoning sacrifice makes a fatal encounter with the holy possible – and behold, we live!

(e) Christ, the sacrament of the world

We can now resume and complete our consideration of the institution of sacrifice as promise and sign. We can also deal with any appropriate reservations about the matter.

It is a fundamental principle of Old Testament sacrificial concepts that no sacrifice which has been made by the transference of the subject can atone once and for all. In the Old Testament, the atoning sacrifice is made in each case *ad hoc*. Israel depends on its being repeated. This is why Israel's need for a repetition of the sacrifice is 'a shadow of the good things to come' (Heb. 10:1). This is also a fundamental principle of Old Testament sacrificial concepts: the substitutionary offering of a life by an animal which has been sacrificed by the transference of the subject cannot express and effect the final healing of humanity. Not even the sacrifice of a single person could express and effect the fact that God removes the sin from human beings; he atones for the world. How could one single person assume liability for the lost wholeness of undivided being and make a substitutionary atonement for all?

What is needed is for that lost completeness to be present again. What is needed is for the whole of creation to be present. And that can only mean that the divine Creator must be present in the form of the creation.

---

[27] Ibid., 106.

Of course, we are mentioning this too late; we are working backwards from effect to cause. We are looking back to the fact that such a presence of the Creator in the creation *has become reality*. We are not making an assumption, but rather confessing the mystery of Jesus Christ when we say that only a completely different 'transference of the subject', only the identification wherein the holy God identifies himself with a person and identifies this person with all of humanity can give to this one person the power to be a substitute for all. In this sense the New Testament tradition very clearly confessed – and this was a stumbling block to Jews and folly to the Gentiles – that it was the Son of God who, in the person of Jesus Christ – himself human – gave up his life for us, for everybody (Gal. 2:20; cf. Rom. 8:32; John 3:16) and thus deserves to be called the sacrifice which is well-pleasing to God (Eph. 5:2) or, again, the one, true Mediator (1 Tim. 2:5). By the blood of this human being the eternal High Priest himself (cf. Heb. 7:20–27) once and for all through the eternal Spirit offered himself without blemish to God (Heb. 9:14, 23, 26).

So now the only-begotten Son of God (John 1:18, 14) can be called most emphatically the Lamb of God who takes away the sin of the world (John 1:29). According to 1 Peter 1:19f. he was recognized before the foundation of the world as being the Lamb without defect or blemish, and so he will be revealed at the end of the age. Since the eternal God has identified himself with this human being, since Jesus Christ the human being is the Son of God, for that reason the whole of humanity is integrated in his humanness. Thus we are all present in the One, so that it is true to say: 'One has died for all; therefore all have died' (2 Cor. 5:14; cf. Rom. 5:12–21). Thus Jesus the human being (the *homo humanus*) is identical with human nature (the *natura humana*), so that Christian doctrine is right to express the mystery of God's becoming human not as him taking on human life *(assumptio hominis)*, but as him assuming human nature *(assumptio humanae naturae)* in the person of the Son of God. In this way the early theologians with their language and thinking about substance and ontology emphasized the universal scope of the identity of the Son of God with the one distinctive person Jesus. In so doing they dared *to think* that Jesus Christ is the *sacramentum mundi* – the generally recognized great Sacrament *per se* (cf. 1 Tim. 3:16). Not only was God shown as reconciling the world in him, but this reconciliation was accomplished in him. This did not come about by a replacement, but, if we may use this term, by the ontologically appropriate substitution. Therefore he is the epitome of the perfect sacrifice, sacrificed once and for all. There is no meaningful sacrifice that can follow.

(f) The death of Christ: God's offering of himself

Compared with the Old Testament institution of sacrifices, there are major changes in the New Testament meaning of the death of Jesus as a sacrifice.

We must note first *the reversal of the order of events* from what goes to make up the sacrificial system in the Old Testament, which has three of these events. In the Old Testament, they must occur *in an order that cannot be altered*: (1) the consecration, which is to be seen as a transference of the subject or of identity; (2) the killing of the sacrificial beast; (3) the incorporation into the Holy which is meant by these two acts. Now, on the other hand, when we interpret the death of Jesus – as Ingolf Dalferth has rightly emphasized[29] – the order is reversed. The goal of

---

[28] Ibid., 101.

[29] I. U. Dalferth, 'Die soteriologische Relevanz des Opfers. Dogmatische Erwägungen im Anschluß an die gegenwärtige Diskussion', in *Freude an der Wahrheit. Freundesgabe zum 50. Geburtstag von Eberhard Jüngel*, W. Hüffmeier and W. Krötke, eds, 1984, 102–28: 118ff.; reprinted in a revised version in I. U. Dalferth, *Der auferweckte Gekreuzigte. Zur Grammatik der Christologie*, Tübingen: Mohr Siebeck, 1994, 271ff. For a reply to Dalferth and the idea of substitutionary sacrifice, see the impressive argument of J. Fischer, 'Glaube als Erkenntnis. Zum Wahrnehmungscharakter des christlichen Glaubens' (*BEvTh* 105, [1989], 76–86). Fischer puts forward a convincing objection to the tendency of the idea of substitution to eliminate that insight, both practical and theoretical (p. 83), which is fundamental to the soteriological effect of sacrifice. This causes what Fischer calls the practical recognition that has the power to translate the sinner to a different existential plane to be further underestimated. However, in my opinion, what Fischer says still is far from making talk of substitution itself obsolete.

the Old Testament sacrifice, which was to incorporate people
into the Holy, now becomes the fundamental act: at the cross
of Jesus Christ, God accomplishes the incorporation of sinful
humanity into his own life, the life of the holy God. This
'incorporation is no longer a soteriological goal; it has become
a soteriological pre-condition of identity transfer . . . , in so
far as God himself has publicly set forth Jesus, by his resurrection, as the place of his saving presence, and has incorporated
us in the person of Christ proleptically into his fellowship'.[30]
This act coincides factually with the execution of the human
Jesus of Nazareth by the powers in charge. But please note: it
is not God who sacrifices the human Jesus – this is not human
sacrifice! No, God so identifies himself with the human Jesus
put to death by humans, that we must affirm that this human
being was God's Son. To put it accurately: God does not
identify himself with the executioners, but with the executed
one. In a manner of speaking, he makes the best of the killing
of a human by humans, when he makes the one killed out to
be a sacrifice and in this one makes himself – in the person of
the Son of God – a sacrifice. God so identified himself with the
crucified one, if we are to follow the earliest Christian Easter
confessions, that it must be said: in this human being God
has come into the world. So here humanity no longer accomplishes the salvific act of incorporating itself into the Holy, as
in the Old Testament sacrificial system – a 'coming to God
by passing through the sentence of death'.[31] Now it is 'God
coming to us . . . , with which humans in faith are consistent,
and in unbelief contradictory'.[32]

So faith is now the transfer of identity by which the individuals
so identify themselves with the fate of Jesus that they know
they have died and been raised from the dead *with him*.
'Faith, considered from the point of view of sacrifice, is the
transfer of identity that corresponds to the Old Testament

[30] Dalferth, *Der auferweckte Gekreuzigte*, 277.
[31] Gese, 'The Atonement', 114.
[32] Dalferth, *Der auferweckte Gekreuzigte*, 277f.

function of the laying on of hands.'[33] Thus the structure of Old
Testament worship (consecration – death – incorporation) is
replaced by the exactly inverse structure of the cross (Christ –
cross – faith), when we understand the death of Jesus Christ, as
do the corresponding New Testament traditions, to be a
sacrifice.

Here we need to observe another vital difference which has
also been pointed out by Ingolf Dalferth. The Old Testament
sacrificial system had *several actants*; on the one hand there is
the high priest, who identifies himself with the sacrificed animal
by the laying-on of hands; then there is the priest who kills the
animal, and finally there is God, who accepts the sacrifice – the
transfer of the subject and the offering up to the Holy. God
reconciles the high priest and allows him to live, snatches him
from a deserved death. In contrast to this, the New Testament
interpretation of Jesus' death as atoning sacrifice recognizes
God and God alone as actant: God acts in Christ by reconciling
the world to himself in Christ. God has exposed himself to death
in the person of his Son. But God also acts in human beings by
awakening faith and thereby granting believers their new
identity as saints – we can also say: as Christians. In the act of
salvation at the cross and when he awakens faith, God acts
alone. In the soteriological act of the cross, there is no *do ut
des* ('I give that you may give'), nor is there any *do quia dedisti*
('I give because you have given'), for 'humans give God nothing
whatsoever, but God, on the other hand, gives them everything'.[34] Indeed, he gives himself, precisely so that we may
say: *God sacrifices himself.* Because we have to speak of *God's self-
sacrifice* (a concept which of course forces us to speak of the
Trinity) it is clear that the sacrificial system of worship has now
basically been cancelled. We may perhaps not go so far as
Dalferth who claims that this model 'has been soteriologically
shattered from within'.[35] But we can, in fact, claim that the

---

[33] Ibid., 276.
[34] Ibid., 282.
[35] Ibid.

sacrificial system of worship has been soteriologically abolished and *ended* from within by the sacrificial death of Jesus. Therefore we had better not say that Christian soteriology is 'possible . . . without this category',[36] but we can say that understanding the death of Jesus Christ as a sacrifice which reconciles humanity, in which God has given himself in the person of the Son, from now on renders impossible any use of the category of sacrifice other than the Christological. The sacrifice on the cross happened once and for all, so that no further meaningful sacrifices can follow. 'His sacrifice means that the time of *being* has dawned in place of that of signifying – of the being of man as a faithful partner in covenant with God, and therefore of his being at peace with God.'[37]

(g) Sacrifice: a metaphor for the Christian life

Peace is, in fact, the category which appropriately encompasses the goal and the outcome of the sacrificial death of Jesus Christ. It expresses two concepts. On the *negative* side, peace means that every human being *really died* on the cross of Jesus Christ (Rom. 6:6–8; 2 Cor. 5:14; Col. 2:20, 3:3) and since the death of Christ the old self no longer has a future. 'I have been crucified with Christ; and it is no longer I who live' (Gal. 2:19f.). This negative side must on no account be seen as purely 'symbolic'. It is not possible to interpret it 'realistically' enough! If Jesus' humanity thanks to his identity with the person of the Son of God integrates the humanity of all human beings, then his death is the death of all of us. And then, in the negative sense, our peace with God is our finish. As representatives of what is old, which, according to 2 Corinthians 5:17 has finally passed away, we have peace with God, as long as on our side we have *passed away*. The old self is now no longer simply old, but hopelessly out of date: a being from the past. In that sense only does it have any 'being'. Or to put it more accurately: only in that sense can it walk abroad, instead of – *requiescat in pace!* – resting in peace.

---

[36] Ibid., 283.
[37] Barth, *CD* IV/1, 281.

Now the meaning of peace in real language (and especially in biblical language) is not this negation, but rather something very positive. The biblical dimension of peace, of *shalom*, can only be reached when this negation of the unholy opens the way positively to the Holy. It is in this sense, says Paul, that as justified people we have peace and access to God (Rom. 5:1). Part of this peace which is Jesus Christ (Eph. 2:14) is the fact that the passing of the old is eclipsed by the coming of the new. 'So if anyone is in Christ, there is a new creation: everything old has passed away; see, everything has become new!' (2 Cor. 5:17). For the same Christ, who was handed over to death for the sake of our sins, was raised again for our justification (Rom. 4:25). It was this positive and real dimension of peace that we had in mind when we were speaking of the immediate presence of the whole, undivided being. As the true atoning sacrifice, Jesus is our peace, because he restores to us that lost wholeness of being which is more than the sum of its parts and which thus deserves to be called *salvation*. To acknowledge Christ's atoning sacrifice and to take delight in it means to be justified by faith and as a consequence to have peace.

If Jesus Christ is himself the perfect sacrifice, then the sacrificial system of worship has been completely abrogated: 'there is no longer any offering for sin' (Heb. 10:18). When Jesus (in Matt. 9:13; 12:7) quotes the prophet Hosea concerning the Pharisees: 'I desire mercy, not sacrifice' (Hos. 6:6), this prophecy takes on the force of a judgement which makes the question of the sacrificial system irrelevant. It no longer has any meaning. With the sacrificial death of Jesus, the category of sacrifice has essentially lost its religious context. It has been reduced to a metaphor.

Of course, in the metaphorical sense, the concept of sacrifice and the whole field of terminology that goes with it is still quite useful for describing the Christian life. But when we do this, it is essential to remember that what is now called 'sacrifice' no longer means a deal where the part replaces the whole. The whole of a Christian's life can be described in a metaphorical sense as a sacrifice. This is consistent with the fact that Christ's sacrifice was also no piece of *pars pro toto* bargaining. The whole of life's context was present in him in an immediate sense. This is how the concept of sacrifice of Paul, 1 Peter and Hebrews applies metaphorically to the Christian life.

Paul is able to exhort Christians, in response to God's mercy, to offer themselves physically 'as a living sacrifice, holy and acceptable to God' and thus to celebrate their whole lives as 'spiritual worship' (Rom. 12:1). The author of 1 Peter challenges Christians to let themselves be built into a 'holy priesthood to offer spiritual sacrifices acceptable to God through Jesus Christ' (1 Pet. 2:5). The addition of the word 'spiritual' makes the metaphorical language quite clear. It is not specific sacrificial offerings that the writer has in mind, but the offering to God of a whole life sanctified by God (1 Pet. 1:15). Now the concept of sacrifice can be applied metaphorically to everything a Christian does in life to serve God. Paul can describe his activity in spreading the gospel as 'priestly service' (liturgy) by which the Gentiles who have come to faith or their faith itself is offered up (cf. Rom. 15:16; Phil. 2:17). But he can also be quite down-to-earth and praise the material support which the church has given him as 'a fragrant offering, a sacrifice acceptable and pleasing to God' (Phil. 4:18).

The double use of the sacrificial concept in Hebrews 13:15f. is most instructive for the metaphorical use of sacrificial terminology in the Christian sense. On the one hand, the church is encouraged through Jesus, who has sanctified them with his own blood (Heb. 13:12) to 'continually offer a sacrifice of praise to God, that is, the fruit of lips that confess his name'. But in the same breath the members of the church are exhorted not to neglect to do good and to share what they have 'for such sacrifices are pleasing to God'. Such a double metaphorical use of the concept of sacrifice sends us through the one expression 'sacrifice' straight to the physical needs of those who are dependent on our good actions, communication and fellowship. Thus a Christology of sacrifice presupposes not only the doctrine of justification but Christian ethics.

4. The exclusive formula 'solus Christus' in the formulations of Trent and Vatican II

The meaning of 'Christ alone' (*solus Christus*) admittedly only becomes sufficiently clear when we use the three other exclusive formulae. These, in turn, have no other function than to guarantee a correct understanding of the 'Christ alone' formula. If, on the other hand, we put the other three formulae aside – by grace alone (*sola gratia*), by the Word alone (*solo verbo*), by faith alone (*sola fide*) – the declaration 'Christ alone' would allow a quick and easy ecumenical agreement. This is because the use of 'alone' in a Christological sense is by no means limited to the theology of the Reformers and their confessions.

Of course, they do express themselves very clearly. In the Smalcald Articles (1537) we read that '[Jesus Christ] alone is "the Lamb of God, who takes away the sin of the world"' and thus that 'it is clear and certain that such faith alone justifies us'.[38] In the *Augsburg Confession* XX, the decisive formula from the *Augsburg Confession* IV, that sinners 'are freely justified for Christ's sake through faith'[39] is expounded as follows: 'our sins are forgiven for Christ's sake, who alone is the mediator [and atoning sacrifice] who reconciles the Father'.[40] Finally, the *Formula of Concord*, in its *Epitome* III, expresses the same meaning, that 'Christ alone is our righteousness'[41] and more precisely, 'the entire Christ according to both natures'.[42]

However, the *solus Christus* formula is by no means confined to the theology of the Reformers. All Christian confessions in their different ways use the expression. So what is important is the context of its use. In order to be correctly understood, does it show a need for the other three exclusive formulae, or can it do without them?

---

[38] *BC*, 292.

[39] *BC*, 30: 'gratis iustificentur propter Christum per fidem'.

[40] *BC*, 42: 'Quod propter Christum recipiamur in gratiam, qui solus positus est mediator et propitiatorium, per quem reconcilietur pater.'

[41] *BC*, 472.

[42] *BC*, 473.

Present-day Catholic theology does not dispute the fact that Christ alone is the basis for our justification. In fact, it aims to emphasize it forcefully. To do this, it is able to refer to the classic document of the Catholic magistrum, the Decree Concerning Justification by the Council of Trent. This document, issued at the sixth session of the Council in 1547, is the first coherent Catholic teaching concerning justification. It appears to show no disagreement with the Reformers' doctrine in the matter of the Christological basis for justification. In chapter 2 the sending of Jesus Christ by the Father has for its ultimate motive the justification of Jews and Gentiles and is founded in a universal sense on the salvation of the whole world in Christ: 'God has sent him forth as a propitiation by his blood through faith for our sins (*see* Rom. 3:25), not for our sins only, but also for those of the whole world (*see* 1 John 2:2).'[43] Accordingly, the Decree frequently emphasizes the fact that we are justified or saved *through Christ* (*per Christum*)[44] or *for Christ's sake* (*propter Christum*).[45] It is noteworthy that Christ is no longer defined as the final cause, *causa finalis* (ch. 7: 'the final cause is the glory of God and of Christ[!]: *gloria Dei et Christi*'),[46] but as the meritorious cause, *causa meritoria*, of justification: 'The meritorious cause . . . [of justification] is the beloved only-begotten Son of God, our Lord Jesus Christ, who . . . merited justification for us by his own most holy Passion on the wood of the cross, and made satisfaction for us to God the Father. The instrumental cause is the sacrament of baptism, which is the "sacrament of faith"; without faith no one has ever been justified.'[47] Since it names only God in his mercy as efficient cause (*causa efficiens*),

---

[43] *TCT*, 231 = *DH* 1522: 'Hunc, "proposuit Deus propitiatorem per fidem in sanguine ipsius" (*Rm 3,25*), "pro peccatis nostris, non solum autem pro nostris, sed etiam pro totius mundi" (*1 Io 2, 2*)'.

[44] *TCT*, 232. [See *DH* 1523, 1525, 1537, 1551, 1552; *per fidem*: 1532.]

[45] *TCT*, 233. [See *DH* 1526, 1533.]

[46] *TCT*, 233 = *DH* 1529.

[47] *TCT*, 233–4 = *DH* 1529: Causa '*meritoria* . . . [est] dilectissimus Unigenitus suus, Dominus noster Iesus Christus, qui . . . sua sanctissima passione in ligno crucis nobis iustificationem meruit (*can. 10*), et pro nobis Deo Patri satisfecit; *instrumentalis* item sacramentum baptismi, quod est "sacramentum fidei", sine qua nulli umquam contigit iustificatio'.

and human beings exclusively as instrumental causes of justification (*causa materialis iustificationis*), this Aristotelian–Scholastic
scheme of causes can be interpreted to say that the justification
of sinners is founded on Jesus alone and that there is no question
of other mediators. In any case, it is remarkable and odd that
the final, published version of the Decree did not take up the
clear wording of the draft made in the previous September,
which said expressly that Jesus Christ 'alone merited the righteousness of God, in order to bestow it upon us'.[48] Was this to
leave open the possibility of some human contribution to the
acquisition of divine righteousness?

The pronouncements of Trent were taken up and enlarged
in Vatican II.[49] Of course, the apparently clear Christological
statements of Vatican II are remarkably relativized by 'secondary
soteriological centres',[50] that are indebted to mariology – which
always has overtones of how one sees the church – and that are
apt to call the *solus Christus* formula into question. What are we
to make of the fact that in the *Dogmatic Constitution concerning
the Church* Mary can be described as 'cause of salvation'[51] and

---

[48] *Concilium Tridentinum: Diariorum, actorum, epistularum, tractatuum*, vol. 5, 1911,
423, 32–4: 'Iustitia Dei . . . Dici etiam potest iustita Christi, quia ut ea nobis
daretur, ipse solus meruit, dum in ligno crucis . . . pro nobis Deo Patri satisfecit.'

[49] See, for example, the Dogmatic Constitution Concerning the Church *Lumen
Gentium*, a. 9 and 14, *LThK.*E I, 1966, 176–81 and 198–201 (= *DH* 4122–4 and
4136–8).

[50] H. G. Pöhlmann, *Rechtfertigung. Die gegenwärtige kontroverstheologische Problematik
der Rechtfertigungslehre zwischen der evangelisch-lutherischen und der römisch-katholischen
Kirche*, 1971, 222.

[51] 'Justly, therefore, do the holy Fathers consider Mary not merely as a passive instru-
ment in the hands of God, but as freely co-operating in the salvation of mankind
by her faith and obedience. As St Irenaeus says: "Through her obedience she
became cause of salvation both for herself and for the whole human race"' (ET
in *The Christian Faith in the Doctrinal Documents of the Catholic Church*, J. Neuner
and J. Dupuis, eds, London: Collins, 1983 [revised edn], #56, p. 209 [hereafter
referred to as *ND* (Tr)]: 'Merito igitur SS. Patres Mariam non mere passive a Deo
adhibitam, sed libera fide et oboedientia humanae saluti cooperantem censent.
Ipsa enim, ut ait S. Irenaeus, "oboediens et sibi et universo generi humano causa
facta est salutis"' (*Dogmatic Constitution Concerning the Church*, a. 56, *LThK.*E I,
332f.). Cf. Irenaeus, *Adversus Haereses* III, 22, 4, *FC* 8/3, 278; W. W. Harvey, *Sancti
Irenaei, Episcopi Lugdunensis. Libros quinque adversus Haereses*, vol. 2, Ridgewood,
NJ: Gregg Press, 1965 (= Cambridge, 1857), 123f.

that it can even be remembered with approval that 'the Blessed Virgin is invoked in the Church under the titles of [not only] Advocate, Auxiliatrix, Adjutrix, [but also] Mediatrix'?[52] Is it an example of rigorous thinking, is it credible, that these titles 'in no way diminish . . . the dignity and efficacy of Christ the one Mediator', as the members of the Council[53] hasten to add? How do we reconcile talking of Mary as mediatrix with the declaration that Christ is the one (single) mediator? How can we guarantee that to say *solus Christus* really expresses nothing apart from this: that God alone (*solus Deus*) and not some person – even Mary – or a human institution – even the church – can take our place in such a way as to make sinners righteous? It is obvious that the exclusive formula *solus Christus* needs to be interpreted by the other exclusive formulae.

II. By grace alone (*sola gratia*)

1. Grace in law and theology

The God who justifies is a *gracious God*. He is in the right by his *grace*. He is in the right in the person of Jesus Christ, in whom God's grace has obtained its rightness. However, when the righteousness of human beings is decided in the person of Jesus Christ alone and when God's grace has obtained its rightness in that person and only in him, then sinners are justified *by grace alone*.

Before we ask more closely what is being highlighted by the exclusive formula *by grace alone*, both in a positive and in a negative sense, it is appropriate to reflect briefly on the theological

---

[52] *Dogmatic Constitution Concerning the Church*, a. 62, *LThK.E* I, 338 (= *DH* 4177): 'Propterea B. Virgo in Ecclesia titulis Advocatae, Auxiliatricis, Adiutricis, Mediatricis [!] invocatur.'

[53] 'All of which, however, have to be so understood that they in no way diminish or add to the dignity and efficacy of Christ the one Mediator' (*ND*, 209: 'Quod tamen ita intelligitur, ut dignitati et efficacitati Christi unius Mediatoris nihil deroget, nihil superaddat' (*Dogmatic Constitution Concerning the Church*, loc. cit.). Yet over against this, Cardinal Ratzinger explained that the concept of mediator should be 'renounced for the sake of clarity' (*Theologische Prinzipienlehre. Bausteine zur Fundamentaltheologie*, 1982, 296).

concept of grace. We do this in order to bring out the special features of the topic of God's grace, as opposed to what is normally called 'grace' or 'pardon'. [*The German word 'Gnade' and its various forms can embrace the English concepts of* grace, pardon *and* mercy (Tr).]

The context for the secular concept of grace or pardon is found in the legal system. An act of pardon in the secular sense is an act under law by which something is granted to the pardoned person, something to which he or she is not actually entitled. In this sense to pardon does not necessarily mean to be compassionate. This can be easily understood by looking at the political institution of pardon as it still exists today in Germany. The President and the State Premiers, the ones who have the right of pardon in the Federal Republic of Germany, have no need to know personally those who are to be pardoned. They make their decision according to documentary evidence. Thus pardon here is condescension in the best sense of the word. Justice condescends, comes down to the unjust. It places the unjust, who have been identified and condemned as such by the law, in a new relationship to the community of justice: through pardon they become remade into people fitted for community. Thus the right of bestowing pardon is an abnormal prerogative of the power of the head of state[54] (or of his or her representative) which does not place the one who is granting the pardon in a personal relationship to the pardoned one. Pardon in this sense does not necessarily mean that the former has his or her heart in what is being done. It does not mean that the act of pardoning is an act of compassion in the strict sense of the word. For example, it could be nothing more than a carefully thought-out political strategy.

On the other hand, when we speak of grace or pardon in the emphatic theological sense, and emphasize the exclusive formula *sola gratia* in the framework of justification, we are also thinking of an act of compassion, of divine compassion, an act

---

[54] Cf. A. Ritschl, *The Christian Doctrine of Justification and Reconciliation: The Positive Development of the Doctrine*, trans. H. R. Mackintosh and A. B. Macaulay, Clifton, NJ: Reference Book Publishers, 1966 (1900), 88.

which involves the heart of the one who is pardoning. Not only does God come down when he justifies the sinner by grace, he has mercy on the sinner. 'He had compassion' (ἐσπλαγχνίσθη), as the New Testament often says, when Jesus is being described as having mercy. This is exactly what is meant when we speak of God's grace in pardon: He had compassion on the people. He had mercy on them. Pardon in the theological sense of the word is not only a quality that completely defines the recipient, it is also a quality that has an unparalleled effect in the core of being of the one who pardons. When we speak of the justification of sinners by grace alone, we are claiming for God that his heart is totally characterized by his grace. And for human beings we are making the claim that only this altogether compassionate heart of God and nothing else can make them righteous.[55]

2. Grace: a fundamental element in the loving fellowship of God and human beings

By grace alone, *sola gratia*, we become righteous in the eyes of God, since we are justified through Christ alone. For Christ alone is the perfect expression and fulfilment of divine mercy. If the exclusive Christological formula excludes our having any other mediator but Jesus Christ (or any other mediatrix), then the exclusive formula of *sola gratia* guarantees that everything God has done for humanity in, through and for the sake of Jesus Christ is an unconditional divine gift. It guarantees that justification is something that has come to us only 'out of his

---

[55] To this extent, but only to this extent, as Ritschl emphasized, 'the attitude of God in the act of justification cannot be conceived as that of Judge' (A. Ritschl, *The Christian Doctrine of Justification*, 90). A judge is to judge, not according to his heart, but according to the law. '[E]very judicial judgment is an analytic judgment of knowledge. The consequent decree of punishment or acquittal is equally an analytic judgment, being a conclusion from the prohibitive or permissive law involved and the knowledge of the guilt or innocence of the person accused' (ibid.). On the other hand, the judgement enacted by God in his compassion for sinners, a judgement which justifies by grace alone, is a *synthetic* judgement issuing forth from creative divine love.

pure, fatherly, and divine goodness and mercy, without any merit or worthiness on my part'.[56] If justification did not come about *sola gratia,* but occurred at least in part because of my own merits and qualities, then it would not be because of Christ alone. It would have a further cause apart from God. The *sola gratia* formula protects and ensures that of *solus Christus.* 'Thus, when we speak of justification "sola gratia", it is all about the article of "Christ alone"'.[57] In the justification event, God alone enters into a new fellowship of being with us by his grace alone. It is a fellowship of love because it is one of compassion. But love can never be earned. God's love for us thus flies the banner '*by grace alone*'. A fellowship of love is by definition a fellowship of choice, except that there is an important distinction between a fellowship of love from human being to human being and one of God to human beings. Human love, *amor hominis,* chooses what is attractive and present. Luther emphasized this clearly when, recalling Augustine, he stated: 'The love of man comes into being through that which is pleasing to it'. The *amor crucis,* on the other hand, God's love revealed in the cross of Jesus, discovers nothing attractive, only sin, so that God's love first creates what is attractive by the act of love: 'The love of God does not find, but creates, that which is pleasing to it.'[58] The love of God, the *amor Dei,* is directed to the unlovable and the ugly and by the act of creative love makes them lovable and beautiful.[59] That is the difference between human fellowships of love and the loving fellowship of God and human beings which is founded on compassion. God has mercy on those who are totally unlovable.

---

[56] As Luther put it in his *Small Catechism,* in the context of creation (*BC,* 345).

[57] E. Wolf, 'Sola Gratia? Erwägungen zu einer kontroverstheologischen Formel', in idem, *Peregrinatio. Studien zur reformatorischen Theologie und zum Kirchenproblem,* Munich: Christian Kaiser, 1962, 2nd edn, 113–34: 122.

[58] M. Luther, *Heidelberg Disputation, LW* 31, 41 = *WA* 1, 354, 35f.: 'Amor Dei non inventit sed creat suum diligibile, Amor hominis fit a suo diligibili.'

[59] Cf. ibid, 57: 'Therefore sinners are attractive because they are loved; they are not loved because they are attractive' = *WA* 1, 365, 11f.: 'Ideo enim peccatores sunt pulchri, quia diliguntur, non ideo diliguntur, quia sunt pulchri.'

3. Sola gratia: a theological controversy

But there is also a danger to be avoided: that of perverting the doctrine of justification through emphasizing *sola gratia*. It is important to define this danger more carefully. Just what is the formula *by grace alone* aiming at?

The exclusive formula makes it possible for the justification event itself to be exclusive through God's grace. It also sees it put into place. That formula clearly excludes human beings from taking an active role in their justification. The expression *sola gratia* is meant to guarantee in a most particular way that sinners are unable to justify themselves and to take any active part in their justification. The *sola gratia* formula highlights the fact that God has no starting point in us when he justifies sinners – no starting point except our sin. And sinners in turn have no starting point but the grace of God when their justification is at stake.

Thus the Reformers lent a *negative* emphasis to the very intention of formulating *sola gratia* in a *positive* way when they declared that sinners are incapable of participating actively in their justification because they have a totally depraved human nature. This was because of original sin in the spiritual sense – in sinners' relationship to God. The claim that there is no free will epitomizes the Reformers' teaching that human nature is completely incapable of acting in a way that pleases God. This claim, that there is no free will where God is concerned, was objectionable to the church of that time, as well as for the humanists. Luther met with immediate opposition from Rome. In the Bull *Exsurge Domini* (15 June 1520), Pope Leo X condemned Luther's claim[60] that 'free will, after the fall, exists in name only, and as long as it does what it is able to do, it commits a mortal sin' as one of the 'errors of Martin Luther'.[61] On 20

---

[60] Ibid., 48 = *WA* 1, 359, 33f.: 'Liberum arbitrium post peccatum res est de solo titulo, et dum facit quod in se est, peccat mortaliter.' [Jüngel takes the ambiguous Latin to refer to 'he' (the sinner) wherever the English translation uses 'it' (free will) – Tr.]

[61] Cf. *DH* 1486.

December, Luther responded by burning the Bull which threatened him with excommunication. He also repeated and honed his argument. At first he called free will (*liberum arbitrium*) something that existed in name alone (*res de solo titulo*). Now he branded it a name without substance (*titulus sine re*).[62] The response of the Council of Trent was to declare: 'If anyone says that after Adam's sin man's free will was destroyed and lost, or that there is a question about a term only, indeed, that the term has no real foundation; and that the fictitious notion was even introduced into the Church by Satan: let him be anathema.'[63] In this context the Council also rejected the assertion 'that all works performed before justification, regardless of how they were performed, are truly sins or merit God's hatred; or that the more zealously a person strives to dispose himself for grace, the more grievously he sins'.[64] For its part, as a result of the internal dispute between Flacius Illyricus and his adherents and Victorinus Strigel and his followers, the Lutheran *Formula of Concord* declared the opposite: 'original sin is not a slight corruption of human nature, but . . . so deep a corruption that nothing sound or uncorrupted has survived in man's body or soul, in his inward or outward powers. It is as the Church sings, "Through Adam's fall man's nature and essence are all corrupt"'.[65] The *Solid Declaration* puts it even more strongly: 'Hence according to its perverse disposition and nature the

---

[62] M. Luther, *Assertio omnium articulorum M. Lutheri per bullam Leonis X. novissimam damnatorum*, 1520, WA 7, 146, 6; cf. 146, 4–6.

[63] *TCT*, 242 = *DH* 1555: 'Si quis liberum hominis arbitrium post Adae peccatum amissum et exstinctum esse dixerit, aut rem esse de solo titulo, immo titulum sine re, figmentum denique a satana invectum in Ecclesiam: anathema sit.'

[64] *TCT*, 243 = *DH* 1557: 'Si quis dixerit, opera omnia, quae ante iustificationem fiunt, quacumque ratione facta sint, vere esse peccata vel odium Dei mereri, aut quanto vehementius quis nititur se disponere ad gratiam, tanto eum gravius peccare: anathema sit.'

[65] *Formula of Concord*, *Epitome*, Art. I in *BC*, 467: 'peccatum originis non esse levem, sed tam profundam humanae naturae corruptionem, quae nihil sanum, nihil incorruptum in corpore et anima hominis atque adeo in interioribus et exterioribus viribus eius reliquit. Sicut ecclesia canit: . . .' (the hymn is the choral by Lazarus Spengler).

natural free will is mighty and active only in the direction of that which is displeasing and contrary to God.'[66]

In the light of all this, there would seem to be an unbridgeable gulf between the views of the Reformers and the Roman Catholic Church about our ability to contribute to our justification. Nevertheless, according to a number of notable theologians in recent times, this is not an accurate impression. Since Hans Küng's[67] attempt to demonstrate the basic compatibility of the Tridentine doctrine of justification and that of the Protestants – mainly represented by Karl Barth – there has been a succession of attempts to reach agreement on the matter. Among these are the official efforts at rapprochement between the German state churches. Not least of these was the revisiting of the mutual condemnations of the sixteenth century, which took place after a visit to Germany by Pope John Paul II. This was undertaken by the 'Joint Ecumenical Commission', which claimed to have solved the question of the doctrine of justification (among other matters), as follows: 'the condemnations uttered at that earlier time . . . are still important as salutary warnings'.[68] The Commission continues by saying that they, however, 'no longer apply to our partner today in any sense that could divide the churches'.[69] There was a strong protest from the Protestants about this. For example, Jörg Baur rejected as 'unfounded'[70] the claim that the mutual condemnations of the sixteenth century about justification could not divide the churches of today. In his polemical essay he even described the procedures of the Commission as 'spiritual poison'[71] as they

---

[66] *Formula of Concord, Solid Declaration*, Art. II in *BC*, 521.

[67] H. Küng, *Justification: The Doctrine of Karl Barth and a Catholic Reflection*, trans. T. Collins, E. E. Tolk and D. Grandskou, London: Burns & Oates, 1964.

[68] K. Lehmann and W. Pannenberg, eds, *The Condemnations of the Reformation Era: Do They Still Divide?*, vol. 1, trans. M. Kohl, Minneapolis: Fortress Press, 1990, 27.

[69] Ibid., 68.

[70] J. Baur, *Einig in Sachen Rechtfertigung? Zur Prüfung des Rechtfertigungskapitels der Studie des Ökumenischen Arbeitskreises evangelischer und katholischer Theologen: 'Lehrverurteilungen – kirchentrennend?'*, Tübingen: Mohr Siebeck, 1989, 109.

[71] Ibid., 42.

apparently altered the meaning of the old texts and thus misguided the consciences of people.

I, myself, cannot always agree with the way the Ecumenical Working Group has interpreted the statements from the sixteenth century. There are times when the seriousness of the controversy as it was in those times is undermined. Present-day Roman Catholic doctrine should not be superimposed on what obtained during the controversies of the sixteenth century. Nor should Protestant theology itself be misconstrued as simply repeating the Reformers' statements of those days. It *could* simply be that the disputes of that age have become obsolete today because we hear and understand the gospel of justification from quite different positions – perhaps even without taking up the confessional positions of yesterday. It could be that better insights into the biblical texts free us from the clashes of the past so that certain statements from earlier times appear today as inadequate definitions of the truth of the gospel.

This is certainly true of Luther's claim that the image of God in human beings has been perverted by sin into an image of the devil: 'Adam was created in the likeness of God, which, by his sin, he condemned to ruin. And [instead] he put on the image of the devil.'[72] For the image of God, according to our present-day exegetical and doctrinal insights, is founded in God alone and is thus removed from the grasp of human beings. However, the Roman Catholic objection will appear plausible if we do the following. Put the correct Reformation argument that sinners have no *free* will in regard to God, that in fact our will is always *occupied* – either by God or the devil – alongside the unsuccessful idea of the image of the devil. Now also take the idea of the total depravity of human beings ('through Adam's fall man's nature and essence are all corrupt') in the sense of *imago diaboli*.

On the other hand, if we begin with the viewpoint that the image of God *cannot* be destroyed, even by sin, because it is founded on God's faithfulness, we will be compelled to make

---

[72] M. Luther, *Über das 1. Buch Mose. Predigten* (1527), WA 24, 50, 8f.: 'Adam ... Dei imagine creatus est, quam peccans perdidit et diaboli imaginem induit.'

different claims. We will have to maintain that the *ontological structures* of humanity cannot be destroyed by sin, but that the *ontic-existential* realization of these ontological structures is totally determined by sin. From here we can then better clarify the idea that the human will is in bondage to God.

An inescapable observation emerges from the altered theological situation of today: sinners simply can do nothing for their own justification. Thus any *active preparation* on the part of sinners for their justification is completely excluded. If this point is conceded, it renders a whole series of Tridentine positions untenable. Quite simply, nothing 'good in the sinner' can be found[73] which could contribute to justification. Except that here everything comes about by grace alone. There is simply no objection to saying that we, like Mary, are *present* and must be *present* with our faith and obedience, when our salvation is at stake. In this respect we can honour Mary as the model of a believer.[74] But there is no question of the believer, or of course of Mary, being a cause of salvation, a *causa salutis*.

4. Either faith or works

Thus any active participation on our part in our own justification is excluded, according to this interpretation of the justification event as occurring through grace alone. More precisely, the claim made by Vatican II and some Church Fathers concerning Mary is excluded. According to that assertion, Mary did not merely have a passive role (Latin: *mere passive*) in the work of salvation. Rather, she participated freely through her faith and obedience in our salvation, so that she was even in herself a cause of salvation (*causa salutis*).[75] The exclusive formula *sola gratia* says a clear no to such positions. No human being – and that includes Mary – was an active participant in

---

[73] The Ecumenical Working Group believes this is what Catholic doctrine does; cf. Lehmann and Pannenberg, op. cit., 42 ['And when Catholic doctrine recognizes some good in the sinner, it does so to the glory of God'].

[74] See below, p. 242.

[75] See above, p. 170.

the justification of sinners except the human Jesus. And it is not even true to say that he participated; rather, what he did was to suffer.

To put it more accurately, it is the concept of any demonstrable achievement or works by us that is excluded by the concept of grace. This exclusion is emphasized by the addition of the exclusive formula *sola gratia*, which follows Pauline usage: 'Now to one who works, wages are not reckoned as a gift but as something due' (Rom. 4:4). There is no room for grace in the context of works; otherwise the essence of works (and also the essence of duty!) would be perverted, together with the essence of grace. It is important to note that the essence of works would be lost if the one doing the work were to receive wages according to grace rather than service. Works and grace do not belong in the same category. In Romans 4:4, Paul is not only excluding the particular case where someone who does a work receives wages 'according to grace'. He is also excluding as nonsensical the possibility that wages could be awarded according to grace: 'The labourer deserves to be paid' (Luke 10:7)! It is perverse to reckon wages by grace.[76] Wages are earned. Anyone paying a higher wage than the work deserves is generous, but not gracious. With the concept of grace there comes about a μετάβασις εἰς ἄλλο γένος, a transfer to another category.

Just as, in Romans 4:4, works in principle excludes any payment according to grace, so conversely the concept of grace excludes that of works: 'But if it is by grace, it is [in principle] no longer on the basis of works, otherwise grace would no longer be grace' (Rom. 11:6)! As long as we think we have to achieve something before God in order to gain God's recognition, we begrudge ourselves the good that God has already planned and bestowed on us in Jesus Christ. As long as we are wanting to be

---

[76] According to grace (κατὰ χάριν) one can be chosen as an heir (κληρονόμος) of the promise (ἐπαγγελία), as Romans 4:16 shows. In that case, the expression κατὰ χάριν will have the meaning 'chosen by grace' (κατ' ἐκλογὴν χάριτος) (Rom. 11:5). However, one is justified by grace (χάριτι) (cf. Rom. 11:6), so that it is true to say: 'By the grace of God I am what I am' (χάριτι δὲ θεοῦ εἰμι ὅ εἰμι) (1 Cor. 15:10).

righteous through works, we remain ungracious to ourselves. And what in the world is worse than such a person? Those who despise the grace of God are of necessity ungracious to themselves. They end up having to despair of God and themselves without being able to really despair. On the other hand, those who trust in God's grace alone no longer have to despair of God (and may even be able to despair of themselves). They have conquered their despair of God. They enjoy God. They also, not necessarily, but probably, enjoy themselves, for they are certain that God is a gracious God.

But God's graciousness also has a negative side. Human achievement is excluded from our relationship with God through the person of Jesus Christ. The defining factor of that relationship is not what we achieve, but what is given to us in Christ. Thus in John 1:14 we read that it was said of the Word become flesh, the only-begotten Son of God, that he was 'full of grace and truth'. And in John 1:16 the relationship with God which has been opened up through him is determined by the basic statement: 'From his fullness we have all received, grace upon grace.' For John immediately clarifies the concept of grace by its antithesis, not the concept of works, but that of the law, which requires works: 'The law indeed was given through Moses; grace and truth came through Jesus Christ' (John 1:17).

John's expression 'grace upon grace' – reduplicating grace as it were – says the same thing in a positive way as the exclusive formula *sola gratia* does in a more restricted way: in order for us to be ready and suited for a relationship to God, we are completely reliant on God's grace. We ourselves can contribute nothing towards our fellowship with God, absolutely nothing. We can only receive. We are in fact involved in our justification in a merely passive way (in Latin: *mere passive*).[77] But this is precisely

---

[77] What is the meaning of the Latin phrase *mere passive*? What does it mean to say that we are excluded from any active participation in our own justification, instead of being rightly included in the event? What does passivity mean as opposed to action? Passivity takes many different forms. We need to define more precisely what we mean by saying that human beings, even Mary, even the human Jesus, take part in justification by passive obedience, or simply passively.

what the Roman Catholic Church has contested. In its latest pronouncement on the matter, the Vatican questions 'the use of the expression "*mere passive*"' and in so doing appeals expressly to the decree on justification made by the Council of Trent.[78]

5. The exclusive formula **sola gratia** in Trent

(a) By grace alone?

It is a somewhat complicated task to define the differences between the position of the Reformers on justification and the corresponding Tridentine pronouncements.

There is a passivity of dead material. The block of marble used by the sculptor is passive in comparison to what the artist is doing with it. 'When, through dead stone to breathe a soul of light, / With the dull matter to unite / The kindling genius, some great sculptor glows; / Behold him straining every nerve intent – / Behold how, o'er the subject element, / The stately THOUGHT its march laborious goes!' (F. Schiller, 'The Ideal and the Actual Life' in *The Poems and Ballads of Schiller*, trans. E. Bulwer Lytton, London and New York: F. Warne, 1887, 269). This is not the sort of passivity under discussion when we talk of passivity, of excluding human activity from justification. Rather, the (Old Testament) model of the Sabbath is in view when we think of an exclusively passive participation in justification. There people are transferred to a very lively, spontaneous and creative inactivity. Of course, not working on the Sabbath is not itself to be seen as a work! We can see here, too, how dialectic the concept of passivity is. Doing nothing can be seen as a work, an achievement. We so much want to act, and now we are forced to do nothing; so we *achieve* the doing of nothing. Obviously, that is not what is meant when the Sabbath is referred to. The Sabbath is the day of creative passivity because it is the day of celebration. And when sinners say, with Mary: 'Let it be with me according to your word' (Luke 1:38), they are hardly asserting that human beings are *giving* a place to God and his acts. All we can claim is that we are *leaving* God the room that he takes, that he creates. This is the spontaneous aspect of passivity: leaving God the room that he takes, that he creates for himself – and for us! To put it yet another way: by justifying us, God opens us up to his Word, which creates fellowship and to his grace, which also creates fellowship. It is not that we open ourselves to God, but that God is the one who opens us up. And we let this opening up of ourselves happen, and we enjoy it. This passivity, full of enjoyment of what comes to us from God, is what we mean when we say that human beings take part *mere passive* (Latin) in their justification and when we contradict the claim that Mary or anyone else has any other than a role *mere passive* in the justification event.

[78] 'Response of the Catholic Church to the Joint Declaration of the Catholic Church and the Lutheran World Federation on the Doctrine of Justification', Clarification 3, www.justification.org (documents) (1998). On this, cf. E. Jüngel, 'Amica Exegesis einer römischen Note', *ZThK*.B.10 (1998), 252–79, in particular 267–70.

Even today there is disagreement about how to evaluate the Tridentine doctrine of justification. On the Protestant side, negative assessments outweigh positive. This is understandable, since the condemnations issued by the Council for reform are mostly directed against the Reformers' doctrine of justification: twenty-nine of the thirty-three canons. But from the very beginning the Protestants objected even to the Council's positive statements about justification. The Lutheran theologian Martin Chemnitz drew up an *Examination of the Council of Trent* which was famous in its time.[79] Even in our own day Karl Barth's *Church Dogmatics* – which sees itself as ecumenically open-minded[80] – makes this devastating judgement:

> The Roman Church adopted an official attitude to the Reformation teaching in the decree of the Council of Trent on justification . . . And, unfortunately, we have to admit that in this decree it laid down its attitude for all time. The decree itself is theologically a clever and in many respects a not unsympathetic document which has caused superficial Protestant readers to ask whether there might not be something to say for it. But if we study it more closely it is impossible to conceal the fact that not even the remotest impression seems to have been made upon its exponents by what agitated the Reformers or, for that matter, Paul himself in this whole question of faith and works. Even more depressing is the reason for this lack of understanding: that what was not only to the Reformers but to Paul the climax of justification in its character as a divine work for man was to them a completely unknown quantity . . . It is difficult to see in the Tridentine doctrine of justification anything better than what Paul meant by another gospel. It has no light from above.[81]

Of course, this has been contradicted by Hans Küng, who claims that Barth's own doctrine of justification – but not only his – agrees with the decree on justification made by the Council of Trent, when the latter is correctly understood: 'today there is a fundamental agreement between Catholic and Protestant theology, precisely in the theology of justification – the point at

---

[79] M. Chemnitz, *Examination of the Council of Trent*, trans. F. Kramer, St Louis: Concordia, 1971.

[80] Cf. Barth, *CD* IV/1, 523.

[81] *CD* IV/1, 625–6.

which Reformation theology took its departure'.[82] If such is the case, then this agreement should be evident in the affirmation by both sides of the *particulae exclusivae*.

As we turn to the decree of the Council of Trent on justification, we ask how God's grace in justification is emphasized. In a purely formal sense, the pronouncements by the Roman Catholic office of doctrine also see justification as coming entirely from God. The pronouncements by the Reformers and the Catholics show superficial agreement on the fact that justifying grace *cannot be earned*. The decree of the Council of Trent on justification expressly declares in chapter 8 on unmerited justification (*gratis iustificari*) that 'nothing that precedes justification, neither faith nor works, merits the grace of justification; for if out of grace, then not in virtue of works; otherwise (as the same Apostle says) grace is no longer grace (Rom. 11:6)'.[83] This statement rejects the view that any human action or work before justification could have any merit. If such actions or works are not completely without value in God's eyes,

---

[82] Küng, *Justification*, 271. Barth's position on Küng's argument is worthy of attention: 'You can imagine my considerable amazement at this bit of news; and I suppose that many Roman Catholic readers will at first be no less amazed . . . All I can say is this: If what you have presented . . . is actually the teaching of the Roman Catholic Church, then I must certainly admit that my view of justification agrees with the Roman Catholic view; if only for the reason that the Roman Catholic teaching would then be most strikingly in accord with mine! . . . If the things you cite from Scripture, from older and more recent Roman Catholic theology, . . . and . . . from the Tridentine texts, do actually represent the teaching of your Church and are establishable as such . . . , then, having gone twice to the Church of Santa Maria Maggiore in Trent to commune with the *genius loci*, I may very well have to hasten there a third time to make a contrite confession – "Fathers, I have sinned." But taking the statements of that Sixth Session as we now have them before us . . . don't you agree that I should be permitted to plead mitigating circumstances due to the considerable difficulty I had trying to discover in that text what you had found to be true Catholic teaching? . . . How do you explain the fact that all this could remain hidden so long, and from so many, both outside and inside the Church?' (H. Küng, *Justification*, xvii–xviii).

[83] *TCT*, 235 = *DH* 1532: 'Gratis autem iustificari ideo dicamur, quia nihil eorum, quae iustificationem praecedunt, sive fides, sive opera, ipsam iustificationis gratiam promereatur; "si enim gratia est, iam non ex operibus; alioquin (ut idem Apostolus inquit) gratia iam non est gratia" (*Rm 11, 6*)'. Here we should note the completely distorted parallel between faith and works!

they still do *not* have the value of a *merit*. Or, to put it as the Scholastics might have: they do not have the value of a *meritum de congruo* (of a merit which is only of a meet and fitting kind, which lacks any real claim to recompense) and certainly do not have the value of a *meritum de condigno* (of a merit which is the basis for a genuine and complete claim to recompense).[84] Here the nominalist view would also be rejected, that *before* justification there is a merit of fittingness of '*facere quod in se est*'.[85]

The passage quoted from the decree of the Council of Trent on justification suggests that the Catholic idea of justification agrees decisively with the Reformers' position; that the only effective cause of justification is the gracious, 'the merciful God, who freely washes and sanctifies'.[86] That is to say, *God alone, solus deus*! And *God alone by grace alone: solus deus sola gratia*.

---

[84] At the Council there was a debate at first over whether it should be denied that human works had any merit at all. The more strict conception of the Thomists was conveyed in such a way by the arguing of the Franciscans, whose position was that of *meritum de congruo*, that, in the text which was decided upon, the Thomists could read their own strict view. On the other hand, the Franciscans could also recognize their own position from the text. We may doubt, with H. Rückert ('Promereri. Eine Studie zum tridentischen Rechtfertigungsdekret als Antwort an H. A. Oberman', in idem, *Vorträge und Aufsätze zur historischen Theologie*, Tübingen: Mohr Siebeck, 1972, 264–94) that the verb *promereri* is to be taken in the sense of 'to merit in the full meaning of the word'. That is to say that no action which precedes justification merits *in the full meaning of the word* the grace of justification, so that the statement only excludes the *meritum de condigno* and not the *meritum de congruo* (that is, it sanctions the conception of the Franciscan theologians in the decree). In any case, one can, as usual, read *promereri* as having the same meaning as *mereri*, so that – and this was what the Council wanted – the Thomists were right to read their idea in the document: justifying grace could be merited (*promereri*) neither in the sense of *meritum de condigno* nor in the sense of *meritum de congruo*. 'In the Council's sense, one of the most welcome features of *promereri* is that it acquires a double meaning because of the wording. It means "*mereri de condigno*" and in general "*mereri*". It becomes ambiguous and both Thomists and Franciscans can recognize their positions in the pronouncement as it is phrased. For that very reason it is superbly suitable as a formula which has the element of mediation about it' (ibid., 293f.). It would lose this feature if it tried to make a clear affirmation of *meritum de congruo*. The Thomists would never have been able to agree to such a thing.

[85] Chapter 7, *DH* 1529.

[86] *TCT*, 233 = *DH* 1529: '*misericors Deus, qui gratuito abluit et sanctificat*'. [Note that 'freely' is used in the official translation to render 'gratuito', whereas Jüngel uses 'ohne unser Verdienst' – 'without any merit on our part' (Tr).]

Adolf von Harnack described the Tridentine decree as 'in many respects remarkably well constructed' and raised a doubt 'whether the Reformation would have developed itself if this Decree had been issued at the Lateran Council at the beginning of the century, and had really passed into the flesh and blood of the Church'.[87] In any case for Harnack the decree could only use such language because the Council itself was a *result* of the Reformation. It was a result of that Reformation which placed the doctrine of justification into the central position in theology and the church, so that there had to be an answer from the Catholic side to this very central question. Of course, this answer had to consider too much at once. On the one hand, it had to treat and where necessary balance out the doctrinal disagreements which were internal to the Catholic Church. Then it had to deal with the accusations from the Reformers that the article on justification had been distorted – and the concept of grace was all it needed! And at the same time it had to place certain key statements of the Reformers under anathema. This was done lavishly in the canons which were attachments to the decree. To accomplish all of that would have been some achievement! Thus the document which seems at first 'not disagreeable' appears on closer inspection to be riddled with compromises, in many respects ambiguous and 'unclear because of its sheer cleverness'.[88] In actual fact, the understanding of grace shown by Trent is fundamentally distinct from that of the Reformers.

(b) Differences in the concept of grace

Perhaps the distinction is most obvious in the odd differentiations in the concept of grace which come about, from motives both characteristic and instructive, because of the Roman Catholic understanding of how justification occurs. In true scholastic fashion, they distinguish between, on the one hand,

---

[87] A. von Harnack, *History of Dogma*, trans. W. M'Gilchrist, London: Williams & Norgate, 1899, vol. 7, 57.

[88] F. Loofs, *Leitfaden zum Studium der Dogmengeschichte*, ed. K. Aland, Tübingen: M. Niemeyer, 6th edn 1959, 557.

prevenient grace (*gratia praeveniens*) which awakens the active contribution of human beings to their own justification and helps them in their free collaboration (*gratia excitans et adiuvans*)[89] and, on the other hand, the 'grace of justification' proper (*gratia iustificationis*).[90] Nevertheless, justifying grace can be lost again through any mortal sin – and this occurs 'even though faith is not lost'.[91] Concerning these mortal sins it is said that (and note the differentiation in the concept of grace which here too takes up space!) 'they can be avoided with the help of divine grace' though they 'separate men from the grace of Christ'.[92] This distinction parallels the fundamental one between, on the one hand, grace which precedes, accompanies and follows justification, and on the other hand, 'justifying grace', which effects justification itself. Grace, grace and grace again! But why is there such a mutiplicity of grace? Why split the one grace of God, and thus split God himself into so many graces working in so many different ways?

According to Hans Küng,[93] these basic distinctions in the concept of grace do not compromise the unity of grace (for which Karl Barth, for example, criticized Trent). Rather, 'they are intended only to present the overwhelming and variegated effect on man of God's sovereign action'. In order to understand them appropriately, we need to hold before us the Tridentine 'description' of 'justification itself' as 'a passing from the state in which man is born a son of the first Adam, to the state of grace and adoption as sons of God (*see* Rom. 8:15), through the second Adam, Jesus Christ our Saviour'.[94] This justification itself is 'not only the remission of sins . . . , but sanctification and

---

[89] 'Awakened and assisted by his grace', *TCT*, 232; cf. *DH* 1525.

[90] *TCT*, 235; cf. *DH* 1532; 1542; 1536.

[91] *TCT*, 240 = *DH* 1544: 'Quamvis non amittatur fides . . . , acceptam iustificationis gratiam amitti.'

[92] *TCT*, 240 = *DH* 1544: 'Letalia [= mortalia] . . . peccata, a quibus cum divinae gratiae adiumento abstinere possunt et pro quibus a Christi gratia separantur.'

[93] Küng, *Justification*, 197–8.

[94] *TCT*, 231–2 = *DH* 1524: 'Translatio ab eo statu, in quo homo nascitur filius primi Adae, in statum gratiae et "adoptionis filiorum" (*Rm 8, 15*) Dei, per secundum Adam Iesum Christum Salvatorem nostrum.'

renovation of the interior man through the voluntary reception of grace and gifts, whereby a man becomes just instead of unjust'.[95]

Seeing justification as a passing into the state of grace (*translatio in statum gratiae*) does not, of course, have any direct logical correlation with the claim of a deliberate acceptance of grace (*voluntaria susceptio gratiae*) if, as was decided in chapter 8 (*DH* 1532) 'nothing that precedes justification . . . merits the grace of justification'.[96] Thus the real difference between the Reformation and the Roman Catholic doctrines of justification is found in this exact spot. It becomes obvious when you ask more directly how we are able to participate in our justification. 'Not at all' is the answer of the Reformers as they dispute any human ability to receive grace by our own free will. In a way, this is also disputed by Trent: we receive grace, not because of our free will, but thanks to the grace of God. But this is done with the help of, or through, our free will. It is explicitly claimed that our free will is not completely lost and destroyed because of sin.[97] So at the end of the day the debate about the correct interpretation of *sola gratia* proves to be about Anselm's question of what theological weight to give to sin.

For the Reformers, human beings are sinners through and through because, as far as the relationship between God and humans is concerned, we are incapable of relating. We are sinners, which means we are 'without fear of God, are without trust in God and are concupiscent'.[98] By the fact of our being sinners we have destroyed our relationship to God, though not God's relationship to us, and we are unable to restore it by ourselves. In this respect we have no free will. On the other

---

[95] *TCT*, 235 = *DH* 1528: 'Iustificatio ipsa . . . non est sola peccatorum remissio . . . , sed et sanctificatio et renovatio hominis per voluntarium susceptionem gratiae et donorum, unde homo ex iniusto fit iustus.'

[96] *TCT*, 235 = *DH* 1532: 'Nihil eorum, quae iustificationem praecedunt, . . . iustificationis gratiam promeretur.'

[97] Cf. *TCT*, 230 = *DH* 1521; canon 5, *TCT*, 242 = *DH* 1555.

[98] *The Augsburg Confession*, Art. 2, *BC*, 29 = *BSLK* 53, 5f. [Translation based on the Latin text (Tr).]

hand, the Catholic Church teaches that we are such sinners that we are able to receive justifying grace *only because of grace*, to be sure, but that is wholly *by our free will*. To that extent we are altogether able to be willing and active participants in our justification. Because of grace (that is, *gratia praeveniens, excitans et adiuvans*) we receive grace (that is, *gratia iustificationis*) but we receive it by an act of free will. This act is not set free simply by grace, but is still a free act of a will which is in theory free, though impaired by sin.

The apparent tautology 'thanks to grace human beings receive grace' is not splitting hairs. It really gets to the heart of things. It makes the curious distinctions in the concept of grace comprehensible. The tautology in grace disappears when we add that voluntarily receiving grace is an act of human free will. Adam's free will, which is not completely extinguished, forms, in a manner of speaking, the constant between the old and the new self. The free will of the old self is like a link to the new self; the Reformers knew no other link than grace *alone*.

It is now possible to make sense of the Tridentine distinctions in the concept of grace. They are *anthropologically determined*, even *anthropologically imperative*. This becomes even clearer when we analyse justification more closely as a transfer into the state of grace. This transfer is only possible when God's grace is so internalized in us that we *have* or *possess* grace. With this doctrine too, Trent is taking up the scholastic tradition. The scholastic background will become clear as we recall Aquinas' model of justification.

(c) Infused grace

Thomas Aquinas described justification as a transmutation (*transmutatio*) of human beings from the state of unrighteousness (*status iniustitiae*) to that of righteousness (*ad statum iustitiae*).[99] In this there is a distinction between two acts which for God occur *in instante*, at the same moment, but for us are

---

[99] Cf. Aquinas, *STh* Iª IIᵃᵉ, q. 113.

seen as occurring in succession. These are the infusion of grace (*infusio gratiae*) and the forgiveness of sins (*remissio peccatorum*). Change in the human being (*transmutatio hominis*) is produced through the infusion of grace by which we are transferred from the state of sin to that of righteousness. This movement, whose goal is the forgiveness of sins, in turn has two anthropological aspects: it represents our *No to sin* and our *Yes to God.*[100]

Now if the change from the state of unrighteousness to that of righteousness is at the same time a movement from our side, whereby we turn against sin and turn to God, there is a risk that our *receiving* of justifying grace will be misconstrued as being our own work. At the very least it would then be taken as a *meritum de congruo*. Since Aquinas cannot entertain such a thought, our volitional participation must again be brought under the heading of grace. That is why there is a distinction between justifying grace properly so called (*gratia iustificationis*), which makes us acceptable to God and is thus called *gratia gratum faciens*, and the divine activity whereby, with a view to justification, God prepares us for or helps us *to prepare ourselves* to receive justification. These acts of grace, which are to be distinguished from justifying grace proper, are called as a group by the name *gratia gratis data*, grace given for free. Not only do they precede justifying grace or *gratia gratum faciens* (grace which makes us acceptable to God); they also follow it in the form of *gratia perseverantiae* (persevering grace). The Tridentine decree on justification goes back to these concepts.

Grace given for free, *gratia gratis data*, is expressed by Trent as grace that precedes all human effort, arouses us to be active for our own justification and assists us in our free participation (*gratia praeveniens, excitans et adiuvans*[101] – also *auxilium* or *divinae gratiae adiumentum*).[102] This grace given for free is limited to individual acts of God where it is given *ad hoc*, so to speak, in order

---

[100] Forgiveness of sins appears to us as the first act, but seen objectively it is the second act. Duns Scotus takes the opposite view and sees only *infusio gratiae* as real *iustificatio*, justification.

[101] Cf. the Decree Concerning Justification, *TCT*, 232 = *DH* 1525.

[102] Cf. ibid., *TCT*, 232 = *DH* 1526.

simply to give assistance (*auxilium*) so that our human free will is rid of the impairment caused by sin. On the other hand, justifying grace proper is infused, poured into us so that it dwells in us in an infused state, as *habitus infusus*. So the so-called theological virtues of faith, love and hope[103] are poured into us at the same time as justifying grace, which is the grace that makes us acceptable in the eyes of God. The righteousness of God can even be seen as a righteousness that he has put in us or poured into us (*iustitia a Deo nobis infusa*) and as righteousness that inheres or dwells in us (*iustitia nobis inhaerens*).[104]

However, there are major theological problems with using such language as 'grace poured into us' and 'grace dwelling in us as *habitus infusus*'. When we talk of grace being poured in, we see it as a possession. Justifying grace is then possessed by us. But grace which we have or possess ceases to be grace. It is little use to say with Bonaventura that such a possession (of grace and thus of God in his grace) is really being possessed by God: 'Having God is being had by God'.[105] Just as human beings cannot in any real sense have or possess themselves, so we cannot *have* or *possess* God or his grace. The impossibility of such a model of having grace is displayed in a particularly blatant manner when we think that grace possessed by human beings can be '*lost*' again, even when faith is not lost! The decree on justification made by the Council of Trent says: 'We must also assert, . . . that the grace of justification, once received, is lost not only by unbelief, which causes the loss of faith, but also by any other mortal sin, even though faith is not lost.'[106] How are we to understand this?

---

103 Together with the four 'worldly' virtues (*fortitudo, temperentia, prudentia, iustitia*), the three theological virtues go to make up the seven cardinal virtues. The theological virtues, along with justifying grace, are poured into us as *habitus infusus*. However, the 'worldly' virtues may be acquired by our own activity (say, by training the corresponding abilities of the soul).

104 Cf. the Decree Concerning Justification, *TCT*, 241 = *DH* 1547.

105 Cf. *Mysterium Salutis*, vol. IV/2, 1973, 674, n. 116; referring to Bonaventura, *Breviloquium* V, 1: 'Habere Deum est haberi a Deo.'

106 *TCT*, 240 = *DH* 1544: 'Asserendum est, non modo infidelitate . . . , per quam et ipsa fides amittitur, sed etiam quocumque alio mortali peccato, quamvis non amittatur fides . . . , acceptam iustificationis gratiam amitti.'

Of course, we can point to Romans 5:5, where it says that God's love is poured into our hearts through the Holy Spirit. Paul can also speak of the Spirit which is 'given' to us (2 Cor. 5:5), so that we 'receive' (Rom. 8:15) and 'have' him (Rom. 8:23; cf. 1 Cor. 2:16). So, too, John says that 'we have all received, grace upon grace' (John 1:16). Accordingly, the Holy Spirit is 'in us' (cf. Rom. 8:9–11). Thus, from a biblical point of view, to talk of the grace of God being in us is not basically wrong. But at the same time in the context of biblical language, the fact of the Spirit, the love and the grace of God being in us means that we are, we live and have our being 'in the Spirit', that is, outside ourselves. So it follows that the Spirit, the love and the grace of God are not at all to be conceived of as a condition or state which has been poured into us and inheres in us (*habitus infusus* and *inhaerens*), but rather as powers and events which are so effectual in us that they bring us outside of ourselves. Justifying grace simply cannot be *possessed* by us in the sense of a *habitus*, for then it would no longer be *the God of grace himself.*

Equally confusing is the Catholic distinction between un-created and created grace (*gratia increata* and *creata*), although this does not appear in the Tridentine documents. Can grace ever be anything other than divine conduct, anything other than *the God of grace himself*? In fact this is precisely what is claimed by Catholic theologians: that justifying grace 'is *per se*, in a strictly supernatural way and fundamentally, God himself, the one who with himself imparts his own being',[107] so that we can really only talk of 'uncreated grace' (*gratia increata*). Rahner adds explicitly: 'From this it will be seen that any conception of grace which might place grace at the disposal of human beings is excluded from the outset. The teaching concerning "inherent" grace (*DH* 1530f., 1561) by no means disputes this or even expresses an opinion about the problem of distinguishing between created and uncreated grace'.[108] Even 'concepts like "inherent", "acci-dental", etc.' must 'be understood in this context as being

---

[107] K. Rahner, 'Gnade', part IV (Systematik), *LThK*, vol. 4 (1960), 991–1000: 994.
[108] Ibid.

completely independent of the question of the difference between "created" and "uncreated" grace'.[109] All the more remarkable, therefore, is the fact that 'there is no consensus in Catholic theology' whether 'we take created grace in the bad sense as an efficient prerequisite and result, caused by God, of un-created grace, imparted by a quasi-formal causality . . . or . . . as an element, launched simultaneously by itself, of this un-created grace . . . or whether we (as has mostly been the case since Thomas Aquinas, although in a most unsatisfactory way and running counter to the final drift of his thought . . .) take "uncreated grace" more or less as a simple result of created grace'.[110]

The statements quoted at the very least make clear how confusing is the distinction between 'uncreated grace' and 'created grace'. It raises more problems than it solves. Moreover, this distinction is not only confusing. It is an example of a mistaken categorization, which misses the essence of grace. No

---

[109] Ibid. [Rahner has 'can', which Jüngel has changed to 'must' (Tr).]

[110] Ibid., 994–5. The view held by Thomas Aquinas (*STh* I^a II^{ae}, q. 110 a. 2 corpus) that sanctifying grace is infused by God into the soul as an habitual gift ('quod aliquod habituale donum a Deo animae infunditur') does allow for the claim that grace is created. However, this is in the sense that we are created in it, i.e. are constituted in a new being out of nothing ('gratia dicitur creari ex eo quod homines secundum ipsam creantur, idest in novo esse constituuntur, ex nihilo' – ibid., ad 3). Catholic exegetes deduce from this that justifying grace which is produced, infused into human beings as a quality of the soul (*qualitas animae*), according to Aquinas 'cannot be called 'created' in the strict sense' (T. A. Deman, *Kommentar*, in *Die deutsche Thomas-Ausgabe. Vollständige, ungekürzte deutsch-lateinische Ausgabe der Summa theologica*, ed. by the Albertus-Magnus-Akademie, vol. 14, 1955, 378). According to O. Pesch (*Theologie der Rechtfertigung bei Martin Luther und Thomas von Aquin. Versuch eines systematisch-theologischen Dialogs* [*WSAMA*.T 4], 1985 [2nd edn], 633), 'the expression *gratia creata* vulgarizes the doctrine of Thomas . . . : Grace is not created like a thing which somehow has existence for its own sake. God himself, who gives himself to us, is salvation and grace; this brings about as its inevitable result a change in the created state . . . Any talk of grace as a created reality in human beings is always only a pointer to God, who gives himself to fellowship'. Along with C. Mueller [and G. Philips] (*The Theology of Grace and the Oecumenical Movement*, trans. R. A Wilson, London: Mowbray, 1961, 22), Pesch points out that 'not until post-tridentine theology does the "production" of grace *in* human beings develop from the trans-formation of human beings *by* grace' (loc. cit., n. 74).

matter what you think about the other distinctions in the Catholic concept of grace, this distinction between uncreated and created grace is unacceptable. They should never even have ventured onto the path of making a distinction and thus considering the possibility of *created grace*. It contradicts the idea of a gracious God for whom grace is an integral part of the self-definition of his own being, so that it cannot even be separated from him as being his creation (*gratia creata*). Only in the person of Jesus Christ are Creator and creation one and yet distinguishable. To pronounce the same difference as relevant to the grace which comes to sinners' aid is just as problematic as the claim 'that there are salvific acts by the unjustified'.[111] It is just as problematic as the claim that 'despite original sin, . . . we are free; we can agree freely with prevenient grace or reject it freely'.[112] It is hard to comprehend that this 'mutual co-operation . . . still does not mean a synergism which divides salvation up', because 'even free agreement itself . . . is the grace of God'.[113]

This points out the real difference between Protestant and Catholic doctrine. The latter sees God's grace in the final analysis as a kind of substitute work: it performs everything that we as sinners are no longer or not yet able to do. It prepares, awakens, prods, transforms, follows and secures, etc. In short, it does a great deal; in fact, it does almost everything.[114] However, when viewed as a work, it is introduced basically as a competitor or parallel structure to human beings, who are required to perform certain religious works. But this obscures divine compassion, which is a decisive element for understanding the biblical concept of grace. Compassion is anything but a work, and it is certainly not a substitute work. Thus a doctrine of grace which sees God's grace as so extremely productive – and there

---

[111] Rahner, 'Gnade', 995.

[112] Ibid., 996. Cf. *TCT*, 222 = *DH* 243; *DH* 247; *DH* 330–9; *DH* 393; *TCT*, 230 = *DH* 1521f.; *TCT*, 250 = *DH* 2002; *TCT*, 250 = *DH* 2004; *DH* 261; *TCT*, 29 = *DH* 3010; *ND*, 52–3 = *DH* 3875–7.

[113] Rahner, 'Gnade', 996–7.

[114] The whole justification event is determined by the question of what must be *achieved* – either by us or by God – so that sinners can be justified.

is no doubt that the Tridentine decree on justification does this – raises the question whether we are talking of anything deserving of the title *grace*.

Our objections to the Catholic understanding of grace can be summarized by the following questions: (*a*) Can God's grace be grasped through the model of performing works? (*b*) Can human beings even without justification experience or even perform 'saving acts'? (*c*) Are we, from an anthropological standpoint, introducing the concept of freedom prematurely if a free and voluntary reception of grace (*voluntaria susceptio gratia*) is to be possible? The biblical point of view is that freedom can only be brought in by our being set free. Certainly we, as slaves to sin, through the liberating act of grace, become freely in charge of all things, but also, as regards the grace of God, we are those who behave as though we are free. From the anthropological standpoint, freedom is founded on being set free. Only when this is grasped will freedom be properly emphasized as the wondrous, lavish and brilliant idea that is meant when the New Testament speaks of our justification.

This understanding of God and of human beings traces our freedom quite unreservedly back to our being set free by God. On this basis the Reformers see grace in the strict sense as divine behaviour which – at least according to Luther – not only *pronounces* us righteous, but also *makes* us righteous. God's grace justifies us by touching us at the *centre* of our existence as external grace (*gratia externa*). That is, it comes closer to us than we are able to do ourselves; and it does this in such a way that it places us *outside* ourselves, even as it touches us in our *inmost* being. It does not remain external, as Trent accuses the Reformers of claiming.[115] Rather, as we shall explain, it is so efficacious in the way it works in human beings that it turns us inside out. It marks us just as fully in our very being as so-called infused and indwelling grace supposedly does. As early Protestant orthodoxy so aptly put it, justifying grace is essentially grace which bestows salvation (*gratia applicatrix*) and not applied grace (*gratia*

---

[115] Cf. *TCT*, 234 = *DH* 1530 and *TCT*, 243 = *DH* 1561.

applicata). For grace is and remains a divine concept, one of divine behaviour, a relational concept. If grace is seen as divine behaviour applied to human beings, then it will be clear that we are two things at once: *simul iustus* (to the extent that God relates to us and we allow ourselves to relate to God) *et peccator* (to the extent that we rashly relate to ourselves). Thus we can neatly summarize the distinction between the two ideas of grace: Catholic doctrine acknowledges grace as a force that brings about a work in human beings – grace does everything!, while the *sola gratia* of the Reformers conveys the idea of sinners being constantly reliant on a gracious God and the unearned, and thus heartfelt, devotion of God to sinners. Grace is God's effectual delight in beloved human beings in defiance of the sin of vile sinners. And grace, when seen as God's delight in human beings, is effectual by making vile sinners fair. Grace is the flooding of God's love into the glut of human guilt. For human beings this delight of God is not an all-accomplishing power, but a liberating freedom from which power is drawn.

(d) Is grace a power active in us?

The contrast between the two different views of grace is most evident in the Catholic doctrine that grace is active in us *as love* and that sinners are only justified through grace active in love. At least, that seems to be the meaning of Canon 11 of the Tridentine decree on justification. This canon anathematizes those who say 'that men are justified either through the imputation of Christ's justice alone, or through the remission of sins alone, excluding grace and charity which is poured forth in their hearts by the Holy Spirit and inheres in them, or also that the grace which justifies us is only the good will of God'.[116] The word 'and' in the expression 'grace and charity [= love]' was pushed through by the Thomists against the Scotists, who

---

[116] *TCT*, 243 = *DH* 1561: 'Si quis dixerit, homines iustificari vel sola imputatione iustitiae Christi, vel sola peccatorum remissione, exclusa gratia et caritate, quae in cordibus eorum per Spiritum Sanctum diffundatur . . . atque illis inhaereat, aut etiam gratiam, qua iustificamur, esse tantum favorem Dei: anathema sit.'

wished to identify grace and love by the use of 'or' (*seu*). But the surprising use of the singular forms of the verbs in 'is poured forth' (*diffundatur*) and 'inheres' (*inhaereat*) shows that grace and love are fundamentally conceived of as one single *habitus infusus*. Here, grace is not grace without love which causes human beings to act. Isn't what is being discussed here as grace in fact a 'christianized principle of performance'?[117]

This question forces us to explain *by grace alone* using the term *through faith alone*. In order to comprehend to what extent we become righteous *through faith alone*, we must understand why we can attain to the righteousness of God *through God's word alone*. For faith comes by the hearing of the Word (Rom. 10:17).

It is possible to express the objections to the Tridentine view of grace by saying, somewhat clumsily, that the decree puts too much emphasis on grace and so fails to see how exclusive faith is. We shall need to return to this. Suffice it to note here that the Tridentine view of grace can be encountered often enough even within Protestant circles, albeit much less well thought through. Compared with the way we see ourselves today, Trent's view is a remarkably progressive one. In this respect the Enlightenment proved indirectly to be on the side of Trent. Even the great Immanuel Kant made his contribution to the Tridentine decree slipping unnoticed into Protestant thinking. He did this with his insistence on moral deeds having their origin simultaneously in a 'good disposition'.[118] In recent times the impression that human beings are essentially active participants has increasingly won the day. This scarcely allows any place for the biblical claim that we are non-participants as far as God is concerned. 'For God's sake, do something brave' – Zwingli's words, so necessary in their time and place have long since become a basis for those who (mis)understand themselves to be Protestants. And all Protestant Christians should check

---

[117] Ebeling, *Dogmatik des christlichen Glaubens*, vol. 3, 222.

[118] Kant's 'Doctrine of Justification' is a web of Reforming and anti-Reform motifs which it is almost impossible to disentangle. Cf. I. Kant, *Religion Within the Boundaries of Mere Reason* in *Religion and Rational Theology* (Cambridge: Cambridge University Press, 1996, 111–17).

whether the criticism levelled at Trent is true of them as well: 'the Tridentine doctrine of justification . . . is admirably adapted to serve as a touchstone to show where we all stand in the matter. There are Protestant doctrines of justification . . . which . . . are far too Tridentine'.[119]

III. By the word alone (*solo verbo*)*

The God of grace, the God who justifies the ungodly is *a God who speaks*. This very fact, that he is not a silent partner, but speaks as he interacts with us, is grace. It would be a graceless God indeed who refused to address a word to us. Even a torrent of angry words would be a blessing compared with a God who met us in silence. Yet grace does not consist only in this simple fact, that God communicates with us by means of language. What is of interest to us now is the particular fact that justifying grace proves itself in the Word, and in the Word alone, to be grace. The God of grace, the God who justifies the ungodly, acts in the justification event *by the Word alone, solo verbo*. But God acts there by the Word alone *in many ways*.

The very expression *Christ alone* implies a Word event. For God is gracious towards sinners when he is gracious towards them in the person of Jesus Christ, the Word of God become human (John 1:14). God has spoken, spoken once and for all, in the person of Jesus Christ, who died for all human beings and was raised from the dead (Heb. 1:2). And he has said what he had to say once and for all in the story of this person. Paul compresses this neatly when he writes: 'in him it has always been "*Yes*"' (2 Cor. 1:19 [NIV]). And this *Yes* of God's happened when God gave his grace its due place and thus set in motion the justification of the ungodly.

---

[119] Barth, *CD* IV/1, 626.

* In this section, the German uses *das Wort*, which, by reason of its having a capital, as do all German nouns, obscures the difference which English would choose to make between 'the word' and 'the Word'. Therefore, there are times when both meanings are in view, and the translation has to make an initial choice which is not exclusive (Tr).

This is how God's speaking comes to have its particular feature of divine *judgement*. More precisely, the justification of the ungodly occurs when God the Father pronounces his *judgement* as a Father on the history of his Son, who became a human being, and simultaneously on the history of *all* human beings. The justification event is a judicial act. The heavenly Father *passes judgement* by *judging* the story of Jesus. And this *judgement* is passed in the form of *a Word that raises from the dead*. It is the resurrection of Jesus by the Father where judgement is passed on the death of Jesus. By his resurrection, his death and he himself are 'justified', as the odd expression in 1 Timothy 3:16 has it. And with the justification of his *substitutionary death* a judgement is also passed *on sinners*: a judgement of *pardon*.[120]

The pardon that comes to us as sinners lends our existence something of a word-shaped structure. Sinners live as *those who have been pardoned*. We live with this pardon. It is ours not only from hearing it, but we have it in our hearts as well. We know that it speaks to us in the depths of our being so that now we make our lives fit in with this pardon. Luther described it is the characteristic of Christians that they take on the *forma verbi*, the *shape of the Word*.[121]

---

[120] Cf. *CD* IV/1, 309: 'the resurrection of Jesus Christ is the great verdict of God . . . concerning the event of the cross. It is its acceptance . . . It is the justification of Jesus Christ . . . And in His person it is the justification of all sinful men'.

[121] Cf. Luther, *Romans*, *LW* 25, 317: 'Thus "the Word was made flesh" (John 1:14) and "He took on the form of a servant" (Phil. 2:7), so that the flesh might become the Word and manhood take on the form of the Word . . .' = *WA* 56, 329, 29f.: 'suam formam relinquere ac formam verbi suscipere'; *Romans*, *LW* 25, 54, n. 16: 'For "the Word became flesh", so that we might be made the Word.' = 'Quia "Verbum caro factum est", ut nos verbum efficiamur', *WA* 56, 329, 29f. Note the parallel to, and the difference from, the well-known statement of Athanasius, *Oratio de incarnatione verbi*, ch. 54, *PG* 25, 192 B: 'The Word became man, that we might become divine.' Andreas Osiander was able to link in with this theosis soteriology when he emphasized that the 'Son of God has come into us by faith and still comes daily in order to be, according to his divine nature, our life, righteousness and salvation' (A. Osiander, *Beweisung, daß ich dreißig Jahre immer einerlei Lehre von der Gerechtigkeit des Glaubens gelehrt habe*, 1552, *Gesamtausgabe* (*Collected Edition*), ed. for the Heidelberger Akademie der Wissenschaften by G. Seebass, vol. 10, 1997, 421–49: 442, 20–2). If it were possible to see this participation in the divine nature of Jesus Christ and thus in God's righteousness

So justification is a Word event in every respect. But how can we say it occurs *by the Word alone?* Is this exclusive term essential? Isn't this an example of typical Protestant fixation on words, consistent with the typical Protestant fixation on the intellect? Doesn't the term *by the Word alone* lead to a church full of head-knowledge? Don't we need to get away from this fixation on words so that we can do justice to the totality of humanness?

We find it a bit embarrassing to answer such questions. They show how little those asking them have understood what the Word can do. But questions like this are again troubling Protestants, and in any case even Dr Faustus found it 'impossible, the Word so high to prize'.[122] So we shall look at these questions in order to recall some essential fundamentals of language. These will clarify in what way the Bible values the Word so highly. It has already been recalled in another context[123] that language is not only a means of information so that our reason may be put into the picture. As is well known, language has many semiotic functions.[124] What concerns us here is the function of the Word that discloses reality and facilitates possibilities.

This function of language, disclosing reality, is one of the oldest insights into the essence of Logos: 'for you will not find thinking without being', says Parmenides.[125] It is not only the poet who senses that 'a thing which lacks the word must go'.[126]

---

which occurs in us as an event of placing us outside ourselves (*ponere nos extra nos*), so that believers are placed by the *Christ in us* (*in nobis*) into a new place of being outside ourselves in Christ (*in Christo extra nos*), it would be possible to interpret theosis soteriology as being genuinely Reformed, that is in *in praedicamento relationis*, not in *praedicamento substantiae* [relationally, not in substance].

[122] Goethe, *Faust* I, 30.

[123] See above, p. 68.

[124] Cf. I. U. Dalferth, 'Zeit der Zeichen. Vom Anfang der Zeichen und dem Ende der Zeiten' in idem, *Gedeutete Gegenwart. Zur Wahrnehmung Gottes in den Erfahrungen der Zeit*, Tübingen: Mohr Siebeck, 1997, esp. 219.

[125] Freeman, *Ancilla*, 44.

[126] S. George, *The Works of Stefan George*, trans. O. Marx and E. Morwitz, New York: AMS Press, 1966, 343. Cf. M. Heidegger, 'Words', trans. J. Stambaugh, in idem, *On the Way to Language*, trans. P. D. Hertz, New York: Harper & Row, 1971, 139–56.

In the Word, being becomes accessible. This is the only reason that the Word is suitable for misuse as lying. The function that the Logos has of revealing reality makes the concept of the Word particularly suited to describe divine revelation. But we have already made it clear that the Logos does not only determine facts, call things by a logical name and give a logical judgement as to what is the case. Beyond this declarative function, it is a fundamental feature of the Logos that it *addresses, speaks to* human beings. This function which the Word has of addressing us is not simply identical with its role of determining and pronouncing. For example, addressing us may also mean saying what must be. It can also be a command. This is something different from labelling a fact. Speaking to us can also mean making promises, which is also different from labelling. Furthermore, the act of speaking to us can be the linguistic expression of an affection where *what* is said is only of secondary importance. Without this being deliberately communicated, it can also say: 'Do not fear, for I am with you' (Isa. 41:10). At times, the fact of addressing can even be more important than what is communicated. This is particularly so when previously either there was no speaking or speaking was refused. In its mere factuality, speaking to us can be a sign of affection or commitment. Of course, its commitment aspect increases when the linguistic content expresses this affection: 'Do not fear, . . . I have called you by name' (Isa. 43:1).

This addressing aspect of the Word gains a special importance when the one speaking not only communicates something but communicates himself or herself. This is when the revealing or disclosing aspect of the Word and its addressing aspect enter into a new partnership. The Word becomes the occasion for self-communication, self-disclosure and self-revelation. And if this self-communication also takes the form of affection from the speaker to the one being addressed, the concept of the Word is especially suited for describing divine revelation.

Together with this addressing aspect, there is another factor which makes the Word a preferred theological category: the possibility of creative speech. The Bible says God is the One who calls into existence the things that do not exist (Rom. 4:17). This must not be misunderstood as attributing a special 'spiritual' manner of creation to the Creator, so that he does not get his hands soiled. Such an idea is contradicted by the fact that the creation texts represent God as *making*. The creating *hand* of God works alongside God's creating *Word*. The week of creation in Genesis 1 is shown quite simply as a kind of working week: the Creator is a creative worker (cf. Gen. 2:7 with Isa. 48:13). Not only the verb *to create* (בָּרָא = *creare*), but also *to make* (עָשָׂה = *facere*) is a technical term in the creation texts. There are indeed a great number of less 'spiritual' models of God at work in creating, which turn up in the margins of the biblical texts. When we think of the findings of studies in the history of religions,[127] we are also reminded to be careful not to wrongly spiritualize the act of creation as a speech event. These studies have shown us that, although the creation is shown in the Bible predominantly as by the Word and by making, there are two other classic models of creation which are found: creation through (procreation and) birth (cf. Gen 2:4a), and creation through conflict (cf. Isa. 51:9f.). Traces of both of these are found in the Bible as well, even though they may be demythologized.

When God's creative activity is described as creating by the Word, there is no question of any sort of desensualizing or spiritualizing. Of course, it is possible that the accounts of creation which are found outside the biblical tradition and which talk of 'creation through a word' *may* tend in this direction. But a Christian doctrine of creation will certainly not follow that tendency. A Christian doctrine of creation quite simply cannot move away from this fact: the New Testament says the Word by which God created the world (John 1:3) *became flesh* (John 1:14). The Christian faith has explicitly identified God's creative Word with Jesus Christ, so that it is said that everything was created through him (1 Cor. 8:6; cf. Col. 1:16f.;

---

[127] Cf. C. Westermann, *Creation*, trans. J. J. Scullion, Philadelphia: Fortress Press, 1974, 39–46.

Heb. 1:2f.). So the Word by which God created the world is recognized by the Christian faith as being Jesus Christ. In turn, this is why the words he utters have a creative and life-bringing effect. Thus God's creative Word can never be understood on the basis of some idealistic contrast between the spirit and the senses. Quite the opposite: in the Word – in the λόγος, as Christians understand it, but also in the word simply as address – the senses and the spirit originate together. Language is the original unity of senses and spirit. In the Word, the spirit is reconciled with the world of the senses. The Word makes the spirit sensuous and permeates the senses with the spiritual without destroying their sensuous character. That is why we are at home in the Word from the beginning and only on that basis are we 'in our world'. That is why the Word affects our whole being: our hearing, our reason, our heart and our conscience. That is why a word can cut right through us.

There is one final matter which should provide food for thought for those who wish to make theology into head-knowledge by splitting the Word from the senses. (And how else could we think, except with our heads?) The very One who announces the reign of God opens the eyes of his listeners: 'Look at the lilies . . .' (Luke 12:27 [paraphrase]). Not only did Jesus have eyes for the lilies of the field, but by his word he opened the eyes of his audience to what the lilies have to say. Remarkably, we are even told in Mark to see what we hear. First, Jesus appeals to the faculty of hearing: 'Let anyone with ears to hear listen!' But then there follows after this appeal to hearing the very strange challenge: 'Look out what you listen to!' (Mark 4:23f. [paraphrase]).[128] Head-knowledge? Inability to see the

---

[128] [Both modern English and Luther's German allow of an idiom which means to be careful, but is based on seeing, as does the Greek βλέπετε (Tr).] If we cannot *see* what we *hear*, then we have not *heard* aright at all. Then even the word risks losing its sufficiency. True words *shape*, but the word, when robbed of its sufficiency, can shape nothing. It does not help us to *depict* anything. We lack any shape or form, we refuse any contact with the word's ability to portray what is real. We arrogantly ignore the fact that there is a solid basis for the claim that there can be too much visualizing. We refuse to allow the word one of those

whole because of fixation on words? It is said of the Catholic Church that it thinks in centuries. It would be a good idea for the Protestant Church to think, if not in centuries, at least by taking a long breath. Then it would not fall prey to every fashionable argument that comes along. The sort of long breath I am talking about cannot be drawn from centuries. It has to be drawn from the Spirit of the Holy Scripture.

However, all that we have considered here about the high place given by the Bible to the Word is still insufficient grounds for claiming that we are justified by the Word alone. What is there that compels us to take this lofty view of the Word in the justification event?

1. Justification of the ungodly as a forensic act

The justification of the ungodly is brought about *by the Word alone* because only the Word can both *pronounce* and *make* us righteous. This is the first thing we need to emphasize as a basis for the exclusive term *solo verbo*.

The Reformers viewed justification as the pronouncement of a judgement over the ungodly. The act which justifies us is a forensic act (*actus forensis*), an act of judgement in the heavenly court (*in foro Dei*). In the *Apology of the Augsburg Confession*, Melanchthon called for the word justify (*iustificare* – in Rom.

---

places where it ought to have some influence. And when we finally notice what is lacking, we repeatedly make a snap decision to blame it on faith in the Word and start to gaze in undisguised envy at the Roman Church, which, as ever, appears glorious: 'And when I saw . . . / And last the holy Pontiff, clad in all / The glory of his office, bless the people! . . .' were the enthusiastic words of Schiller's Mortimer, who then bade farewell to the church which had raised him: 'It tolerates no image, it adores / But the unseen, the incorporeal word' (F. Schiller, *Maria Stuart*, in *The Works of Frederick Schiller*, London: G. Bell & Sons, 1877, 220). We do not do this; we remain staunch Protestants and supply what has been seen to be lacking with all sorts of tom-foolery. But if faith in the Word alone is to change the world, then what needs to be regained is not the enthronement of bishops and the college of cardinals in all the pomp of liturgy in St Peter's Square, not the liturgical tom-foolery with which we replace it in our church, none of this. It is quite simply a matter of *learning to see what we hear.*

5:1) to be interpreted according to forensic usage. Thus it would denote an acquittal and declaration that the accused was innocent: 'In this passage "justify" is used in a judicial way to mean "to absolve a guilty man and pronounce him righteous".'[129] But since in this case the accused is the guilty party, he cannot be acquitted and declared innocent on the basis of his own righteousness, but only on the basis of the righteousness of another – that of Christ – which is communicated to him through faith.[130] For this reason, Melanchthon described the forensic act of the justification of the sinner as *imputatio alienae iustitiae*, as the imputation or reckoning of someone else's righteousness.[131] The expression *imputatio* is meant to render the New Testament phrase 'to be reckoned as righteousness' (λογίζεσται εἰς δικαιοσύνην = *reputare ad iustitiam*) (Rom. 4:3, 5). Because of this and similar statements, Melanchthon has been referred to, praised or attacked as representing a purely forensic, imputative, declaratory and extrinsic doctrine of justification.[132] We shall leave the problem of the historical facts here and limit our concern to stressing *what it was* that the forensic view of justification was targeting and *how it must not* be misunderstood, even if Melanchthon is said to have misunderstood it.

The intention of the forensic view of justification is to highlight the justification of sinners as an event by which they are accepted by God as righteous purely on the basis of God's righteousness – a righteousness completely extraneous to them – as it has been shown in the person of Jesus Christ. Thus

---

[129] *BC*, 154 = *BSLK* 219, 43f.: 'Iustificare vero hoc loco forensi consuetudine significat reum absolvere et pronuntiare iustum.'

[130] Cf. *BC*, 154 [cont'd]: 'and to do so on account of someone else's righteousness, namely, Christ's, which is communicated to us through faith' = *BSLK* 219, 44f.: 'sed propter alienam iustitiam, videlicet Christi, quae aliena iustitia communicatur nobis per fidem'.

[131] Cf. *BC*, 154 = *BSLK* 219, 46.

[132] Karl Holl ('Die Rechtfertigungslehre in Luthers Vorlesung über den Römerbrief mit besonderer Rücksicht auf die Frage der Heilsgewißheit', in idem, *Gesammelte Aufsätze zur Kirchengeschichte*, vol. 1: Luther, 1948 (7th edn), 111–54: 128) even went so far as to say, in italics: '*Melanchthon ruined the Lutheran doctrine of justification.*'

believers are described as those who 'are made acceptable to God because of [the] imputation [of God's righteousness]'.[133] This ensures that sinners can do nothing towards their own justification and, what is no less important, that they can never internalize the righteousness that is foreign to them or make it their own so that it passes into their possession. I am always accepted by someone else. I always have to gain my acceptance before a group.[134] So recognition can never be 'had' as a possession by the one who is accepted or recognized. Those who are justified must resort to a tribunal outside themselves (*extra se*). There is nothing about them or in them – not even justifying grace poured into them – which can make sinners righteous. In the reality of the state of the justified there are no concessions to be made. They are righteous purely and simply because they are *pronounced* righteous. And they are only pronounced righteous because God's righteousness, which is extraneous to them, is attributed, imputed to them. So in the strictest sense, God's righteousness comes to them *from outside*, it is *outward*. Sinners are righteous externally to themselves: *extrinsece Iustificantur semper*.[135] Sinners are righteous externally to themselves in the same sense that the Word is an external One, coming from the outside into our innermost being and responding and relating to what has happened outside us (*extra nos*) in Christ. So it is the Word alone that can come from outside into our innermost being in such a way as to move us to the place where we should be, where we have the right to be together with God. The doctrine of justification by the Word alone (*solo verbo*) is aimed at emphasizing this external relationship of justified sinners.

Everything depends on a correct understanding of this external relationship of justified sinners and of the external Word that forms its basis. Clearly what is excluded is any view of the righteousness of God as being in any way earned and possessed. Similarly out of the question is any understanding of justification as a process by which we are involved other than by

---

[133]   *BC*, 154 = *ApolCA* IV, *BSLK* 219, 52: 'accepti Deo propter imputationem'.
[134]   See above, p. 6.
[135]   Luther, *Romans*, *LW* 25, 257. See above, p. 122, n. 52.

hearing and believing. We must not hold any view which sees justification as a process of salvation whereby we co-operate in any way at all with God. Any notion of justification as a condition which can be kept and maintained by human achievement or good works is excluded.[136] Also untenable is the idea that justification is a process of maturation that can be checked empirically by reference to certain human situations or actions. We must further rule out the thought that we can in any way prove our righteousness before God by referring to ourselves, instead of pointing only and exclusively to Christ crucified. Thus it is abundantly clear what views are excluded.

---

[136] Thus the *Formula of Concord* rejected the Tridentine idea that 'our works either entirely or in part sustain and preserve either the righteousness of faith that we have received or even faith itself' *BC*, 557. The Strasbourg Institute for Ecumenical Research tried to blunten this statement by means of an unbelievable series of contortions (cf. Th. Dieter, 'Eine erste Antwort auf neuere Kritiken an der "Gemeinsamen Erklärung zur Rechtfertigungslehre"', *epd-Dokumentation* No. 1/1998, 1–13: 7f.), and Harding Meyer, former director of the Institute, went so far as to claim that the *Formula of Concord* was passing judgement on something the Tridentine decree on justification had never asserted. He maintained that the latter did not say 'sustain and preserve', but rather 'increase' the righteousness received (H. Meyer, 'Ja ohne Vorbehalt. Konsens in der Rechtfertigungslehre erreicht', *EK* 31 [1998], 37–40: 39f.; cf. on this E. Jüngel, 'Unglaubliche Irreführungen. Wie Protestanten über ihren Glauben getäuscht werden', *EK* 31 [1998], 93–6: 94). But what do we read in Canon 24 of the Tridentine decree? 'If anyone shall say that the justice received is not preserved [!] and also increased before God through good works, but that those works are merely the fruits and signs of justification obtained, but not the cause of its increase, *anathema sit* (*TCC* , 401) = 'Si quis dixerit, iustitiam acceptam non conservari [!] atque etiam non augeri coram Deo per bona opera . . . anathema sit' (*DH* 1574). I mention this embarrassing situation because it is typical of the defence of the Tridentine position by Lutheran theologians in the interest of ecumenism. There is nothing wrong with a Protestant attempt to understand the Tridentine decree on justification better than it understood itself! But we must do it honestly. We must defend what is there. *The Joint Declaration* reiterates basically the only part of the Catholic doctrine of justification that was condemned by the Lutheran Confessions, saying that it is still Catholic teaching. And then it goes on to assert that the condemnation in the Lutheran Confessions no longer applies to the Roman Catholic doctrine of justification as expounded in *The Joint Declaration*. This is one of the scandals in the history of theology of which that *Declaration* will go on to serve as an example. To accept this amounts to a sacrifice of the intellect on the part of any theologian. But enough of these shameful attempts to excuse ecumenism from due intellectual honesty! What concerns us here is to expound the doctrine of justification positively.

But there will immediately be a loud objection to this doctrine that it throws the baby out with the bathwater. How can we speak seriously about justification when it is nothing but a forensic act which only forgives sinners their sin by imputing a purely extraneous righteousness to them, that is, it only *pronounces* them righteous? How can we take God's justifying judgement at all seriously when the extraneous righteousness of God remains *external* to sinners instead of being *poured into* them, imparted to them, as a power that *transforms*? Isn't God treating us *as though* we were righteous when in fact we are not? Is this some sort of 'as though' theology? Isn't God even fooling himself with such a justification *by the Word alone*? Is God himself still righteous when he says that the unrighteous are righteous without first *making* them righteous?

Quite a few of the Council of Trent's condemnations express these objections to the purely forensic and extrinsic view of justification. The clearest is Canon 11, which has already been quoted: 'If anyone says that men are justified either through the imputation of Christ's justice alone, or through the remission of sins alone, excluding grace and charity which is poured forth in their hearts by the Holy Spirit and inheres in them, or also that the grace which justifies us is only the good will of God: let him be anathema.'[137] This condemnation expresses the objection that we can only speak seriously of justification of sinners when it describes a righteousness which may be encountered *in human beings*, which allows of being righteous and not only of being considered as righteous.

This argument is by no means restricted to Roman Catholic prejudice against a purely forensic and extrinsic interpretation of justification. It is also to be found in various forms among Protestant theologians. Its presence forces us above all to define more closely the divine Word which issues the verdict that sinners are righteous. Protestant theologians of the nineteenth and twentieth centuries raised the question of whether the verdict that justifies is an analytical or a synthetic one. Analytical

---

[137] See above, p. 196, n. 116.

judgements (subject–predicate) are, according to Kant, merely 'elucidatory' judgements, because they do not 'through the predicate add anything to the concept of the subject; rather, they only dissect the concept, breaking it up into its component concepts which had already been thought in it (although thought confusedly)'. On the other hand, synthetic judgements are those which 'add to the concept of the subject a predicate that had not been thought in that concept at all and could not have been extracted from it by any dissection'. 'Hence . . . analytic judgements are those in which the predicate's connection with the subject is thought by [thinking] identity, whereas those judgements in which this connection is thought without [thinking] identity are to be called synthetic.'[138] According to this, God's justifying judgement would be an analytical one, if it uses the predicate 'righteous' of a person already made righteous. If the justifying judgement were an analytical one, it would be guaranteed that the statement 'the sinner is righteous' would not be turning a blind eye, that God would not be lying to himself in the act of declaring us righteous. But God's justifying judgement in this sense simply cannot be an analytical one, since in that case it would *follow* the justification event. This would mean that justification did not occur by God's word alone.

This is why Albrecht Ritschl called God's justifying judgement a synthetic one and thus expressed the fact that 'justification . . . must be thought of as a resolve or act of the Divine will. For every act of the will moves analogously to the synthetic judgment; especially can a creative act of God's will only be understood in this form. But such an act is conceived when God through the revelation in Christ receives those who are separated from Him by sin into fellowship with Himself, to the establishment of their salvation'. This creative act of pronouncing righteous consists in this, 'that to the sinner whom God makes righteous there is

---

[138] I. Kant, *Critique of Pure Reason* (Unified Edition), trans. W. S. Pluhar, Indianapolis/ Cambridge: Hackett, 1996, 51. [Square brackets as used in Pluhar's tr. to indicate his expansions (Tr).]

added a predicate not already included in the concept "sinner"'.[139] Karl Holl's objection to this was that Ritschl 'the great systematician' had 'not thought his idea out completely. He had forgotten to consider that every act of the will follows a particular *goal* and that when it is an act of God's will the goal is always reached'.[140] For 'what God intends is already completed before his eyes, as soon as he wishes it. What is to come to light at the *end* is already *present* for him, the Timeless and Almighty One, at the beginning, that is, when he "pronounces the judgement"... For God, the sick person is already well, because he knows that he can heal him. This self-assuredness of God' implies that God sees 'in the sinner whom he justifies the just person he will form out of him'.[141] And on this condition, but only on this one, it is more accurate to say that God's 'justifying verdict is analytical'.[142]

What is crucial is not whether we can call the justifying judgement synthetic – with Ritschl – or analytic – with Holl, accepting his special conditions. From a purely logical standpoint, Ritschl should be correct with his assertion that the justifying judgement is synthetic. In addition, there is every objective evidence for this. However, the vital thing is that this judgement has creative power because it is God's Word. As the creative Word of God, it effectively pronounces sinners righteous. This is the Word, as Paul says in the oft-quoted phrase of Romans 4:17, which calls into existence the things which do not exist. It works according to the rule given in Psalm 33:9: 'For he spoke, and it came to be; he commanded, and it stood firm.' This is also the rule to be applied if we are to understand the forensic judgement of God as he pronounces sinners

---

[139] Ritschl, op. cit., 80.

[140] Holl, *Die Rechtfertigungslehre in Luthers Vorlesung über den Römerbrief*, 125, n. 1.

[141] Ibid., 124f.

[142] Ibid., 124, n. 2. Using the quite different assumption that 'if we follow Paul the *declaring* righteous cannot be regarded as the basis of the righteousness of believers but already presupposes this', W. Pannenberg (*Systematic Theology*, vol. 3, 223–4) claims that the verdict of justification is an analytical one. However, this view is hardly Pauline. Even Romans 4:17 disproves it.

righteous. This forensic act *is* the effective act of making the ungodly righteous. It *is*! *Imparted* righteousness is what we must discuss here, despite Melanchthon's timidity. It is not something which differs from *imputed* righteousness; it neither precedes nor follows it. The *imputation of extraneous righteousness* (*imputatio alienae iustitiae*) can only be rightly grasped when it is seen as God *granting* divine righteousness in such a way as to *effectively change* the *being* of humans. If sinners are pronounced righteous by God's judging Word – which is also pre-eminently creative in its judging power – and thus *recognized* by God as being righteous, then they not only *count* as righteous, they *are* righteous. Here we must again remind ourselves that *the Word alone* can in this way do both things at once: a *judgement* and a *creative Word* – a *pardon* and *a Word which sets us free.*[143]

2. The renewal of the inner person

Do we, then, have to maintain, with Trent, that 'justification itself . . . is not only the remission of sins, but sanctification and renovation *of the interior man* through the voluntary reception of grace and gifts, whereby a man becomes just instead of unjust . . .'[144]

The free decision of human beings for justifying grace is made possible by prevenient, awakening and preparatory grace. In our attempt to explore the Tridentine view more closely, for the moment we shall put to one side the fact that this free decision (*voluntaria susceptio gratiae*) is meant to move us across from the state of the unrighteous to that of the righteous. This matter has already been debated when we discussed *sola gratia* and is very problematical because it is so accommodating to the way people today see their freedom in decision-making. If we

---

[143] We should remember that the pardons of this world often have the unpleasant disadvantage that the pardoned person has to be taken into political protective custody. We may think of the name Martin Niemöller in this regard.

[144] *TCT*, 233 = *DH* 1528: 'Iustificatio ipsa . . . non est sola peccatorum remissio . . . , sed et sanctificatio et renovatio interioris hominis per voluntariam susceptionem gratiae et donorum, unde homo ex iniusto fit iustus. . . .'

overlook such problematical information, the claim that the justification of sinners is after all the renewal of the inner person can, under certain conditions, be interpreted in the best light and, thus viewed, can also represent the Protestant view. There is a clear precondition for such a favourable interpretation, and that is that any discussion of renewal of the inner person must be seen quite categorically from the point of view that God's Word declares us righteous. What renews the inner person is the external Word, which addresses us from outside ourselves and grants us God's righteousness. If any discussion of the gracious renewal of the inner person (*renovatio interioris hominis*) is to be acceptable to Protestant theology, it must never be seen as complementary, as an alternative or as completing the extrinsetist view of justification. It can only be seen as a refinement of the definition of the external reference of justified sinners.

This occurs when we take the justifying Word of God seriously as one that *speaks to us creatively*. Such a Word can never remain 'external' to those addressed. Together with the righteousness of God that brings it to us, it touches us so greatly that it touches us more closely than we can touch ourselves. It becomes to us something more inward than our inmost being: *interior intimo meo.*[145]

However, now we need to emphasize again that the justifying Word that so addresses and touches sinners does not let us remain in ourselves; it calls and places our inner being outside ourselves. If our inner being were to stay put, it would not be justified. This is what creatively defines those who are in concord with God: they come out of themselves in order to come to themselves – outside themselves, among other persons, and above all with the person of the wholly other God. And this is our human sin: that we want to come to ourselves by ourselves – instead of outside ourselves. So, leaving the relational riches of

---

[145] This is the element of truth in T. Mannermaa's interpretation of Luther: *Der im Glauben gegenwärtige Christus. Rechtfertigung und Vergottung. Zum ökumenischen Dialog*, 1989.

our being, we press forward into relationlessness. The Word of justifying grace essentially interrupts sinners in this urge towards relationlessness as it speaks creatively to us. It calls us out of ourselves as it comes so close to us, as it speaks and relates to what is outside ourselves, to what has been definitively moved by God's righteousness. It speaks and relates to the cross and resurrection of Jesus Christ as they are outside us. The justifying Word from the cross addresses our inner being in this exterior aspect of our existence so that there we may come to ourselves and thus really, effectively be renewed. 'Anyone who is in Christ is a new creation' (2 Cor. 5:17 [alt. (Tr)]). In the next section we shall see how this comes about through faith. For the moment we need to highlight the creative, renewing strength of the justifying Word by which alone God in his grace reaches our inner being and effectively makes us righteous.

So the justifying Word remakes our human existence anew, by relating us to Jesus Christ and there bringing us to ourselves, outside ourselves (*extra se/extra nos*). Thus this external reference is not something inferior and superficial, but a relationship which defines us in our inmost being.[146] We are simply not ourselves when we are only by ourselves. We cannot find ourselves by 'going into ourselves'. We must come out of ourselves in order to come to ourselves. In a very clear sense we are called out of ourselves by the Word of justification: 'By faith he rises above himself unto God'.[147] By faith we are able to 'rise above ourselves' because the Word of justification addresses us in such a way

---

[146] No doubt Calvin was also influenced by this insight when he refuted Osiander's doctrine of justification. The latter countered Melanchthon's concept, which saw justification as purely imputed, by saying that justification is a making righteous (*iustum efficere*), not only in the presence of God, but also in us, thanks to an indwelling of the righteousness of Christ (*inhabitatio iustitiae Christi*). Cf. A. Osiander, *De unico mediatore Jesu Christo et iustificatione fidei*, 1551, *Gesamtausgabe*, vol. 10, 1997, 49–300: 195; J. Calvin, *Institutes of the Christian Religion*, III, xi, 5ff., ed. J. T. McNeill, trans. F. L. Battles, Philadelphia: Westminster, 1975 (1960), vol. 1, 729ff.

[147] M. Luther, *Reformation Writings of Martin Luther*, 2 vols, trans. and ed. by B. L. Woolf, London: Lutterworth, 1952, I, 379.

that we know we are related to the person of Jesus Christ and of God who acts in him. This is why we can speak of justification as a renewal of our inner persons who are also placed outside ourselves. It is impossible to imagine a more thorough-going renewal. So righteousness imputed to sinners is also righteousness which is imparted to them and renews them – *by the Word alone.*

To be more specific, this is how effectual justification works in sinners who have become related to justification by the Word of justification which has addressed them. They are given a role in Jesus' story, not only in his resurrection, but in his death. Baptized into Christ's death, we are buried with him so that, as Christ was raised from the dead, we too may walk in newness of life (Rom. 6:3f.). Thus the justifying judgement is effectual in two senses: it kills the old nature, which is crucified and buried with Christ, in order immediately to bring into being a new person (Rom. 6:5; 2 Cor. 5:17). In this way one person is both things at once: a sinner, who is passing away, delivered up to nothingness with the crucified Christ, and a justified person, called into existence with the resurrected Christ and in the midst of becoming. Now, in this sense – although we must note that there is an *imbalance* here – human beings who are pronounced righteous are *simultaneously righteous and sinners.*

3. Righteous and sinners at the same time

At this point it will be good to examine Martin Luther's famous and indeed infamous formula, that a Christian is at the same time righteous and a sinner: *simul iustus et peccator.* We encounter this terminology relatively early in Luther's writings.[148] He then held to it consistently, though using a variety of phrases.[149] The Council of Trent made at least indirect reference to Luther's formula when, in Canon 25 of the *Decree on Justification*, it

---

[148] Cf., for example, Luther, *Romans, LW* 25, pp. 63, 260; and *Galatians* (1519), *LW* 27, 230.

[149] Cf. in his early works, for example, *Die dritte Disputation gegen die Antinomer*, 1538, *WA* 39/I, 508, 5–9.

rejected the idea that 'a just man sins'.[150] We may leave open the question whether the Tridentine condemnation of Luther's idea is at all correct. The fact remains that the formula *simul iustus et peccator* is still unacceptable to the Roman Catholic Church today. In its statement on *The Joint Declaration on the Doctrine of Justification*, the Catholic Church again pronounced Luther's formula (which is interpreted positively in the *Joint Declaration*) to be unacceptable to Catholics. It expressly disavowed the facts which this formula expresses. It even located the major difficulty 'preventing an affirmation of total consensus between the parties on the theme of Justification'. This is without any doubt to be found in 'the formula "at the same time righteous and sinner"' which is 'for Catholics ... not acceptable'.[151] Is the formula really so important that it divides the churches? What does it mean?

Luther's claim that Christians are *simultaneously righteous and sinners* seems paradoxical. No doubt he deliberately emphasized this apparent paradox[152] so as to allow the intended meaning to

---

[150] 'If anyone says that a just man sins at least venially in every good work, or (what is more intolerable) says that he sins mortally, ... let him be anathema', *TCT*, 245 = *DH* 1575: 'Si quis in quolibet bono opere iustum saltem venialiter peccare dixerit, aut (quod intolerabilius est) mortaliter ... : anathema sit.' Cf. 'Hence, it is clear that they are against the correct doctrine of religion when they say that the just man commits a venial sin in everything he does ... , or (what is more intolerable) say that he merits eternal punishment. They also are incorrect who state that the just sin in all their works if, in those works, ... they look for an everlasting reward ...' *TCT*, 237 = *DH* 1539: 'Unde constat, eos orthodoxae religionis doctrinae adversari, qui dicunt, iustum in omni bono opere saltem venialiter peccare ... , aut (quod intolerabilius est) poenas aeternas mereri; atque etiam eos qui statuunt, in omnibus operibus iustos peccare, si in illis ... mercedem quoque intuentur aeternam.'

[151] *Response of the Catholic Church to the Joint Declaration of the Catholic Church and the Lutheran World Federation on the Doctrine of Justification*, Clarification 1. [Jüngel makes the 'major difficulty' a singular, whereas both the German and English forms of the document have 'major difficulties' ('die größten Schwierigkeiten') being found in Paragraph 4.4 'The Justified as Sinner' (Tr).] Cf. E. Jüngel, 'Amica Exegesis einer römischen Note', *ZThK.*B 10 (1998).

[152] Luther evidently sees 'paradox' as expressing the biblical claim that what is foolish to the world is wise in the eyes of God. Luther clearly stated that the arguments which he defended in the *Heidelberg Disputation* were 'theological paradoxes' (Luther, *Heidelberg Disputation*, *LW* 31, 39).

seem inconsistent: 'It is no doubt a wondrous thing [*mira res*]. If you can find logic here, then you are welcome. Two [predicates] which contradict each other in one subject and at the same time.'[153] At any rate, that would contradict the declaration that contradiction is forbidden. Yet Luther by no means saw the claim that we are *simultaneously righteous and sinners* as an absolute paradox. Rather, he interprets what seems to be a paradox in such a way that its dialectic remains, while the dialectic assertion can and must be read as a logically meaningful statement. This is managed by claiming that the same subject, of which at the same time both contradictory predicates *righteous* and *sinner* are said to be valid, exists simultaneously under two different jurisdictions. I exist on the one hand before God who justifies me, and on the other hand before my own Self.[154]

Luther's example of the Lord's Prayer shows what this is all about. The Lord's Prayer is the prayer of Christians, yet it asks for forgiveness of sins:[155] 'If you are holy, why are you crying out [for God]? Because I feel sin clinging to me, that is why I pray: Hallowed be Thy name, Thy kingdom come. O Lord, be gracious to me. And yet you are holy. And yet . . . are you holy? In this sense, to the extent that I am a Christian, I am righteous, devout and belong to Christ, but to the extent that I look back [*respicio*] to myself and my sin I am miserable and the greatest of sinners. So it is true to say: in Christ there is no sin, and in our flesh there is no peace and no rest, only perpetual struggle.'[156] Only death will end this struggle. These few

---

[153] M. Luther, *Die dritte Disputation gegen die Antinomer*, 1538, WA 39/I, 507, 21–508, 2: 'duo contraria in uno subiecto et in eodem puncto temporis'.

[154] Cf. Ibid., 564, 6f.: 'in different respects we are called righteous and sinners at the same time': diverso respectu dicimur iusti et peccatores simul.

[155] Cf. idem, *Defense and Explanation of all the Articles of Dr Martin Luther which Were Unjustly Condemned by the Roman Bull*: 'the Lord's Prayer alone is enough to show that all of us are still sinners, for all the saints must also pray, "Hallowed be thy name . . ."', *LW* 32, 24.

[156] Idem, *The Third Disputation Against the Antinomians*, 1538, WA 39/I, 508, 2–8: 'Si sanctus, cur clamas? Quia sentio peccatum adhaerens mihi, et ideo oro: Sanctificetur nomen tuum, adveniat regnum tuum. Ah domine, sis mihi propitius. Attamen es sanctus. Attamen es sanctus? Ita, in quantum christianus,

sentences explain adequately what we mean when we say that a Christian is at the same time righteous and a sinner. They explain adequately why this claim when it is rightly understood is theologically correct and indispensable.

We must note first of all that Luther was led to make this claim by his exposition of the Scripture. In defence of the proposition that a Christian is *simul iustus simul peccator*, we could point to the undeniable everyday experience that even a justified person remains in some ways a being of the flesh and constantly suffers from a bad conscience. This experiential element permeates Luther's argument: *sentio* – I feel – that sin is clinging to me. But our experiences are capable of many interpretations, especially those experiences we have with ourselves. In order to feel that our sins are clinging to us we first need to have had the completely different, spiritual experience of having our sins forgiven. But nobody ever has this experience without referring back to the Scripture, which testifies to God's justifying Word. And it is precisely this Scripture, which has so testified, that now tells sinners they are still sinners. Luther refers to 1 John, which claims on the one hand that those who have been born of God do not sin (1 John 3:9), but on the other hand that we deceive ourselves if we say we have no sin (1 John 1:8). Luther says that the whole Scripture basically testifies to this. He believes that Romans chapter 7 is particularly convincing in this regard.[157]

Of course, Luther has no intention of claiming that the justified *want* to be sinners. That would be absurd. Those who are justified want to be together with God. But sin, for its part, desires to be with the justified. Luther clarifies this in the text we quoted when he speaks of 'sin clinging to me' (*peccatum adhaerens mihi*). It is not that Christians cling to sin, but that sin

---

eatenus enim sum iustus, pius et Christi, sed quatenus respicio ad me et ad meum peccatum, sum miser et peccator maximus. Ita in Christo non est peccatum et in carne nostra non est pax et quies, sed pugna perpetua.'

[157] Cf. Ibid., 507, 14–19. Like other Reformers, Luther saw Romans 7:14–25 as summarizing the Christian life. On the other hand, modern exegetes generally see this text as a Christian looking back to his pre-Christian life.

clings to them so closely that they cannot help identifying it as their own sin (*meum peccatum*).[158] As sin clings to us it makes our Self do the opposite of what that Self wishes to do. Paul describes the process as a struggle between flesh and spirit in the Christian: 'for these are opposed to each other, to prevent you from doing what you want' (Gal. 5:17). Here we are reminded of what he says about our life before we were Christians in Romans 7:15 and 23. But there is an important difference to note. The Self before Christ is ruled by sin and the law of sin; it is '*under* sin' (Rom. 3:9) and '*under* the law' (Rom. 6:14), so that sin is the power that totally and inescapably determines their present life. On the other hand, sin, in clinging to Christians, also determines our present being, but it can only have influence on the present life of Christians in the sense that it has already been condemned to pass away and thus be given over to the past. Sin has no future. Just as the old Adam who accompanies Christians to the end of their lives must pass away, so also sin's power ends with death, not before. But when it does end with death, that end is irrevocable. Thus Luther was wont to describe Christians' *being righteous* in terms that pointed to an *unlimited future*: the righteous have *promise* and *hope* on their side; there will be a day when they are completely righteous. In *this* sense it is true to say that saints are sinners in fact, but in the hope which anticipates the future they are irrevocably righteous.[159] Just as a sick person who has undergone a successful treatment is still vividly aware of his or her illness, yet on the other hand is well on the way to health in the doctor's eyes and can even be called healthy, in the same way a Christian is *righteous and a sinner at the same time*.[160] There is an *inceptive* or beginning aspect to being righteous,[161] but it is a beginning that determines our *whole*

---

[158] Ibid., 508, 2f.6.

[159] Cf. idem, *Romans*, 'they are sinners in fact but righteous in hope', *LW* 25, 258 = *WA* 56, 269, 30: 'peccatores in re, Iusti autem in spe'.

[160] Cf. idem, *Romans*, *LW* 25, 160; idem, *Die dritte Disputation gegen die Antinomer*, 1538, *WA* 39/I, 564, 1f.

[161] Cf. idem, *Romans*, *LW* 25, 160; idem, *Die Promotionsdisputation von Palladius und Tilemann*, 1537, *WA* 39/I, 204, 6.

existence. It is not putting things off until a future date: 'we are already in fact completely righteous'.[162]

The fact that for the Christian sin only has influence on the present as a power which belongs to the past makes Luther say that Christians look back on their sin (even though it is quite present): 'to the extent that I . . . look back on my sin, I am . . . the greatest of sinners'.[163] Looking back to oneself means looking back to a Self which wants to come to itself by itself and thinks it is able to do so. And that is precisely the sinner[164] who has no future.

Luther's formula must be used to bring out this theological imbalance between our being simultaneously righteous and sinners. Only then is it possible and necessary to emphasize the equally serious reality of the sinful state of Christians. If this theological imbalance is not clearly highlighted, the Reformers' formula is likely to mean nothing more than this: 'despite all the talk of renewal, everything remains as it was'.[165] The justification of sinners risks losing its eventfulness. Grace is likely to stop abounding more than sin (Rom. 5:20). This would make Christian life an insoluble paradox. But we must consider this misunderstanding cleared up.

If it is indeed cleared up, then it is with some rigour that we must highlight the dialectic of the Christian life. Christians are not only fully righteous, they are also fully sinners.[166] We are not talking of two partial aspects (not partially righteous and

---

[162] Idem, *Die dritte Disputation gegen die Antinomer*, 1538, WA 39/I, 563, 14: 'sumus revera et totaliter iusti'.

[163] Idem, 508, 6f.: 'quatenus respicio . . . ad meum peccatum, sum . . . peccator maximus'; cf. ibid., 564, 3f.: 'Sic etiam revera sumus et totaliter peccatores, sed quod ad nos respiciendo: we are thus as well in truth completely sinners, but this is as we look back to ourselves.'

[164] Cf. idem, *Romans*, *LW* 25, 257: 'The saints are always sinners in their own sight, and therefore always justified outwardly . . . I use the term "inwardly" (*intrinsice*) to show how we are in ourselves, in our own eyes, in our own estimation': *Sancti Intrinsece sunt peccatores semper . . .* Intrinsece dico, i.e. quomodo in nobis, in nostris oculis, in nostra estimatione sumus (*WA* 56, 268, 27–32).

[165] Ebeling, *Dogmatik des christlichen Glaubens*, vol. 3, 155.

[166] Cf. M. Luther, *Die dritte Disputation gegen die Antinomer*, 1538, WA 39/I, 563, 14–564, 4: 'sumus revera et totaliter iusti . . . revera sumus et totaliter peccatores'.

partially unrighteous: *partim iustus, partim iniustus*).[167] It is rather a question of two aspects of a complete whole. In both cases we are looking at the whole person. But to the extent that the complete person is a sinner, his or her true completeness is disturbed: this person is now 'only' the Self wanting to come to itself by itself and thinking it can do so. This person is a Self without being a Self with God. This person may be said to be forcing his or her own completeness by self-actualization: a totalitarian completeness, a totalitarian *homo totus*. By contrast, the Self gains its true completeness by allowing itself, by the justifying Word of God, to be called and placed away *from* itself, outside itself – away *to* the one, with whom it comes to itself without any compulsion and thus finds its true completeness. And this true completeness is its being as a righteous person.[168] It is extremely important that God's justifying judgement – what we call imputation, which attributes God's righteousness to sinners – be always understood as the creative Word which calls and places sinners outside themselves. This Word, by its power to displace the human Self, also makes that Self righteous and makes it sure of its righteous standing: 'And this is the reason why our theology is certain: it snatches us away from ourselves and places us outside ourselves.'[169] The fact of being sinners and righteous at the same time is shown by the same Self existing in two different existential places: on the one hand by itself, on the other hand in Christ and thus with God. 'I am a sinner in and by myself apart from Christ. Apart from myself and in Christ I am not a sinner.'[170] And it is apart from myself in Christ that I find myself, I become a *complete person*.

---

[167] Cf. ibid., 563, 10.

[168] Idem, *Romans*, *LW* 25, 267: 'only outside of herself [Luther is referring to the Church in the Song of Solomon (Tr)] is her fulness [completeness] and righteousness' = *WA* 56, 279, 31: 'extra se esse plenitudinem et Iustitiam suam'. On the question of philosophical and theological concepts of completeness, cf. E. Jüngel, 'Ganzheitsbegriffe – in theologischer Perspektive' in *Der 'ganze Mensch'. Perspektiven lebensgeschichtlicher Individualität (FS für Dietrich Rössler zum siebzigsten Geburtstag; APRTh 10)* ed. V. Drehsen et al., 1997, 353–67.

[169] Luther, *Galatians*, *LW* 26, 387 = *WA* 40/I, 589, 8: 'Ideo nostra theologia est certa, quia ponit nos extra nos.'

[170] Idem, *The Private Mass and the Consecration of Priests*, *LW* 38, 158.

There is a further important insight for the correct under-standing of the formula *simul iustus et peccator*: the fact that there is a conflict within this simultaneity. The twin existential positions 'in myself' and 'in Christ' do not get along with each other. The one who is righteous in Christ fights with himself or herself, against the Self that wants to come to itself by itself: 'perpetual conflict: *pugna perpetua*'.[171]

The theological imbalance between being righteous and being a sinner works itself out in this conflict. The side of being righteous gains the upper hand; the righteous make progress in righteousness: 'this act is in progress'.[172] The conflict shows that justification is still not completed. 'We are not now what we shall be, but we are on the way. The process is not yet finished, but it is actively going on. This is not the goal but it is the right road. At present, everything does not gleam and sparkle, but everything is being cleansed.'[173]

And because the justified are still under way, they are perfectly aware of the sin that still clings to them. That is why they pray for forgiveness of sin. In doing this, each knows that he or she is rightly to be described as the greatest of sinners, *peccator maximus*. This is true not only for the individual Christian, but for the community of the saints, the church. It too is both justi-fied and a sinner: 'there is no greater sinner than the Christian Church'.[174] Luther establishes a fundamental connection between the holiness of the church and its existence as a sinful entity: 'How can that be, that it is holy and sinful at the same time?' His answer: 'It believes in the forgiveness of sins and says

---

[171] Idem, *Die dritte Disputation gegen die Antinomer*, 1538, WA 39/I, 508, 8; cf. idem, *Die erste Disputation gegen die Antinomer*, 1537, WA 39/I, 376, 9–12: 'Faith fights against sin . . . sin fights against faith': 'fides pugnat contra peccatum . . . Peccatum contra fidem pugnat'.

[172] Idem, *Die Promotionsdisputation von Palladius und Tilemann*, 1537, WA 39/I, 252, 7: 'hic actus in progressu est'. Cf. Idem, Psalm 68, *LW* 13, 20; idem, Psalm 51, *LW* 12, 343.

[173] Idem, *Defense and Explanation of all the Articles*, 1521, *LW* 32, 24.

[174] Idem, 'Sermon on Easter Sunday', 9 April 1531, WA 34/I, 276.7f.: 'Non est tam magna peccatrix ut Christiana ecclesia.' What follows takes up my remarks in the essay 'The Church as Sacrament?' in *Theological Essays*, trans. J. B. Webster, Edinburgh: T&T Clark, 1989, 189–213.

"Forgive us our trespasses". Nobody says that unless he is holy.'[175] Those who are holy first make an appropriate petition for forgiveness of sins; that is the proof of their holiness. 'Therefore the Christian and the Christian Church are the true sinners, because they truly acknowledge their sins. The Pope, the cardinals and others have no sin at all; they are not tormented in their consciences.'[176] On the other hand, those who really believe feel themselves to be full of faults because in faith they recognize the discrepancy between themselves and their faith, between the truth of the faith and the life of the believer. Luther says this is just as true of the church as it is of the individual Christian.

This statement 'there is no greater sinner than the Christian Church' makes an extremely high claim for ecclesiology. It claims that the church is basically the community of *believers*. Believers are people who know that they are sinners because they allow their sins to be forgiven. They make the claim that they are people who are justified and recognized by God. That is the highest claim it is possible for a human community to make about itself.[177]

---

[175] Luther, op. cit., 276, 8f.: 'Quomodo haec est Sancta et peccatrix? Credit remissionem peccatorum et dicit: "debita dimitte". Hoc nemo dicit, nisi qui sit sanctus.'

[176] Ibid., 276:11–13: 'Ideo Christianus et Christiana ecclesia sind die rechten sunder, quia vere agnoscunt peccata. Papa, Cardinales et alii non habent peccatum omnino, non torquentur in conscientiis.'

[177] Luther's explanation that the very holiness of the church, consisting of *faith* in the remission of sins, is what makes the church into a 'righteous' sinner, coincides with and yet is distinct from the traditional idea of the church as a *casta meretrix*, a chaste prostitute. This is an image that emerged in the early church, based both on the Old Testament metaphor of Israel's adultery (especially in the prophets, where it is a picture of judgement!), and on the New Testament passages about women who were sinners receiving mercy (Luke 7; John 8; cf. Matt. 21:31f.; cf. also H. U. von Balthasar, 'Casta Meretrix' [ch. trans. by J. Saward] in idem, *Explorations in Theology III: Spouse of the Word*, San Francisco: Ignatius Press, 1991, 193–288. The idea is that the church as the Bride of Christ is *ecclesia casta* [chaste], but in its earthly reality it is and always will be *meretrix* [a prostitute], so that it is *casta meretrix*. To use the language of the Song of Solomon 1:5, it is black (suntanned), but, as in Song 4:1ff., 6:4ff. 7:6f., it is still beautiful. Because of its unity with the bridegroom it is without

As we come to the end of these considerations, a pressing question is raised. Is this carrying over of the simultaneous character of being righteous and sinful to the church what makes the Roman Catholic Church shrink from the Reformers' formula? In any case, the rejection of the formula by the Roman Catholic Church is not necessarily conclusive. It needs to be acceptable by Rome as well as a statement about the dialectic of Christian existence. But that would force a revision of that church's ecclesiological self-understanding. In this regard, the

_____

spot or wrinkle (Eph. 5:27), yet in its empirical appearance it is full of spots and wrinkles. Nevertheless, we are to think in this respect only of certain sinful members of the church as 'the dirty feet in the body of Christ' (H. U. von Balthasar, 'Casta Meretrix', 283; cf. Jerome, *Adversus Jovinianum*, 2, 29, *PL* 23, 326; Caesarius of Arles, *Sermo* 83, 3, *PL* 39, 1907; and Ambrose, *Epistula* 41, 26, *PL* 16, 1120, according to von Balthasar, loc. cit.), while the church itself is hardly affected by its dirty feet. Even von Balthasar closes his impressive study by quoting approvingly Emile Mersch, saying that the church is indeed 'made up of sinners' whose 'prayers are the prayers of sinners': '"Forgive us our trespasses" . . . Sin is in the Church . . . like the weeds in the field that are forever obstinately encroaching' (E. Mersch, *The Theology of the Mystical Body*, trans. C. Vollert, St Louis and London, 1951, 305ff., quoted by von Balthasar, op. cit., 287–8). Yet to the extent that the church is seen as the continuation of Christ, it is the source of holiness and is thus without fault (von Balthasar, loc. cit.). So here we see holiness excluding sin. However, this is not what Luther meant. His amazing claim that there is no greater sinner than the Christian church has its roots elsewhere. The difference is noticeable when one compares Luther's statements with a passage from the encyclical *Mystici Corpus* of Pius XII: 'if at times there appears in the church something that indicates the weakness of our human nature, it should not be attributed to her juridical constitution' (*scil.*: 'and certainly not to her mystical essence' [note by the author], 'but rather to that regrettable inclination to evil found in each individual [*lamentabilis singulorum ad malum proclivitas*]'. Thus, the church itself is not really affected by such weakness. Rather, as it continues: 'Certainly [*absque ulla labe*] the loving Mother is spotless in the Sacraments, by which she gives birth to and nourishes her children; in the faith which she has always preserved inviolate; in her sacred laws imposed on all; in the evangelical counsels which she recommends; in those heavenly gifts and extraordinary graces through which, with inexpressible fecundity, she generates hosts of martyrs, virgins and confessors. But it cannot be laid to her charge if some members fall, weak or wounded' (C. C. Ihm, ed., *The Papal Encyclicals 1939–1958*, 1981, 50). Hans Küng said what would appear to be the contrary when he unambiguously affirmed the question 'Is there a Catholic "simul iustus et peccator"?' and referred expressly to the Roman Mass (cf. Küng, *Justification*, 225–36).

German-speaking Catholic bishops have expressed themselves with agreeable clarity.[178] The question is: Can the Vatican follow them?

4. The ruling that justifies rules a basic line of separation

The justifying judgement – the ruling that justifies – is an efficacious one. It brings about a far-reaching distinction in the being of humans. Paul hinted at this in 2 Corinthians 4:16 when he wrote that our outer nature (that is, the one that *cannot* get outside itself!) is wasting away, while our inner nature (that is, the one that *is* able to leave itself!) is being renewed day by day. This serves as a *reminder*, though nothing more than a reminder, that our old Adam has been crucified with Christ and that we are therefore a new creation in Christ, who has been raised from the dead. The ruling that justifies rules a basic line of separation, dividing one and the same person into old and new, inner and outer, flesh and spirit, life under the law and life under grace, etc. The divided person exists not as half and half, but as both aspects complete. This becomes quite clear when we interpret this essential soteriological division in a temporal sense. The justifying judgement distinguishes and sets up two opposites: the being of the person as it is determined by that person's past and as it is determined by the person's future. It also makes a closer distinction and contrast. On the one hand there is the power that determines the being of the person, the power of his or her guilt-laden past which is self-made, and which, by the death of Jesus Christ, has been forever condemned to perish and is therefore perishing. On the other hand there is the future, with all its eschatological possibilities, which has been granted to us by God and can thus never date. It has already

---

[178] The Berlin Bishops' Conference, the German Bishops' Conference and the Austrian Bishops' Conference issued a joint 'Wort der Bischöfe zum Verhältnis von Christen und Juden aus Anlaß des 50. Jahrestages der Novemberpogrome 1938', which stated that 'the Church, which we confess to be holy and venerate as a mystery, is also sinful and in need of repentance' ('Die Last der Geschichte annehmen', *Die Deutschen Bischöfe: Hirtenschreiben*, Erklärungen 43, ed. by the Secretariat of the German Bishops' Conference, 20 October 1988, 7).

been opened to the believer by the resurrection of Jesus from the dead. The past, as it makes a claim to define our present, is a *power*, an *incredible power*.

To be defined by the past means above all to be defined by the context of human life in its deeds and works. It means to be defined by one's own deeds, misdeeds, achievements and failures and by the deeds, misdeeds, achievements and failures of other people and groups and their institutions. Thus I am precisely what I and others (with their institutions) have made of me. I am what I – and not only I – have done.

On the other hand, to be defined by the future as it comes from God means to conceive oneself anew as a person coming from the God who communicates himself in the judgement that justifies and addresses the sinner. Then I am precisely what God's Word makes of me. In the midst of the indissoluble context of persons and works I am distinct from all my works and from the works and effects of other people, groups and their institutions. I am so distinct that the work no longer makes up the person, but the person becomes free to act responsibly.

From what we have explained regarding the formula *simul iustus et peccator*, it should be clear that the essential division which the justifying judgement makes does not set up some sort of balance between the two sides that are being distinguished (the old and new natures, flesh and spirit, being defined by the past or by the future). This judgement says *No* to one side and *Yes* to the other. That is the meaning and purpose of the soteriological ruling that divides: we are removed from the dominance and the compulsions of the power of sin. We are set free from the claim of an ungodly past which is condemned to destruction (but which loves to linger). Now, instead, we live wholly for the future which is granted to us by God's Word. The meaning of *simul* – at the same time, simultaneously – can only be this: that a power which is condemned to destruction and has actually perished is *still* trying, with at least some measure of success, to press its totally illegitimate claims to dominance, when the sole legitimate Lord is already ruling with the authority of a freedom that sets others free.

Here we must make the cautious note that not everything from the past has to be excluded from this domain of freedom. By no means! The basic division of which we have been speaking, between being defined by our self-made past or by God's future, in no way condemns to destruction *everything* that has happened and has been. Rather, the justifying judgement makes a further distinction *within the past* between what has promise and a future (e.g. acts of freedom which, by setting others free, point beyond themselves!) and what has no promise or future simply because it is *past*, and thus has no promise or future. This is how the creative Word of the God of grace gives even the past – a part of the past – a new future that cannot date.

5. By the gospel alone

Everything that has been said about the exclusive formula *solo verbo* would be completely misunderstood if we were to claim that the Word in general had some kind of exclusive importance for justification. What has been said is aimed in every respect at excluding the achievements of human beings from the justification event. What can be said for human activity is that it too is brought about by a Word: by the demanding Word of the law. So there must be a further differentiation within the category of 'Word'. Obviously, the function of an exclusive formula is not to be attached to the 'Word as such, but . . . to a particular Word . . . So we must make a distinction between Word and Word if the meaning of *solo verbo* is to be clarified'.[179] It is *the gospel alone* by which sinners are justified. 'The Word of the Gospel is, in contradistinction to that of the law, that Word which does not presuppose reality, but puts it in place. For this reason it is not brought about by deeds only. Rather, its own reality can only be distorted by the belief that it must be brought about solely by deeds.'[180]

---

[179] Ebeling, *Dogmatik des christlichen Glaubens*, vol. 3, 223.
[180] Ibid.

The relevance of this distinction between law and gospel for justification can be explained by looking at the different ways in which the law on the one hand and the gospel on the other hand affect the human conscience. This will make it completely clear why only the gospel can justify sinners.

It is in their conscience that human beings experience the fact that the law *convicts and identifies them as sinners.* Thus we also need to speak of the conscience in connection with human justification, because the conscience is the relevant court for human beings. Here the human Self is the accessory to itself, its own witness, prosecutor and judge. In my conscience I know myself to be one who acts or has acted. Through this action my conscience places itself in such a relationship to itself that its own identity is at stake.

My conscience is firstly an accessory to itself. I know myself to be one who acts or has acted in a particular way. But along with this fact of being an accessory there also comes a knowledge of the norms of behaviour that should govern my Self, so that the conscience, knowing what I am doing, at the same time judges whether what I am doing is in accordance with these norms. In Paul's usage, the conscience is not something like the voice of God speaking to us. Nor is it a 'fundamental knowledge of good and evil' or a 'moral court which puts the brakes on'[181] certain behaviour. It is, as Luther put it so powerfully: 'not the power to do works, but to judge them' ('non . . . virtus operandi . . . sed . . . Iudicandi').[182] Kant comes to a similar conclusion: 'Now it is . . . not conscience, which judges whether an action is in general right or wrong . . . Conscience does not pass judgment upon actions as cases that stand under the law'. Rather, it is in conscience that 'reason judges itself, whether it has actually undertaken, with all diligence, that examination of actions (whether they are right or wrong), and it calls upon the human being himself to witness *for* or *against* himself whether this has

---

[181] H.-J. Eckstein, *Der Begriff Syneidesis bei Paulus. Eine neutestamentlich-exegetische Untersuchung zum 'Gewissensbegriff'* (WUNT, 2nd series, 10), Tübingen: Mohr Siebeck, 1983, 312.

[182] Luther, *The Judgment of Martin Luther on Monastic Vows, LW* 44, 298.

taken place or not'.[183] In the conscience the human Self brings itself before its own bar and judges itself on the basis of its deeds. In this sense it is '*the moral faculty of judgment, passing judgment upon itself*'.[184] In order to pass judgement on itself, this faculty of judgement must, as regards itself, insist rigorously on truth. In our consciences we human beings are truthful.

This is always subject to the condition that we are told what is good and what is required of us. The Bible says that it is God who tells us what is good (cf. Mic. 6:8). According to Kant it is practical reason that makes the laws. Whichever way it may be, the conscience only knows what it is told.[185] And at the same time it knows, as an accessory does, what the Self is doing or has done. The conscience unites these aspects of knowledge and being an accessory into a judgement, which in turn decides whether the Self is in agreement or in disagreement with itself. That is how in the conscience the being of the person is at stake.

At any rate, this is what happens when the being of the person is reduced to the being of the Self as it acts, as an *actant*. When human beings know themselves only as actants, when they see themselves according to the motto 'I am my deeds', then every deed that is judged by the conscience also raises a question mark over the personhood of human beings. In a manner of speaking, the unjust deed comes in between me and me; it splits me up. Thus the conscience becomes an accessory to its split Self. And this is exactly the position the Self finds itself in when it has

---

[183] Kant, *Religion Within the Boundaries of Mere Reason*, 203.

[184] Ibid.

[185] The conscience always has to rely on 'an external word, since it only speaks what is spoken to it (either contradicting or agreeing)' (G. Ebeling, 'Das Gewissen in Luthers Verständnis', in idem, *Lutherstudien*, vol. 3, 108–25: 111). E. Wolf said something similar ('Gewissen zwischen Gesetz und Evangelium. Erwägungen zur Frage nach der Freiheit des Gewissens', in idem, *Peregrinatio*, vol. 2, 104–18: 116: 'Conscience only exists together with the Word of God: a terrified conscience under God's Word of wrath; a consoled conscience under the gospel'). Cf. M. Luther, 'Sermon of 31 January 1524', WA 15, 426, 27: 'Cor et conscientia oportet habeat verbum, vel bonum vel malum: The heart and the conscience must have a Word; either a good one or a bad one.' Cf. idem, *Operationes in Psalmos*, 1519–21, WA 5, 259, 18f.: 'Quale enim est verbum, . . . talis conscientia: For just as the Word is, . . . so also is the conscience.'

been identified by the law as being sinful. As has been explained, the law,[186] as distinct from the gospel, makes demands on us as *doers*, those who perpetrate actions. It says: 'Thou shalt . . .' This demand provides a benchmark for it to judge everything I do. But as the law only ever addresses human beings as those of whom a demand is made, it reduces the being of the person to that of a doer. It turns human beings into the sum of their deeds. Thus it places impossible, hopeless demands on them.

We then become absolutely *terrorized* (a strong term, but necessary) in our consciences by these impossible demands born of our own guilt. The Reformers spoke of the 'terror of the law (*terror legis*)'[187] and of the 'terrorist acts of the conscience (*terrores conscientiae*)'[188] when we are once stricken in our conscience by the law and identified as sinners, the conscience is experienced as 'an evil beast which makes a man take a stand against himself'.[189] For acting against their conscience breaks up the sense of identity of those who do it. When acting (or being passive) against the conscience really 'becomes an irrevocable part of the personality', the cryptic saying is justified: 'only those who are able to kill themselves can have a conscience'.[190]

The end of this conscience – albeit a bad conscience[191] – is the gospel of justification. It is only the gospel that can set us free from our bad consciences when the law has identified us as

---

[186] We need to note again at this point that we are talking of the law as distinct from the gospel. That is, we are not discussing the Old Testament Torah, which does not differentiate, where the New Testament makes a clear distinction. Nevertheless, in what we are discussing – as Werner H. Schmidt has pointed out to me – the distinction between gospel and law runs parallel to the basic Old Testament distinction between God's deeds and human action.

[187] Cf. M. Luther, 'Sermon of January 1, 1545', *WA* 49, 654, 16.

[188] Cf. *ApolCA* IV, *BSLK* 163, 41. [Latin only. The German version (p. 164, lines 3–4) is a very free paraphrase, and introduces new elements (Tr).]

[189] M. Luther, *Lectures on Genesis*, 1535–45, *LW* 7, 331: 'Conscientia est mala bestia, quae facit hominem stare contra se ipsum.' Luther quotes this sentence as a 'saying . . . of a certain Cardinal (dictum . . . Cardinalis cuiusdam)'.

[190] N. Luhmann, 'Die Gewissensfreiheit und das Gewissen', in *AÖR* 90 (= *NS* 51) (1965), 257–86: 269.

[191] M. Luther, *Dictata super Psalterium*, 1513–16, *WA* 4, 67, 38: 'omnis conscientia mala: every conscience is a bad conscience'.

sinners. Luther even goes so far as to interpret being freed from a bad conscience as being free from any conscience at all. The gospel so touches the conscience that it is not tranquillized,[192] but rather cancelled and relieved of its post. When Luther talks of the *freedom of the conscience* (*libertas conscientiae*), he has in mind this tremendous fact, which has only a very tenuous connection to what today enjoys protection from the Constitution under the title of 'freedom of conscience'. We should not be led to minimize the radical nature of this pronouncement by the fact that Luther's other expressions for describing the same fact are avoided. So, for example, he is able to ascribe a *good conscience* even to the justified. But the vital *good conscience*, which he so often mentions, is for him not a moral phenomenon, but is directly equivalent to faith in Christ: 'faith in Christ is a good conscience'.[193] Faith is nothing but a good conscience.[194] In this context and in similar contexts faith is always faith in the justification of sinners: of sinners who are identified as sinners by their bad conscience which has been given a voice by the law. A *good* conscience is not then to be seen as an alternative to a *bad* one. Rather, it is the conscience united with Christ and thus freed from its guilt: 'the blood of Christ produces a good conscience. This only comes about through a conscience sure of the forgiveness of sins. Where [this assurance] is lacking, the conscience is restless'.[195] 'Restless' in this context means that the conscience is in its element as a bad conscience, that it lets itself be terrorized by the law and itself becomes a terrorized conscience. The gospel puts an end to this conscience. It sets us free from the terrorized and terrorizing conscience and in doing

---

[192] The gospel is definitely not an 'opium to conscience', *pace* Kant, *Religion Within the Boundaries of Mere Reason*, 117, n.

[193] M. Luther, *Heidelberg Disputation*, 1518, *LW* 31, 67 = *WA* 1, 372, 34: 'fides Christi est conscientia bona'.

[194] Cf. idem, *I John*, 1527, *LW* 30, 281 = *WA* 20, 718, 19f.: 'fides nihil aliud est quam bona conscientia'.

[195] Idem, 'Sermon of 5 January 1538', *WA* 46, 128, 24–6: 'Christi sanguis facit bonam conscientiam. Hoc non fit, nisi certa conscientia de remissione peccatorum. Ubi non, conscientia inquieta'; cf. *LW* 54, 64: 'For this did God permit his Son to die, that we might have a good conscience.'

so sets us totally free from the conscience.[196] This freedom, seen as freedom from the conscience, is described by Luther as *evangelical* freedom.[197]

However, at this stage we are once again faced with the dialectic of Christian life, where Christians are simultaneously sinners and justified. For, although 'this highest article: to know that we are free in Christ' and although the contrary, that is knowing the article concerning the cancellation of the law 'mightily consoles the conscience',[198] even in Christians the conscience keeps fixing on sin: 'the conscience wants to have dealings with sin'.[199] Although 'the conscience must have no dealings with the law [which prosecutes and condemns]',[200] it evidently does keep returning to its fundamental function of judging deeds and prosecuting and condemning the perpetrators on the basis of their deeds. If the conscience of even Christians can be so reduced to the level of a wild beast, seeking to range Christians against their own selves, then it is valid to 'summon God against the conscience'.[201] It is even valid

---

[196] The so-called good conscience is thus, as Ritschl so trenchantly affirmed: 'only . . . a way of saying the absence of a bad conscience', A. Ritschl, 'Über das Gewissen' in idem, *Gesammelte Aufsätze*, NF 1896, 177–203: 186). And this means, when we take it to its logical conclusion, that the conscience is only the phenomenon of conscience when it is a bad one. Martin Heidegger finds in this sense 'the "good" conscience is neither a self-subsistent form of conscience, nor a founded form of conscience; in short it is not a conscience-phenomenon at all' (M. Heidegger, *Being and Time*, trans. J. Macquarrie and E. Robinson, London: SCM Press, 1962, 338). P. Tillich comes to a similar conclusion ('Das religiöse Fundament des moralischen Handelns' in idem, *Gesammelte Werke*, vol. 3: *Das religiöse Fundament des moralischen Handelns. Schriften zur Ethik und zum Menschenbild*, ed. R. Albrecht, 1965, 13–83: 58.

[197] Cf. Luther, *On Monastic Vows*, *LW* 44, 298.

[198] M. Luther, *Galatians*, 1531, WA 40/I, 670, 2–5 [version by Tr. The *LW* translation varies from the Latin, but see *LW* 26, 445]: 'Summus articulus: nosse, quod in Christo liberi, – sic per Antithesin est necesse scire articulum abrogationis legis, quia hoc valet ad confirmandam nostram doctrinam et valde consolatur conscientiam, si scias te liberum a lege et eam abrogatam.'

[199] Ibid., 214, 4f.: 'conscientia vult cum peccatis zuthun haben'.

[200] Ibid., 214, 1: 'conscientia nihil habeat commercii cum lege'.

[201] Idem, *Operationes in Psalmos*, 1519–21, WA 5, 93, 37: 'contra conscientiam deum invocare'.

to fight with the conscience to the point of accusing it of lying: 'You are lying; Christ is right, not you.'[202]

Let us summarize. This is why we say that justification occurs *by the Word of the gospel alone*. Because it so unites with Jesus Christ human beings who have been named as sinners that they are able conscientiously to have no conscience. Because it so speaks to human beings who are terrorized by their consciences that they can allow themselves to be seen by God.

6. Word and sacrament

As a conclusion to our reflection on the exclusive formula *by the Word alone* we may briefly point out that it can by no means imply any sort of reduction in the importance of the sacraments. *By the Word alone* in no way means *by excluding the sacraments*. Regardless of the problems which go with the expression 'sacraments', we must assert the complete contrary: the very fact that God brings about *by the Word alone* what his Word promises becomes a concrete reality in baptism and the Lord's Supper. The sacraments are not acting in competition with the effectual divine Word. They are only sacraments to the extent that the effectual divine Word turns into an action in the world (as do eating and drinking in the case of the Lord's Supper, or the use of water in the case of baptism), and so becomes a concrete reality. 'It is not the water that produces these effects, but the Word of God connected with the water, and our faith which relies on the Word of God connected with the water. For without the Word of God the water is merely water and no Baptism.'[203] Faith does not trust in the water, but only in 'the Word of God in the water'. That is why Luther freely used Augustine's phrase:

---

[202] Idem, 'Sermon of 28 June 1528', WA 27, 223, 8–12: 'You must not believe your conscience and feelings more than the Word that was spoken by the Lord who accepts sinners . . . this is how you can fight with your conscience: by saying: You are lying; Christ is right, not you' ('Du must nicht conscientiae tuae und fulen plus credere quam verbo quod de domino praedicatur, qui suscipit peccatores . . . ita potes pugnare cum conscientia, ut dicas: du leugst, Christus hat war, non tu').

[203] *Small Catechism, BC*, 349.

'This means that when the Word is added to the element or the natural substance, it becomes a sacrament, [it becomes itself the visible Word]',[204] and the added explanation: 'that is, a holy, divine thing and sign',[205] or, as the *Württemberg Confirmees' Manual* puts it: 'a divine Word-Sign'.[206] That is why the Lutheran Confessions insist that the sacraments are only 'rightly administered' when they are 'administered according to the gospel'. In the same way, the sermon is only real proclamation when 'the gospel is preached in its purity'.[207] On the human side, *faith* is the equivalent of the gospel, so that even the sacraments are only effective as sacraments when the Word of divine commitment in the sacrament is laid hold of in faith.

Thus there can be no question of damaging the significance of the sacraments by emphasizing the exclusive formula *by the Word alone*. The contrary is true: only where there is a correct understanding of the God who justifies as the One who acts *by his Word alone* can the sacraments also be rightly understood. If they are 'administered according to the gospel', in the sacraments we become properly aware of how the justifying Word, coming as it does from outside us, touches us in our innermost being so deeply that we simply do not stay in ourselves, but come to ourselves 'in Christ'. For in baptism we are incorporated into the body of Christ. And in the Lord's Supper believers gather together at the Table of the Lord, whose body was given and whose blood was shed for them. Of course, we are not justified by baptism, but by faith as it affirms the Word of justification.[208] But in baptism, believers allow

---

[204] *Large Catechism, BC*, 438 [words in brackets altered (Tr)] = A. Augustinus, *In Joannis Evangelium Tractatus LXXX*, 3, *CChr. SL* 36, 529, 5–7: 'Accedit verbum ad elementum, et fit sacramentum, etiam ipsum tamquam visibile verbum.'

[205] *Large Catechism, BC*, 438.

[206] *Kirchenbuch für die Evangelische Landeskirche in Württemberg*. Part 2: *Sakramente und Amtshandlungen*. Section volume on *Die Konfirmation*, 1985, 53.

[207] *Augsburg Confession, BC*, 32.

[208] To this extent, Wolfhart Pannenberg's claim that baptism 'has a place when we think about the basis of justification' is problematical. And it is more than problematical when the theology of the Reformers is criticized for not having the same opinion as the Council of Trent, which 'rightly put baptism at the heart of its justification decree' (Pannenberg, *Systematic Theology*, vol. 3, 233). Rightly?

themselves to be so tied by God to their justifying faith and to its basis and object that they are irrevocably united in the church to the body of Christ.[209]

Thus, sacramental actions need to be seen from the point of view of the gospel. The action accomplished here is anything but a human one. Schleiermacher gives us the most appropriate term when he speaks of a *representative action*,[210] which has

---

Pannenberg's claim presumes that it is not the ungodly, but believers who are justified (ibid., 223f.; cf. The report on a lecture given by Pannenberg in January, 1999 at the *Münchner Collegium Oecumenicum*, where he is said to have explained – and I quote the *Evangelisches Sonntagsblatt für Bayern* of 31 January 1999, No. 5, 15 – 'that is why the believer (not the ungodly) is justified'). By 'justification' the forensic act of declaring righteous is understood here; it is to be distinguished from 'the righteousness of faith' (*Systematic Theology*, vol. 3, 234). Now, the righteous of God (δικαιοσύνη θεοῦ) is not to be interpreted only as a *genitivus auctoris*, but at the same time as a *genitivus subiectivus*; thus we have to distinguish between it and the act of justification (δικαιοῦν). But this must not be done in such a way as to claim that the object of God's justifying act is not the ungodly, but the believer. Even such an exegete as H. Schlier, who claims that 'δικαιοῦν' is fundamentally accomplished 'in the individual case by baptism', sees this δικαιοῦν as 'purely and simply the validation of divine justification by God's action' and not as justification of the believer (H. Schlier, *Der Brief an die Galater* [*KEK* 7], 14th impression, 1971, 89). Moreover, one of the more recent commentaries on Galatians makes the claim concerning 'Schlier's presentation of Paul's theology of baptism' that it is a 'misrepresentation' (H. D. Betz, *Galatians: A Commentary on Paul's Letter to the Churches in Galatia*, Philadelphia: Fortress Press, 1979, 188). And U. Wilckens, who is referred to by Pannenberg (*Systematic Theology*, vol. 3, 224, n. 402), in the context to which the footnote refers, mentions several times the justification of *sinners*, of *iustificatio impiorum* (U. Wilckens, *Der Brief an die Römer* [*EKK* VI/1], 1978, 181–208). In addition, the context of faith and baptism which Wilckens rightly emphasizes (ibid. [VI/1], 1980, 52–4), and to which Pannenberg also adverts, likewise does not say that baptism is part of the fundamental context of justification. Rather, Wilckens says it is only among early Christians in baptism that 'all of the various elements of the process of conversion came together', without our knowing 'anything more precise' about 'why and in what order a convert was brought from the first occasion of being moved by preaching . . . to baptism into the Christian life' (ibid., 54). To claim that Paul believed in the justification of the believer and not of the ungodly is erroneous. What does it say in Romans 4:5?

209 Cf. E. Jüngel, 'Zur Kritik des sakramentalen Verständnisses der Taufe', in idem, *Barthstudien*, (*ÖTh* 9), 1982, 295–314: 304–12.

210 F. D. E. Schleiermacher, *Die christliche Sitte nach den Grundsätzen der evangelischen Kirche im Zusammenhange dargestellt*, in *Friedrich Schleiermacher's sämmtliche Werke*, ed. L. Jonas, Section 1, vol. 12, 1843, 525f. [English by Tr].

nothing to do with the production-oriented workaday world of which we are all compelled to be a part. Representative action is a sabbatical action by which we are relieved of the burden of ourselves. What is represented is precisely what the gospel promises. The Latin word *repraesentatio* may be thought of as being a representation which actualizes or recalls something to mind. Both the Protestant and the Catholic churches use this concept of representation in their pronouncements on sacramental action. The Lutheran confessions say that those who preach the gospel and administer the sacraments in accordance with the gospel represent not themselves, but the person of Christ. They offer Word and sacrament in Christ's stead.[211] In the pronouncements of the Roman Catholic Church at Trent concerning the Mass it says that Jesus left to the church in the form of the Mass 'a sacrifice . . . that was visible. This sacrifice was to represent the bloody sacrifice which he accomplished on the cross once and for all'.[212] For the members of the Council the sacramental representation seems to be accomplished in such a way that Jesus Christ is the subject of the representation, that he realizes his own representation in the priest's action.

These statements about how the sacramental action represents Jesus should allow of a fundamental agreement between the Lutheran Church and the Roman Catholic Church. This is that Jesus makes himself present in the sacrament, that he is *really the one at work* in the sacramental action, who makes us into *receivers*. However, what he *does* is nothing other than a *being* in the *action* of the Word, that is, in the Word of the gospel. That is why any alternative between a church of the Word and a church of the sacraments is completely inappropriate and misses

---

[211] Cf. *BC*, 173: 'For they do not represent their own persons but the person of Christ . . . When they offer the Word of Christ or the sacraments, they do so in Christ's place and stead' = *ApolCa* VII, *BSLK* 240, 42–7 [Latin only at this point. (Tr)]: 'repraesentant Christi personam . . . , non repraesentant proprias personas . . . Cum verbum Christi, cum sacramenta porrigunt, Christi vice et loco porrigunt'.

[212] *TCT*, 291 = *DH* 1740: 'visibile . . . relinqueret sacrificium, quo cruentum illud semel in cruce peragendum repraesentaretur eiusque memoria in finem usque saeculi permaneret . . .'

the essence of the Word of the gospel as well as the essence of the sacraments. It is quite indicative that the great Catholic theologian Karl Rahner could even say: 'the Eucharist is . . . the absolute instance of the word'.[213] The prime meaning of the exclusive formula *solo verbo* is Word and sacrament.

IV. By faith alone (*sola fide*)

The God who is gracious and pronounces ungodly human beings righteous is a God who makes *faith* possible and craves *faith*. 'For these two belong together, faith and God.'[214] Only faith can allow God to be God. This is why the exclusive formula *by faith alone* is the point of the justification article.[215] It emphasizes positively how human beings, very clearly excluded

---

[213] K. Rahner, *Theological Investigations*, vol. IV, *More Recent Writings*, trans. K. Smyth, London: Darton, Longman & Todd, 1966, 283. [Translation altered. Cf. the original in context: K. Rahner, 'Wort und Eucharistie', in idem, *Schriften zur Theologie*, vol. 4 (3rd edn) 1962, 313–55: 351: 'Die Eucharistie ist in aller Wahrheit das Sakrament des Wortes schlechthin, der Absolutfall des Wortes überhaupt'. (Tr)]

[214] *Large Catechism, BC* 365.

[215] In the *Joint Declaration*, the Lutherans decided not to specifically include the exclusive formula *by faith alone*. This is disconcerting enough. But it is one of the most macabre aspects of the dispute about the *Joint Declaration* that the Lutheran apologists – bishops, church officials, members of church assemblies, even professors of theology – justified this step by saying that Melanchthon had already left out the exclusive formula *by faith alone* in the article on justification in the *Augsburg Confession*. And since Melanchthon made the claim concerning the teaching of the first 21 Articles of the *Augsburg Confession* that it was 'not contrary or opposed to . . . [even that] of the Roman church' (*BC*, 47), they said that it was not only permitted, but in point of fact required to remove the exclusive formulae from any consensus of both churches reached today. What are we to say to this? As it is, the exclusive formula is lacking in the *Augsburg Confession*, Article IV. But in the next article but one, on 'The New Obedience', it says, using a quotation from the early church, that we have 'forgiveness of sins . . . through faith alone' (*BC*, 32). And in the article which is so decisive for the issue of justification, on 'Faith and Good Works', we read that our reconciliation with God 'happens only through faith' (*BC*, 42). Since, as Melanchthon thought, the first twenty-one articles are also acceptable to the Roman Catholic Church, we ought to be able to say from the Lutheran perspective that the *sola fide* formula is acceptable ecumenically. *But what about Trent?* A number of the Lutheran apologists who drafted the *Joint Declaration* apparently feel more strongly bound to it than to the *Augsburg Confession*.

from the justification event by the other three exclusive formulae *Christ alone, by faith alone, by the Word alone* are now included positively in the occasion of their justification by a life-act which they accomplish themselves. As believers, and only as believers, they are involved from where they are in their own justification. As believers they become involved in God's Word. As believers they allow themselves to partake of God's grace. As believers they profess their faith in Jesus Christ. As believers they are justified sinners.

Here too, the use of the exclusive term is appropriate. We shall examine immediately below what is excluded here. But first we must explain that human beings are positively included in the occasion of their justification by the fact that they believe. But why and how? Why and how is faith *justifying faith, fides iustificans*? Why and how is it that very faith which justifies human beings? What is human faith that it can achieve such great things?

The simplest answer to the question of the nature of human faith is that faith is the human '*Yes*', the affirmation, coming from the heart, to the definitive *affirmation* from God which comes to us in the occasion of our justification. It is the human '*Yes*' to that clear and already accomplished *negation* by God which we have because of that definitive *affirmation* in Jesus Christ. Believers say *Yes* to God's Word, to God's judgement, to the judgement of God which condemns sin and condemns the sinner to perish, but also acquits us, because it acquits sinners. Believers agree that God's condemning and acquitting judgement is already accomplished in the person of Jesus Christ. It has been accomplished to such a degree that a sinner's death lies behind us and the life of the just lies before us, *right now*. Faith is our heartfelt affirmation of the death and resurrection of Jesus Christ. It affirms Good Friday and Easter Sunday as being the two great events which are decisive for all human beings. Because it is this heartfelt affirmation, faith is *justifying faith*, it is *fides iustificans*.

This fundamental information concerning *justifying faith* will now be expanded along several lines.

1. Faith: self-discovery and self-forgetfulness

The first thing to be emphasized is the fact that faith is *trusting with the heart*. Human beings believe *with the heart* (Rom. 10:9). The faith of human beings is their *heartfelt Yes* to Jesus Christ and to the divine judgement that has been passed and enacted. *This Yes comes from the heart,* because the divine judgement has come into the heart of believers, striking them in the centre of their existence. By such a formulation we are presupposing a biblical anthropology whereby the heart is the *life centre* of human beings, and in it *decisions are made concerning the whole person.*

The affirmation, the *Yes* that the believer says to God's judgement, is not just some arbitrary word which could just as well be replaced by some other word. Rather, by this *Yes*, which we need to see as the foundational word of faith, the whole person, human existence as a whole is expressing itself. The *Yes* of faith is the most concentrated expression of human existence. When we believe, our whole existence becomes a single *Yes* by which we are affirming God's decisive judgement over all human existence and thus over our own existence. But who is really making the decision here? Who makes the decision in my heart? Do I make the decision about myself?

Faith is frequently understood as being a human decision for God, whereby the human Self makes its own fundamental decision about itself. Faith has been interpreted as a free and fundamental decision of the human subject. This decision has been seen to be a foundational act of human freedom, as 'a single act, once and for all' which is meant to be the 'self-fulfilment of a single subject', whereby the subject commits itself 'in the once-and-for-all entirety of its whole history'. This presupposes that 'freedom is not an eternal ability to reconfigure in eternally fresh forms'.[216] Rather, it is the ability of the subject to come to its own 'finality and irrevocability'. 'Freedom does not exist so that everything can constantly take on a new form; it exists so that something can really have validity and

---

[216] Rahner, *Grundkurs des Glaubens*, 102.

inevitability.' We have absolutely no intention of saying anything against Karl Rahner's interpretation of freedom, which he is also able to state as being: 'the ability to establish what is necessary, what is permanent, what is final'.[217] Still, we must ask whether the *Yes of faith* – which, in fact, similarly aims at what is final – can be seen as this kind of *free decision by the subject* by which the subject fulfils itself. For faith would then still remain my deed, the deed in which I *am*.

Rudolf Bultmann – to name another great theologian – apparently saw things as did Karl Rahner when he defined faith in a prose which is much plainer (but none the easier to understand for all that): faith is 'the free deed of obedience in which the new self constitutes itself in place of the old. As this sort of decision, it is a deed in the true sense: In a true deed the doer himself is inseparable from it, while in a "work" he stands side by side with what he does'.[218] No doubt Bultmann the exegete means the Pauline concept of faith when he says: 'it is evident that "faith" has the character of obedience and is an act of decision'.[219] Yet it is the systematician in the exegete who tells us: 'but one's being is constituted in action, and it is *called in question* and called to decision *by this very question of belief*: here man is asked what – or who – he wishes to be. Man does not stand behind his decision to believe, but in it'.[220] So is faith that free act of deciding by a human being on which 'being a Christian' is based? Bultmann would be a poor Pauline expositor

---

[217] Ibid., 103.

[218] Bultmann, *Theology of the New Testament*, 316. Bultmann thus distinguishes between work and deed, between *ergon* and *praxis*. For him a work is defined – rather analogously to the Aristotelian concept of ποίησις, whose τέλος is located outside the productive act – as the doer of the work standing next to his work. A deed, for Bultmann – rather analogously to the Aristotelian concept of πρᾶξις, whose τέλος is located within the act – is defined by the doer of the deed having his being in the deed. Bultmann's doctrine of justification could be interpreted maliciously as saying that human beings are indeed justified without works of the law, but by their free deed [act], which as a genuinely free deed can only be the deed of their faith.

[219] Ibid., 317.

[220] R. Bultmann, 'Grace and Freedom' in idem, *Essays, Philosophical and Theological*, trans. J. C. G. Greig, London: SCM Press, 1955, 168–81: 180.

indeed if he did not have second thoughts. He is aware that faith is not a human work and that the believer can see 'his act of belief . . . simply as a God-given free act', so that it is true to say: 'it *is only divine grace that is responsible for man's real freedom.* For real freedom does not even consist in freedom from the determination of the will by the outward conditions of life to which decision and action are subject; rather is it in freedom from ourselves – from ourselves as we are in every "now", as people who come out of their past and are determined by it.'[221] And this is what Bultmann does say, after all: it is the 'grace of God' and not faith that renews our whole existence: 'In renewing our whole existence it liberates us in a radical sense . . . In this way dependence on God's grace, and being given over to it, far from limiting our freedom, actually makes us in a real sense free.'[222]

If this is the case, that the grace of God renews our whole existence and first and foremost sets us free into our own freedom, then faith simply cannot be understood as that human act of decision by which the being of the justified is established or by which the new self is established in place of the old. Those who adopt this formulation interpret justification according to the transcendental idealism of Kant and Fichte and thus miss an essential feature of justifying faith. Faith justifies sinners for the very reason that it agrees with God's justifying judgement – not on the basis of a *weighing up between Yes and No,* but (to use Bultmann's term) *in obedience* to God's Word. For obedience, a No to God's judgement is simply impossible. It is out of the question from the outset; its very nature excludes it from consideration.

However, we do not need to look to Bultmann's high view of obedience[223] in order to be able to clarify the fact that faith is

---

[221] Ibid.

[222] Ibid., 181.

[223] As is shown by Paul's language, which speaks of 'the obedience of faith' (Rom. 1:5) or obedience to the good news (Rom. 10:16; cf. 2 Thess. 1:8) and of obedience to Christ (2 Cor. 10:5), it is no doubt right to speak of obedience to Christ, but this can easily lead to a misunderstanding of the concept of faith in the direction of authoritarianism.

not some sort of self-reconstruction of the new nature in the act of decision, by which the Self decides about itself. If you are dying of thirst and drink from a fresh spring you are doing something other than fulfilling obedience. Similarly, it is not correct to call it obedience when someone happily empties a full cup (Ps. 23:5). By responding with a heartfelt *Yes* to God's effectual justifying judgement, we are affirming that a gracious decision has already been made concerning us and that the justified and thus new nature is *already established* by this *effectual divine decision*. We *discover* ourselves as new people, constituted by God. Faith is a self-discovery that begins at the same time as we discover God. It is the discovery of a self-renewal that affects the whole person. Those who *discover* themselves as new persons cannot *make themselves* into new persons; nor can they *decide* to exist as such.

So Paul sees life lived 'by faith in the Son of God, who loved me and gave himself for me' in such a way that 'it is no longer I who live, but it is Christ who lives in me' (Gal. 2:20). Even Bultmann interprets this verse as saying that the believer, by living 'with Christ', lives 'no longer as "I", but in such a way that Christ is a new "I" in him'.[224] Thus faith acknowledges the fact that a decision has been made in the person of Jesus Christ about the human Self. Faith is that *Yes* made by the whole person, by which those who have been awakened from slumber affirm that they *have been awakened* and that they are now able to and indeed must make their discovery as people who are wide awake, as people of the light and day, not of the night and darkness (1 Thess. 5:5). That *Yes* which we are to see as being faith is the *discovering understanding* of the divine decision about human beings, which is now being made by human beings. By expressing our entire existence in this heartfelt *Yes* to God's judgement, we are admitting that the first thing was for our hearts to be conquered, that we needed first of all to be set free to speak this affirmative *Yes*. Thus faith is the self-discovery and experience of the Self that has been set free unto freedom. Now,

[224] Bultmann, 'Points of Contact and Conflict' in *Essays*, 133–50: 141.

this self-discovery and experience is an action in life which must be accomplished by myself – and this is no doubt what Rahner and Bultmann meant. It is the act of saying *Yes* to my own negation and affirmation by God.

Faith is the heartfelt human *Yes* to God's Word, as Mary shows when she answers the angel's promise: 'let it be with me according to your word' (Luke 1:38). Those who can speak like this have discovered themselves as human beings who, without any of their own effort or collaboration, are experiencing what God has decided. Mary epitomizes the faith that joyfully asks: 'Thy will be done on earth as it is in heaven', the faith that is totally certain of that request being *fulfilled* in her own life.

2. *Faith as assurance of salvation*

Faith, the heartfelt *Yes* to God's judgement, is the foundational act of a life lived definitively outside itself. Faith thus follows the movement of the Word that justifies sinners. In faith we agree that God's justifying Word is calling, taking and placing us outside ourselves. In faith we *go* outside ourselves, that is, in conformity with the divine decision that affects us. In faith we comprehend the movement of our own justification which has already taken place in Jesus Christ, and it is in that comprehension – and not in some other way! – that we also complement that comprehension. As those who have been moved, we move; as those who have been moved by the grace and the Word of God, we move in accordance with this movement of divine grace and the divine Word. Believing, we *trust* God and thus *entrust ourselves* to the movement of grace and God's Word. That is why the external righteousness of God becomes in faith our own righteousness. For, as we believe, we allow ourselves to be transposed to the place which is *our rightful place,* that is where we, as human beings, are in our rightful human place: with God and his righteousness – with the God who is gracious to us and who, out of his grace, has suffered the judgement of a sinner condemned to death in order to bring *new, justified life* to light out of the darkness of such a death.

That is where I come to myself. *That* is where I am righteous. *Outside myself* I am in full possession of myself. If such a thing as Christian mysticism existed, it would consist of some such crossover of the inward and the outward, whereby the God who speaks to me in the act of justification calls me out to him in a fellowship of life. Of course, such fellowship can only be a fellowship along the way. The mystical union would not be the goal, but the way. Furthermore, it would be a way where the world was not shut out, but viewed from a new perspective. It follows that this would be a way where our senses might not – as is otherwise the case in mystical exercises – be excluded, but rather would be heightened, so that we would have eyes to see, ears to hear – to hear and be amazed. It would be a mysticism of *opened* eyes[225] and *opened* ears.

One of the special features of this fellowship of life along the way with God is that, in one sense, the human Self *forgets itself.* Self-discovery and self-forgetfulness are by no means mutually exclusive. Rather, in Christ we discover ourselves in such a way that our own Self is able to forget itself. That is why Paul could make such an apparently paradoxical assertion: in faith I live in such a way that 'it is no longer I who live, but it is Christ who lives in me' (Gal. 2:20). This should not be seen as being a self-sacrifice. It most certainly should not be seen as heroic. Rather, self-forgetfulness, when correctly understood, comes about all by itself on the basis of the most intimate closeness to another Self. Faith as self-forgetfulness is the most intensive form of certainty of God.[226] But this certainty of God is, in the context of justification, nothing other than *assurance of salvation.* In faith we become *sure* of our own justification and our own salvation and thus of our own *election* by God, *because* faith has this structure based outside itself.

---

[225] So mysticism should probably not be traced back to μύειν ('to close the eyes'). For the concepts on which these ideas are based, I am grateful to Dorothee Sölle and Johann Baptist Metz.

[226] On this cf. E. Jüngel, 'Gottesgewißheit' in idem, *Entsprechungen: Gott – Wahrheit – Mensch* (*BEvTh* 88) (2nd edn), 1986, 252–64: 262.

At this point we need to emphasize the following: justifying faith, which is trust in God, is at the same time *assurance of salvation*. It can even be said to be *assurance of election*. It is the assurance of being chosen as a child of God by God and of being provided with all the privileges of a child of God. Justifying faith externalizes certainty of salvation and removes fear of rejection. 'Rejection, if accepted, would be a contradiction.'[227] That is why assurance of election is not some kind of *add-on* that can be split off from justifying faith. Assurance of election is not added on to faith; faith *is* this assurance. So the assurance of faith is nothing but the assurance of having been put in the right by God: the right of being unshakably together, as a child with God as Father. The believer 'has the right of a son in relation to God as God has the right of a father in relation to him – the right to a being with Him, the right to immediate access to Him, the right to call upon Him, the right to rely upon Him, the right to expect and to ask of Him everything that he needs. This right of sonship is the essence of every right of man. And the promise of this right is the completion of the justification of sinful man.'[228] Believing means to have a calm assurance of this right of the child and to use it.

Thus it is difficult to understand Trent's polemics 'Against the Vain Confidence of Heretics', when it claims 'no one can know with the certainty of faith, which cannot be subject to error, that he has obtained the grace of God'.[229] Did they simply

---

[227] Ebeling, *Dogmatik des christlichen Glaubens*, vol. 3, 235.

[228] Barth, *CD* IV/1, 600.

[229] *TCC*, 390 = *DH* 1534: 'Nullus scire valeat certitudine fidei, cui non potest subesse falsum, se gratiam Dei esse consecutum.' This statement is even more incomprehensible, since Trent itself expressly claims that 'faith is the beginning of human salvation, the foundation and root of all justification' *TCC*, 389 = *DH* 1532: 'fides est humanae salutis initium, fundamentum et radix omnis iustificationis'. At this council too Cardinal Cervini expressed the opinion (on 21 December 1546) that faith is always the root and foundation of the whole of justification 'both in the preparation for and in the moment of justification, as well as in its outworking and increase' (according to E. Stakemeier, 'Trienter Lehrentscheidungen und reformatorische Anliegen' in G. Schreiber, ed., *Das Weltkonzil von Trient*, 1951, 77–116: 100). Nevertheless, these statements concerning the function of faith as the foundation of justification, which sound so like those of

wish to express the idea that doubt is always part of faith? By raising questions about the assurance of faith (*certitudo fidei*) did they wish in fact to issue a warning about trusting in the flesh (*securitas carnis*), which is only too common in relation to God? Do they have in mind a subjective self-assurance and self-confidence which is no part of faith when they say in Canons 13 and 14: 'If anyone says that, to attain the remission of sins, everyone must believe with certainty and without any misgiving because of his own weakness and defective disposition, that his sins are remitted: let him be anathema';[230] and: 'If anyone says that man is absolved from his sins and justified because he believes with certainty that he is absolved and justified; or that no one is truly justified except him who believes he is justified, and that absolution and justification are effected by this faith alone: let him be anathema'?[231] If this is a defence against an unwarranted self-assurance that has completely subjective motives and is thus baseless, we could certainly be given to wonder about it. For we are not justified because of our faith (*propter fidem*), but through our faith (*per fidem*). Otherwise, faith and assurance of faith would be a work to be achieved. That would mean that the doctrine of justification by faith alone would be turned into its opposite. The Reformers had nothing at all like this in mind when they claimed that faith is sure of its object. They expressly excluded such an idea. Even Luther aims

---

the Reformers, are again made relative when that same decree on justification disputes whether faith as such can unite us perfectly with Christ without the addition of hope and love: 'For faith, unless hope and charity be added to it, neither unites a man perfectly with Christ nor makes him a living member of his body' (*TCC*, 388 = *DH* 1532: 'Nam fides, nisi ad eam spes accedat et caritas, neque unit perfecte cum Christo, neque corporis eius vivum membrum efficit.')

[230] *TCT*, 243 = Can. 13, *DH* 1563: 'Si quis dixerit, omni homini ad remissionem peccatorum assequendam necessarium esse, ut credat certo et absque ulla haesitatione propriae infirmitatis et indispositionis, peccata sibi esse remissa: anathema sit.'

[231] *TCT*, 244 = Can. 14, *DH* 1564: 'Si quis dixerit, hominem a peccatis absolvi ac iustificari ex eo, quod se absolvi ac iustificari certo credat, aut neminem vere esse iustificatum, nisi qui credit se esse iustificatum, et hac sola fide absolutionem et iustificatum perfici: anathema sit.'

at a strict differentiation between the assurance of faith and a
merely subjective confidence (which, of course, only too readily
makes use of so-called objective bases and facts for the purpose
of self-assurance). As Luther says: 'Confidence cancels out faith:
securitas . . . tollit fidem'.[233]

Now, it is the exact opposite, the assurance of faith, *certitudo
fidei*, which excludes false confidence, *securitas*. So, to that extent,
what Trent was fighting against was not Christian faith (which
is impossible to imagine without assurance of faith), but rather
unbelief and its presumptuousness, self-fulfilment and vainglory.
Is that what the members of the Council had in mind?

Unfortunately, we suspect that this was *not* their meaning. It
is to be feared that they meant exactly what they said. In that
case their statements are not only hard to understand, they are
intolerable. In that case they must be firmly rebuked. It is vital
then to correct a church which issues such condemnations. That
church must be reminded that believers simply are not sure of
themselves all by themselves, but rather they are sure of God
and his grace outside themselves and with God.

The self-forgetfulness of the believer, rightly understood, is
what should be taken as the criterion for deciding between presumptuous self-confidence (*securitas carnis*) and the assurance
of faith (*certitudo fidei*). In faith, believers are – as the Mystics say
– liberated from themselves. They are free of themselves and
thus oblivious to themselves. This is precisely the opposite of
presumptuous self-confidence. When they are oblivious to
themselves, believers can make a new start in every respect. That
means they can make a new start with themselves as well.

3. 'Faith makes the person'

As faith – the human, heartfelt *Yes* to God's judgement – allows
us to come out of and be liberated from ourselves so that we
become oblivious to ourselves, our personhood is made anew.
This does not happen as an immediate result of faith, but comes

---

[232] M. Luther, *Die fünfte Disputation gegen die Antinomer*, 1538, WA 39/I, 356, 25.

about through the Word of God, which faith follows. So it is only to that extent that it can be said to result from faith. Since faith says with Mary: 'Let it be with me according to your word', we can also make the claim that 'faith makes the person: *fides facit personam*'.[233] Of course, this statement only gives to faith the significance of making persons because faith allows God to be God and thus allows God's working to be manifest. So 'faith makes the person' means 'that the person is made by God through faith'.[234] This contradicts a tradition which has had a powerful effect for a long time. The contradiction is summarized pithily by Luther in these words: 'The work I do does not make the person into the person I am: *opus non facit personam*'.[235]

Even in Luther's early works we find the rejection of this opinion, which went back as far as Aristotle.[236] Luther expressed this contradiction most clearly in his *Disputation Against Scholastic Theology*: 'We do not become righteous by doing righteous deeds but, having been made righteous, we do righteous deeds.'[237] In the previous year, in a letter to Spalatin, Luther had given a name to the authority he was combating: 'For we are not, as Aristotle believes, made righteous by the doing of just deeds, unless we deceive ourselves; but rather – if I may say so – in becoming and being righteous people we do just deeds. First it is necessary that the person be changed, then the deeds [will follow].'[238]

The point which Luther is combating is found in Aristotle's *Nicomachean Ethics*: 'so too we become just by doing just acts'.[239] It expresses a common opinion which it apparently did not occur to anybody to dispute. Thus, apparently we are what we make of ourselves. Luther did not contest the fact that Aristotle's

---

[233] M. Luther, *Die Zirkulardisputation* de veste nuptiali, 1537, *WA* 39/I, 283, 1.

[234] Ibid., 283, 15f.: 'quod persona sit facta per fidem a Deo'.

[235] Ibid., 283, 9.

[236] Cf. E. Jüngel, 'On Becoming Truly Human. The Significance of the Reformation Distinction Between Person and Works for the Self-Understanding of Modern Humanity' in *TE* 2, 216–40.

[237] Luther, *Disputation Against Scholastic Theology*, *LW* 31, 12.

[238] Luther, *Letter to George Spalatin, 19 October 1516*, *LW* 48, 25.

[239] Aristotle, *Nicomachean Ethics*, *BGB* 9, 348–9.

statement seemed plausible 'to a philosophical and worldly forum'.[240] What he did dispute, however, was that the true being of a human person can be revealed and determined by any wordly forum at all. No wordly tribunal can decide what sort of a person I really am. The right of judgement about our person-hood has been taken from all earthly individuals and courts. The only One competent to pass judgement on the being of persons is the One who made persons into persons. And that is God alone. Plausible though it is that human persons can make something of themselves, just as strong a case can be made against our ability to make ourselves. What human persons make from themselves is completely different from what makes a person into a person. There is no validity in the plausible pronouncements of worldly tribunals which say that we are what we make of ourselves when it is personhood that is being decided. When is is a matter of deciding what makes us human, only the Creator of human persons is competent to judge. And the concept of Creator negates the possibility of human persons making themselves. In the eyes of other people I may well be what I am making or have made of myself. I may even seem to myself to be the product of my deeds. But before God I am quite simply not in the position of making anything of myself. That is why Luther, when conceding their rights to the plausible pronouncements of worldly tribunals, adds bluntly: 'but this is not how it happens with God'.[241]

Of course, these abrupt words are not aimed *at* human beings. For Luther, the fact that it is quite different with God is much more closely connected to the fact that human beings in the context of the world remain exposed to the amibivalence of being human or inhuman, of discovering the truth of our being or of missing it. We are unable to escape this ambivalence by ourselves. We cannot by ourselves attain to the unambiguity of our being. Rather, the ambivalence to which we are exposed

---

[240] M. Luther, *Die Zirkulardisputation* de veste nuptiali, 1537, *WA* 39/I, 282, 10: 'Haec valent in foro philosophico et mundo. . . .'

[241] Ibid., 282, 10f.: 'sed non sic fit aput Deum'.

expresses our alienation from ourselves. The human person is, as Luther and tradition put it: 'a corrupt nature: *corrupta natura*';[242] to put it in biblical terms, we are *sinners*. That is why it is good for us not to have control over our personhood. We have been removed from ourselves *for our own good*.

In this sense we need to home in on the fact that it is *by the faith alone* which justifies us that we become *sola fide* justified and thus new persons. The exclusive formula *by faith alone (sola fide)*, when seen from this point of view, provides a neat summary of the doctrine of justification which can appear so complex. It expresses strikingly the fact that it is not by human activity that we co-operate in our own justification. Even the works of human love have no contribution to make here – for it is certain that it is that very faith which brings forth such works of love.

Thus it was a distortion of Paul's doctrine of justification when, using the Latin translation of Galatians 5:6b ('faith, through which love is active'), the implication was made by taking an Aristotelian interpretation of the expression *fides caritate formata* ('faith, formed through love') that faith only becomes real faith (finding its shape and thus being realized) through the deeds of love. This was then carried further to imply that only faith which realized itself as love, only faith showing itself exclusively in loving acts, could justify human beings. The fact that works cannot make the person is also valid for the works of love. And it is totally incomprehensible when Trent anathematizes anyone who 'says that men are justified either through the imputation of Christ's justice alone, or through the remission of sins alone, excluding grace and charity which is poured forth in their hearts by the Holy Spirit and inheres in them . . .'.[243] It is impossible to understand when a similar anathema is applied to anyone who, as a logical consequence of the above, 'says that justifying faith is nothing else than

---

[242] Ibid., 282, 27f.

[243] *TCT*, 243 = *DH* 1561: 'Si quis dixerit, homines iustificari vel sola imputatione iustitiae Christi, vel sola peccatorum remissione, exclusa gratia et caritate . . . anathema sit.'

confidence that divine Mercy remits sins for Christ's sake, or that it is confidence alone which justifies us'.[244]

On the basis of this anathema alone the Roman Catholic Church must revise its claim to infallibility, if it does not wish to also earn the unfortunate reputation of having placed the apostle Paul under anathema. 'A Church which maintains that its official decisions are *infallible* can commit errors which are *irreformable.*'[245] It can only be hoped that the recommendation to declare the sixteenth-century condemnations as irrelevant for today[246] will be an initial step towards rethinking the claim to infallibility of the Catholic Church's official teaching.

We must stress that human beings are not justified by even the most valuable of their works, that they do not become new creatures even by the most noble of deeds. It is by faith alone. Let us also ask once more why the gospel of justification of sinners excludes so rigorously any human participation in our justification.

The most obvious response to this must surely recall the simple fact that human beings in need of justification are *sinners.* That is why they can contribute nothing to their justification except to be present in a purely passive sense.[247] However, we cannot be happy with a negative appraisal which is correct but insufficient. 'That we are good for nothing is true, but it is not so relevant that the confession of this truth has independent significance.'[248] Thus faith alone justifies and excludes all human works and deeds because it recognizes and affirms that God has already acted, that God in Jesus Christ has already been at work in a definitive sense, that God has already accorded us effectually the privilege of existing in relationship to him and thus

---

[244] *TCT*, 243 = *DH* 1562: 'Si quis dixerit, fidem iustificantem nihil aliud esse quam fiduciam divinae misericordiae peccata remittentis propter Christum, vel eam fiduciam solam esse, qua iustificamur: anathema sit.'

[245] Barth, *CD* IV/1, 626.

[246] Cf. Lehmann and Pannenberg, *The Condemnations of the Reformation Era* (n. 68 above), vol. 1, 186.

[247] Calvin, *Institutes*, III, 13, 5.

[248] Barth, *CD* IV/1, 628.

forevermore being persons who are recognized. 'It can be said of the believer at all times and in all circumstances: "What hast thou that thou didst not receive?" (1 Cor. 4:7), and: "By the grace of God I am what I am" (1 Cor. 15:10). What is he in relation to Jesus Christ, to his own justification . . . except the recipient of it . . . ?'[249] Believers come into being as recipients. Those who start to believe have already received. And this very positive fact, that faith is always a receiving faith, a gift, is *the greatest thing of all.* Faith cannot be *increased* by any deed. Faith – as it depends upon God in Christ, as it makes human beings into *persons* who welcome and receive *themselves* as a gift and thus irrevocably become *accepted* – that faith is our grateful *Yes* and *Amen* to God's own *Yes* and *Amen*, which has come into being in Jesus Christ (2 Cor. 1:19f.). There can be no additions made to this *Amen*.

4. The fellowship of believers as the fellowship of the saints: the universal priesthood of all believers

Having examined the exclusive formula *sola fide*, we must now point out a very important consequence for the life of the church. We refer to the *universal priesthood of all believers*, which is founded on justification. Enormous emphasis was given to this aspect of the Christian life by the Reformers; it was crucial to their understanding of the church. It is not an optional conclusion that may be drawn from the article on justification. It is an essential implication of that article.[250] It is not going too far to claim on the basis of the universal priesthood of all believers what is true of the whole justification article: that the church stands or falls with it.

---

[249] *CD* IV/1, 631.

[250] It was Luther's doctrine of justification 'which directly gave birth to his new concept of the Church' (K. Holl, 'Die Entstehung von Luthers Kirchenbegriff' in idem, *Gesammelte Aufsätze zur Kirchengeschichte*, vol. 1, 288–325: 289). And it was the 'fundamental principle of universal priesthood' that enabled the Reformer 'to deduce positive guidelines for the order of the visible Church from his view of the invisible Church' (ibid., 318).

Now, we can only make this claim because it is a fundamental part of the justification event that Jesus Christ gives believers a role in his priestly office. That does not mean a role in his priestly self-sacrifice, but a role in the proclamation and portrayal of the fact of that priestly self-sacrifice. Evangelical doctrine which is true to the New Testament must therefore start from the basis that Jesus Christ is the one and only High Priest. He has completed his priestly work of self-sacrifice for our salvation without any human co-operation. He so performs his priestly office that he makes all those who believe in him to be priests of the kind who witness to humanity about the completed work of Christ and who grant and offer to humanity the salvation which has been accomplished through this work of Christ. Just as Jesus put an end to the institution of cultic sacrifice, so he also as a result put an end to priesthood seen from the cultic point of view. In its place he put the universal priesthood of all believers.[251] Faith itself is now true worship of God.[252] Thus within the Christian church the differentiation in categories between priests and laity must be rejected.[253]

The Reformers rejected the distinction between priests and laity on the basis that justified sinners participate by faith in Jesus' royal and priestly offices. Jesus exercises his priesthood so as to make us priests in a very specific sense of the word. Based on the Old Testament ordering of priesthood and firstborn, Luther can even say that by faith we are born in baptism as priests: 'This priesthood cannot be made or ordered. No priest is made here. He must be born a priest . . . I mean of

---

[251] Cf. M. Luther, *The Freedom of a Christian*, *LW* 31, 354–5; *The Second Helvetic Confession* in J. H. Leith, *Creeds of the Churches*, Atlanta: John Knox Press, 3rd edn, 1982, 154.

[252] Cf. *ApolCA* XV, *BSLK* 300, 8f. : 'they knew nothing of the highest form of service to God [cult], which is called faith' [From the German. The English of *BC*, 217 translates the Latin. (Tr)]

[253] Luther, *The Babylonian Captivity of the Church*, *LW* 36, 3–126: 115–16. Cf. Schleiermacher, *The Christian Faith*, 465: 'Now just as . . . Christ is the climax of the priesthood . . . so He is also the end of all priesthood . . . But at the same time, the high-priesthood of Christ has passed over to the fellowship of the faithful, so that Christians as a whole are called a priestly nation.'

course the new birth by water and Spirit. This is how all Christians become priests of the Highest Priest.'[254] Thus one cannot become a priest by some institutional act of the church. It is Jesus himself who gives believers their role in his priestly office: 'Thus Christ has made it possible for us . . . [to] . . . boldly come into the presence of God . . . and . . . pray for one another . . . and do all things which we see . . . in the outer and visible works of priests. Who then can comprehend the lofty dignity of the Christian? By virtue of his royal power he rules over all things, death, life, and sin, and through his priestly glory is omnipotent with God. . . .' But 'to this glory a man attains . . . by faith alone'.[255]

An unmediated, *immediate* relationship with God goes with this universal priesthood of all believers whereby we 'rule with God'. Nevertheless, it is vital that what the new Protestantism was in the habit of over-praising as the discovery of the 'immediacy of the individual's relationship to God' be on no account misunderstood in the individualistic sense. Priesthood is a thoroughly social phenomenon.

> [One is always a priest for others.] Luther never understands the priesthood of all believers merely in the 'Protestant' sense of the Christian's freedom to stand in a direct relationship to God without a human mediator. Rather he constantly emphasizes the Christian's evangelical authority to come before God on behalf of the brethren and also of the world. The universal priesthood expresses not religious individualism but its exact opposite, the reality of the congregation as a community. The individual stands directly before God, he has received the authority of substitution. The priesthood means 'the congregation' and the priesthood is the inner form of the community of saints.[256]

The universal priesthood of all believers is an *honour* which has been granted to human beings. However, at the same time, it is a *necessity* for both the justified and the 'world'. Jesus' priestly

---

[254] Luther, *Fastenpostille*, 1525, *WA* 17/II, 6, 31–5.

[255] Luther, *The Freedom of a Christian*, *LW* 31, 355–6.

[256] P. Althaus, *The Theology of Martin Luther*, trans. R. C. Schultz, Philadelphia: Fortress Press, 1966, 314–15. [The first sentence is not included in this translation. (Tr)]

work must be proclaimed, both to unbelievers and to believers as they dwell in the dialectic of being righteous and being sinners. For no human being can say of himself or herself that Christ was offered up for our sin and raised for our righteousness. Nor can faith say of itself that faith alone justifies. It must be said to us. Faith comes from hearing and only from hearing. Without the exclusive formula *solo verbo* that of *sola fide* would have no basis, just as *solo verbo* would have none without *solus Christus*. The apostle's argument is very clear (Rom. 10:17).

'You will ask, "If all who are in the church are priests, how do these whom we now call priests differ from laymen?"'[257] Answering this should cause no fundamental problems for the universal priesthood of all believers. We ought not even to appeal to the apostolicity of the church. The *institutionalization* of the apostolate in the form of *the apostolic succession of bishops*, and from there to the Apostolic Seat, shows a failure to understand what is rightly granted the church when it is called a holy, catholic and apostolic church. Likewise the claim, which is inferred from the idea of apostolic succession, that the only priest in the full sense of the word is one ordained by a bishop. True apostolic succession is to follow in witnessing to the truth of the gospel as it is in the canon of the Holy Scriptures. The apostles have not been replaced by bishops, but by the canon. Apostolic succession thus means following the proclamation of the gospel, according to the Scriptures, together with the corresponding practice of the sacraments. All believers are basically qualified to do this.

However, so that witnessing to and offering salvation in Jesus Christ, for which all believers are qualified, may occur in an orderly fashion, Protestant teaching says that God has instituted the ministry of the church within the framework of the universal priesthood of all believers. This is pre-eminently the 'ministry of teaching the gospel and administering the sacraments'.[258] That is why 'nobody should publicly teach or

---

[257] Luther, *The Freedom of a Christian, LW* 31, 356.
[258] Cf. *The Augsburg Confession* V, *BC* 31.

preach or administer the sacraments . . . without a regular call', that is, without a proper call to this office.[259] However, in regard to all other believers, those called to such an office have no special authority (*potestas*) or an irrevocable standing (*character indelebilis*) granted to them in any special sacrament of ordination (*ordo*). Even the superintending (episcopal) offices have no supplementary *potestas*.

Thus God's institution of church ministry is not meant to supply a lack in the universal priesthood of all believers. Quite the contrary, it is to direct the spiritual riches of that priesthood along well-ordered paths and thus make them available to all. Christian life does not need a ministry to give it direction because it is too poor or weak, but because it is too rich. The ministers of the church perform in a substitutionary way the service that is entrusted to and required of the whole church.[260] As they perform it they do so face-to-face with the church and thus point to that face-to-face aspect of the gospel and the church, which only comes to fruition when the gospel is preached and heard *in* the church.[261]

[259] *The Augsburg Confession* XIV, *BC* 36.

[260] Cf. *Barmer Theologische Erklärung*, Thesis IV: 'The various offices in the Church establish no rule of one over the other but the exercise of the service entrusted and commanded to the whole congregation. We repudiate the false teaching that the Church can and may, apart from this ministry, set up special leaders equipped with powers to rule' *CC*, 521.

[261] It should be noted here with respect and satisfaction that even the German Catholic bishops have recognized that Jesus' priesthood has a unique and once-and-for-all meaning and on this basis have arrived at a noteworthy interpretation of the priestly office in the church. The bishops declare that the priesthood of Jesus Christ has a unique and once-and-for-all meaning, which is the 'service of the gospel', whereby 'Christ's sacrifice becomes present for us in the form of the Word' (*Schreiben der Bischöfe des deutschsprachigen Raumes über das priesterliche Amt. Eine biblisch-dogmatische Handreichung*, 1970, 25). However, it was quite different in the determinations of Trent concerning the sacrament of the consecration of priests: 'In conformity with God's decree, sacrifice and priesthood are so related that both exist in every law. Therefore, in the New Testament, since the Catholic Church has received the holy and visible sacrifice of the Eucharist according to the institution of the Lord, it is likewise necessary to acknowledge that there is in the Church a new, visible and external priesthood.' Accordingly, it continues, Jesus gave 'to the apostles and to their successors in the priesthood . . . the power [*potestas*] of consecrating, offering, and

Finally, let us underline the importance of the term *sola fide* simply by recalling a peculiarity of New Testament language. In contrast to our customary modern expression, in the New Testament all believers are *saints*. They are addressed as 'the saints' or those 'called to be saints' (cf. Rom. 1:7; 1 Cor. 1:2 and elsewhere). They also apparently call themselves saints. This is an important fact, which can be illustrated by a reference to Dietrich Bonhoeffer. He reports a conversation with a young French pastor, where they asked each other what they wanted

---

administering his body and blood, and likewise the power of remitting and of retaining sins' (*TCT*, 329 = *DH* 1764: 'Sacrificium et sacerdotium ita Dei ordinatione coniuncta sunt, ut utrumque in omni lege exstiterit. Cum igitur in Novo Testamento sanctum Eucharistiae sacrificium visibile ex Domini institutione catholica Ecclesia acceperit: fateri etiam oportet, in ea novum esse visibile et externum sacerdotium . . . in quod vetus translatum est . . . Hoc autem ab eodem Domino Salvatore nostro institutum esse . . . , atque Apostolis eorumque successoribus in sacerdotio potestatem traditam consecrandi, offerendi et ministrandi corpus et sanguinem eius, nec non et peccata dimittendi et retinendi'). In the tradition of these pronouncements, the new *Codex Iuris Canonici* also says that 'The only minister who, in the person of Christ, can bring into being the sacrament of the Eucharist, is a validly ordained priest' (*The Code of Canon Law in English Translation*, London: Collins, 1983, 166 = *Codex Iuris Canonici*, Canon 900 #1: 'Minister, qui in persona Christi sacramentum Eucharistiae conficere valet, est solus sacerdos valide ordinatus'). Yet it is obvious that in this context they are not especially talking about authority (*potestas*) that is granted by the sacrament of consecration of priests. It is no doubt as a result of Vatican II that 'the constricting of the post-Tridentine theology of priesthood' (but probably that of Trent itself) opened up (cf. B. J. Hillerbrand, '"Ich bin es nicht". Grundlegendes zur Aufgabe des priestlichen Dienstes', *Diakonia* 29 [1998], 173–81: 177). It is true that even Vatican II claimed that the common priesthood of all believers and the official priesthood are different 'essentially and not only in degree'. Still, not a few commentators see the intention of Vatican II in the statement that follows immediately, which says that not only consecrated priests, but also the priesthood that is common to all believers has a part in the priesthood of Christ (*Dogmatic Constitution on the Church*, art. 10, *LThK. E I*, 18: 'Sacerdotium autem commune fidelium et sacerdotium ministeriale seu hierarchicum, licet essentia et non gradu tantum differant, ad invicem tamen ordinantur; unum enim et alterum suo peculiari modo de uno Christi sacerdotio participant: the common priesthood of the faithful and the ministerial or hierarchical priesthood are none the less interrelated; each in its own way shares in the one priesthood of Christ' (*The Basic Sixteen Documents; Vatican Council II: Constitutions, Decrees, Declarations*, ed. A. Flannery, NY: Costello, 1996, 14).

to do with their lives. Bonhoeffer's friend answered that 'he would like to become a saint'. Despite coming from a Protestant, this is a somewhat Catholic response. Bonhoeffer, greatly impressed by this answer, nevertheless contradicted him and said: 'I should like to learn to have faith.' The immense contrast between these two responses only became apparent to him later, as he remarks. He first had to discover 'that it is only by living completely in this world that one learns to have faith', and that *learning to have faith* means completely abandoning 'any attempt to make something of oneself, whether it be a saint, or a converted sinner ... In so doing we throw ourselves completely into the arms of God, taking seriously, not our own suffering, but those of God in the world ... That, I think, is faith'.[262]

In point of fact, between these two responses a great gulf is fixed. For those who say: 'I'd like to learn to have faith' are *really* saints. They are saints who realize that *holiness* does not mean *sinlessness*. It means gratitude for God's suffering and for the justification of sinners which stems from this. From such gratitude grows the *ability* to *ask* every day: 'Forgive us our trespasses.'

In addition, in many passages of the Council texts, the office of the priest is defined by preaching, so that it is not permissible to restrict the service of the priestly office to the cultic, 'priestly-sacerdotal realm' (B. J. Hillerbrand, loc. cit., 179). It is clear that there are other quite different interpretations of Vatican II, including recent Vatican statements, and it is with quite a deal of hope that I quote Karl Lehmann's call to see 'the sacramental powers of celebrating the Eucharist and the forgiveness of sins ... from a deeper perspective', one that allows the distribution of 'the one office of tasks and structures given in the Church ... among many subsidiary offices or persons' (K. Lehmann, 'Das dogmatische Problem des theologischen Ansatzes zum Verständnis des Amtspriestertums', in F. Henrich, ed., *Existenzprobleme des Priesters*, 1969, 121–75: 165; in addition, see very balanced explanations by K. Lehmann: 'Dogmatische Vorüberlegungen zur "Interkommunion"', in J. Höfer et al., eds, *Evangelisch-katholische Abendmahlsgemeinschaft?*, 1971, 77–141). In this call by Lehmann there is a hint of a genuine rapprochement in the way the two churches see the office of ministry.

[262] D. Bonhoeffer, *Letters and Papers from Prison: The Enlarged Edition*, ed. E. Bethge, trans. R. Fuller et al., London: SCM Press, 1971, 369–70.

Furthermore, it is extremely important to note that we never find 'the saints' in the New Testament as individuals. It is a mark of New Testament usage that the expression 'called to be saints' can be used along with 'church' (cf. 1 Cor. 1:2). This explains why the expression 'saints' is only used in the plural. The New Testament only knows the 'collective' form, the community of saints. The singular is different; its usage is restricted to a Christological sense. Only Jesus Christ is the Holy One in himself. All others are saints only in the sense that they have been *made so*. However, it is true to say of them that they are always the community of the saints.[263]

But they are saints only in the faith. Thus the Latin technical term *communio sanctorum* or *congregatio sanctorum* can be translated in the *Augsburg Confession* as 'the assembly of all the believers'.[264]

The fact that holiness is not a heightened faith may perhaps be best expressed by saying that the gathering of believers is marked by *joy*. Joy cannot be heightened. What it does is to heighten the passing moment so that it becomes a genuine *presence*. Generally we experience the present as a fleeting *now*, which is quite unable to be really *present*: it disappears in the blink of an eye. But with *joy*, the present itself becomes present. And in the particular joy of the saints gathered together as the community of believers, their presence becomes so present through the presence of Jesus Christ that they are able to discover and affirm him and themselves as co-present persons (cf. 1 Thess. 1:6; 2 Cor. 2:3; 8:2; Rom. 14:17; 15:13 and elsewhere). This is joy in the presence of the freedom that starts with the presence of Jesus Christ. It has its most concentrated expression in the celebration of communion in the worship service, when the presence of Jesus Christ has the incomparable effect of making believers into people who are *present*. The

---

[263] Cf. Ebeling, *Dogmatik*, vol. 3, 339: 'It is not the individual who is a saint; it is those who belong to the eschatological *ekklesia* who are the saints.' From this standpoint we may critique the Roman practice of canonizing individuals.

[264] *BC*, 32.

earliest church celebrated the presence of Jesus Christ in the Lord's Supper 'with glad and generous hearts' (Acts 2:46), because there had been a sovereign, an unsurpassable occurrence in the indicative mood among them: the indicative mood of the gospel which justifies the ungodly was sending forth its rays of light among them.

By now it should be self-evident that from such faith deeds of gratitude proceed quite spontaneously. These are deeds freely performed. Yet they arise of necessity from the gratitude of faith; they cannot help coming out of persons who are grateful to God. In thankfulness, freedom starts to press the issue. Faith, which is nothing other than receiving, is a taut coil springing creatively into action for the common good. For believers know that since God has done enough for our *salvation*, we can never do enough for the *good* of the world. So we are justified by faith alone, but faith never stays alone; it *strives* to, it *has* to become active in love: 'faith alone is never alone'.[265] There is no more liberating basis for ethics than the doctrine of justification of sinners by faith alone.

[265] Cf. P. Althaus, 'Sola fide nunquam sola – Glaube und Werke in ihrer Bedeutung für das Heil bei Martin Luther', *Una sancta. Zeitschrift für interkonfessionelle Begegnung* 16 (1961), 227–35.

6

LIVING BY GOD'S
RIGHTEOUSNESS

The gospel interrupts the world's reality with a supreme statement in the indicative mood. It is a gracious statement of God's righteousness which quite simply does not come from this world's reality and cannot be made understandable to it. The church lives on the basis of this statement. However, without any innate understanding of it, the world also lives from this indicative statement, constantly placing itself under the pressure of imperatives. The church, in its ultimate shape as God's serving community, *celebrates* this indicative statement and *proclaims* it, so that the world may learn what really lies at the basis of its life.

Like any other indicative, the indicative of the gospel is a *reality*, a reality made possible and brought into being by God himself. But part of the supremacy of this indicative statement is that it is more than a tautological reality. It is a reality that opens up *new possibilities*. 'The one who is righteous through faith *will live*' (Rom.1:17; Hab. 2:4). And real living life always means a life lived among genuine possibilities.

What the possibilities are that are released through the supreme indicative of the gospel must be explained anew in each concrete situation. However, it may be helpful to outline at least some of the elements that show in what direction this indicative is pointing. Readers will derive greater pleasure from expanding the few indications given here through their own spontaneous efforts than would be the case if the inferences were to be drawn for them. For, as has been shown, in faith we become discoverers.

I. Setting us free from a sham existence

The gospel helps human existence to achieve its truth potential. In this it is distinct from what we normally call religion. Religion is the final legitimation of meaning. Every meaning longs for a final meaning that religion has to grant and preserve: 'In the beginning was meaning.'[1] However, it is not the meaning of life, but the truth of our lives that becomes apparent when we believe our sins are forgiven.

This is not to say that the so-called question of meaning has nothing to do with the doctrine of justification. In the negative sense, the Bible leaves no room for doubt: a life without justification becomes meaningless – just as meaningless as the life of Cain became after his own judgement on himself. Without justification, despair lodges even in the inmost heart of joy. 'For despair the most cherished and desirable place to live is in the heart of happiness. . . .' Quite often, it needs nothing more than 'a subtle, almost carelessly dropped allusion to some indefinite something'[2] in order to call forth despair from the inmost heart of joy. When we have no understanding of justification we remain 'in despair not willing to be ourselves, or in despair willing to be ourselves'.[3] Whichever way we are, consciously or unconsciously *despairing*, and thus in the midst of subjective happiness, we are *objectively* unhappy. The justification of human beings by God is aimed at this *meaningless* existence. Our justification is in response to an all-pervasive *loss of meaning*. Yet that is only one side of the problem of meaning in the context of the doctrine of justification. The doctrine definitely has to do with the *negative* side of the problem, the *loss of meaning* in life. 'Without this article the world is nothing but death and darkness' – and meaningless. Luther was right in his claim. Justification reveals the *loss of meaning* for which we are to blame. But it does not have to do with the problem of meaning in such a

---

[1] Goethe, *Faust* I, line 1229.
[2] Kierkegaard, *The Sickness Unto Death*, 25.
[3] Ibid., 77 [altered].

way that it responds to the loss of meaning with a religious *giving* or *establishment* of *meaning*.

Faith in the *overcoming* of our self-made darkness and the all-dominant power of death through the death of Jesus Christ is something other than a religious establishment of meaning. Although justification has a great deal to do with the *question* of the meaning of life, since it casts doubt on the objectivity of sinners' self-actualizing existence and thus confirms that it is meaningless, nevertheless it does not fulfil the religious (or non-religious) *need* for meaning by giving religious meaning. Justification is something other than satisfaction of needs. It is something more like transforming needs. In the context of justification, the question of meaning undergoes a completely *dialectic* treatment. It is *superseded*, in both a positive and a negative sense. So also the gospel of justification of the ungodly takes on an undeniably dialectic relationship to religion. For religion presents itself in a sociological sense as the ultimate legitimation of meaning. To the extent that meaning itself has a legitimating function, religion appears as the meaning of meaning, as the 'ultimate meaning'. Yet when religion is the ultimate legitimation of meaning, it is a human work. So it stands in contrast to the justification of human beings by faith alone *without* the works of the law.

This becomes quite clear when we explain that meaning is an anthropocentric category. Human beings *postulate* meaning in order to be able to live. We *manufacture* meaning by so reducing the excessive complexity of the world[4] that we are able to fit in with the world. What is meaningful is meaning *for human beings*. The quest for meaning thus calls the world and then God before the bar of human beings. Only what is able to be justified *before me* has meaning. Here is where the quest for

---

[4] Cf. N. Luhmann, 'Sinn als Grundbegriff der Soziologie' in J. Habermas and N. Luhmann, eds, *Theorie der Gesellschaft oder Sozialtechnologie – Was leistet die Systemforschung?*, 1971, 25–100: 34. Cf. also N. Luhmann, *Die Wissenschaft der Gesellschaft*, 1990, 109f., 546, 620; idem, 'Identität – was oder wie?' in idem, *Soziologische Aufklärung*, vol. 5, 1990, 14–30; idem, *Soziologie des Risikos*, 1991, 26f.; idem, *Das Recht der Gesellschaft*, 1993, 126f., 214f., 255.

meaning stands in final, stark contrast to the doctrine of justification. For when we are talking about justification, the question is not how the world – or even how God – can stand *before me*, nor is it how *I* can stand *before myself*. The question is how I, and my world, can stand *before God*.

In addition, *meaning* must facilitate our ability to act. Even when meaning is taken to go beyond experience, human beings are to be seen fundamentally as *those who act* in the context of the question of meaning. This goes with our modern understanding of ourselves as being – whether in the moral, economic or technical sense – *doers, makers* and *actors: I am my deed*. Against this, the Christian doctrine of justification sees human beings fundamentally as those who can do nothing towards their salvation. Not that our acts are irrelevant to the problem of justification! But the doctrine of justification goes deeper than that. It does not stress our being from the point of view of our doing. It stresses our doing from the point of view of our being. It is not the question of *meaning* that goes with that of our *being*. It is the question of the *truth* of human life.

The Christian faith is distinguished from all other systems of meaning by its deep interest in the truth of human existence. In this respect it is also distinct from all religions and from its own religious objectivization. If it is nonetheless to be described as a religion or if it describes itself as such, despite any reservations it may have on the subject, it must insist on *differentiation in the way religion is described*, a differentiation which does justice to its deep interest in truth and the priority of truth over the question of meaning. This is not our task here. We are aiming at clarifying the fact that everything sociological (both in the general and in the religious sense of that word) about the Christian faith which can be shown as a *manifestation of meaning*, is, according to the way Christianity sees itself, an *interpretation or representation of truth*. The Christian faith sees itself as a reflection of an event not produced by it, an event which is identical to the truth *that decides human life*. Here the quest for the *meaning* of life must change, as far as the Christian faith is concerned, into the quest for the revealed truth of life. Paul calls this truth the 'truth of the gospel' (Gal. 2:14). John identifies it with Christ (John 14:6). John's paralleling of *truth* with the *way* and the *life* shows that truth for the believer means a power which holds definitive sway over *how life is lived*, even over life and death. Accordingly, John 8:32 says of truth: *it will make you free*. The justification of the ungodly, which is the truth that sets us free, speaks negatively about those *fatal lies* that may perfectly well appear as offers of meaning. A life lived from God's righteousness will thus be lived *in freedom from that sham existence* in which sinners are entangled and in which they threaten to be destroyed.

This sham existence takes various forms: individual and collective, profane and religious, political and economic. It exists in the intimate depths of human life, but also on a global scale. It can spread both locally and in the wider community. As a general rule, it can only be discovered in each concrete, individual case. Nevertheless, it is possible to identify at least some of its global manifestations. These are the ideologically constructed lies that are able to tyrannize entire societies and nations when the necessary means of power are available.

Among these – to give but one instance – is the lie which implies that the old Adam can renew himself, if he only believes in himself, whether generically, or as a member of a class or a race. This lie can be given impetus by following Feuerbach, Nietzsche or Marx. This leaves open the question of how much these three are misunderstood or perhaps understood only too well. Fascist and so-called socialist dictatorships have also set up their 'ten commandments' in order to create a new humanity – totalitarian political systems putting law in the service of race or class. All those who wish to create a new humanity will have to make new laws of this sort, since they need to *completely* take over and control human beings for the sake of the desired changes. The totalitarian claim of these law-givers in itself takes on pseudo-religious qualities that are distinguishable from true fear of God in that they put their totalitarianism into effect by the use of the lie as a terror tactic. For since no earthly power can *truly* make a new person from the old Adam, this totalitarian claim can only be maintained with the aid of a lie, and the lie can only be maintained with the aid of terror. In doing this, the totalitarian state that has such a quasi-religious concept of itself deceives not only its citizens, but also itself. In such a situation, justification of the ungodly means recognizing the liberating truth that only God can make a new creature from that old Adam which we all *are* and, sad though it is to say, which we all *remain* until our dying day. This new person then becomes engaged in an honest struggle with the old Adam. Those who are set free by this truth believe in God, but they no longer believe in themselves or in any sort of promises that require them to believe in themselves. And this very faith in God will have consequences for political life. The question may well arise whether there was not a fundamental link between the break with the pseudo-socialist sham of the former German Democratic Republic and the Christian groups that had decided to *live* their faith in the political arena as well.[5]

It will be possible to *uncover* all these sham forms of existence, whether writ large or small, and then to *be set free* from them, only when we give *truth* that place of honour which justification helps human life to have. Such truth, however, *comes about of itself.* It does so in the church in the form of a life lived in the service of God.

II. A life lived in worship

Our justification is a change from death to life, but the new beginning that occurs here as in every new birth *cannot be brought about by us.* Being born, like being resurrected from the dead, is something we can only be involved in with no active

---

[5] Note should be taken of the fact that belief in justification is often also effective in the secular area in ways not always easily comprehensible even to insiders. This in itself is worthy of a study!

participation on our part. You can't bring yourself to life. You can't beget yourself. Nor can sinners do anything to make themselves righteous before God and thus gain a part in the relational riches of divine life. Only God can bring about the new beginning that comes with the joyous change from death to life. Faith is us coming into this new beginning, and believers are rank beginners. They begin an existence that they have not brought into being. And they take delight in this new existence that has been given them. So, living by the righteousness of God is, first of all, nothing more than being here in a new way and enjoying it. Faith is the most complete exclusion of all human self-actualization. For believers trust in God at work. And this trust in God, as far as we are concerned, consists quite simply in enjoying our new existence.

But can we western Christians, with our equating of our existence and our actions, with our habit of measuring a person's value by his or her achievements, ever grasp this again? Can we ever start to be Christians, not only in earnest, but *joyfully* – that is, *at all*? People who take no delight in the existence given them are by definition not Christians. Instead of being those who *do* and *have*, can we ever again become those who *are*, those who stand amazed at themselves? Can we ever rediscover ourselves as God's children? As *newborn children* who can contribute absolutely nothing towards their own existence? Will we ever find out that all our action has to come out of a *non-action* if it is to be helpful and not be an action that is destructive even because of its success? The working week survives in an unfathomably deep sense on the basis of the *Sabbath rest*. It is by no means an accident that Christians have identified the Sabbath with *Sunday*, when we celebrate the resurrection of Jesus Christ, and have moved it back to become the *beginning* of the week. This is to make it clear that *being* and *letting be* is the basis of all activity. There will only be 'justice, peace and the preservation of the creation' when our actions proceed from this kind of *being* and *letting be* and keep returning to it – just as the working week starts with and comes back to Sunday.

We human beings are incessantly busy, exploiting the world around us and turning others into mere resources with our bustling, working and achieving and our moral self-realization.

In the concept of the weekly *day off* we have an *institution* that enables us to make a fundamental break and stand back and look in amazement at all this. It is an institution where we discover ourselves as those who receive, and God as the one who gives. This institution is the 'day of the Lord', or more specifically *worship*. Here there is such a fundamental break with the reality that dominates sinners that it becomes possible for there to be something new. In worship God becomes of interest to us for his own sake, as the eternally creating Father, as the Son who for our sake suffered and conquered death, as the Holy Spirit, who links Father and Son to each other in the bond of love and links us into the divine fellowship of mutual otherness. And as God becomes of interest to us for his own sake, we also learn to discover the world as his creation and ourselves as his children. In worship we find that the world is not the work of our hands, but of his, and that we need to care for it and nurture it. So we will only be able to rule over the earth when we overrule our need to rule, so that our ruling turns from an empire back into a dominion. In worship we are addressed as persons who are more than the sum of their deeds. In worship we find ourselves as a community of justified sinners whose first act is not some achievement, but praise and thanksgiving. In worship we find ourselves to be free of our past; we find we cannot stop rejoicing in our own freedom. So much so that – as Luther once remarked – we would gladly walk on our heads for sheer joy.[6]

Worship must, of course, extend into the workaday world. Justification cannot be limited to a liturgical relevance. It must also be lived out in everyday life to transform the whole of life into a 'reasonable worship' (Rom. 12:1). Those who live by the righteousness of God will also behave accordingly in their

[6] M. Luther, 'Sermon of 19 October 1533', *WA* 37, 176, 7.

everyday lives. Those who walk on their heads for sheer joy see the world differently, from a new perspective.

III. The primacy of personhood

The most important aspect of this new perspective and of the behaviour which goes with it is that we affirm and emphasize *the absolute primacy of persons over their works*. Not only in the spiritual sense, but in every sense. Those who live by the righteousness of God know that we ourselves do not need to set our own recognition in motion. To be justified means to be irrevocably recognized as a person. Those who live by the righteousness of God will also respect others as persons who have been thus recognized by God, notwithstanding all their possible achievements and successes, despite all their deficiencies and failures. It is not what people make of themselves that defines them; it is the fact that God has made righteous people from sinners that defines our eternal and thus our temporal life. Those who live by the righteousness of God will see in every human being more than just a doer of *deeds* or *misdeeds*. Justification prohibits us from identifying the greatest deed or the worst misdeed with the Self that does it. It demythologizes the myth of the supermen who outdo themselves by their own successes. It lets us see, behind the façade of the self-righteous who confuse their selfhood with their work, people deserving of pity. But equally, it demythologizes the myth of the *monsters* who by their misdeeds make others into non-persons and it allows us to find, even in the worst of cases, behind some sad story the human being on whom God himself has had mercy. Those who live by the righteousness of God find no hopeless cases. They recognize in every case a person who has experienced divine mercy and is thus worthy even of human pity – just as we all are. There are such things as inhuman deeds. And there is a huge number of them. But God's righteousness prohibits us from extending inhuman deeds so categorically as to have their subject identified with them and thus be declared inhuman. The category of 'inhuman' is itself inhuman.

It is obvious that such an absolute primacy of persons over their works needs to be brought out in many ways. We shall content ourselves with three points.

(a) It was not only in western Christendom of days gone by that the *state penal system* with its whole arsenal of barbarous punishments stood in stark contradiction to Christian justification. We are still waiting today for a reform that would make a fundamental split in the undisputed connection between person and deed by addressing prisoners as people who are separable from their deeds. It is no doubt true that there are not a few people who have been condemned and imprisoned because of their misdeeds, who, for their part, are unresponsive to such a distinction. This is often the case with politically motivated crimes. But what are we doing, we who have the legal right and good fortune to live outside prison? What is our society doing, what are the church and the state doing to make such people responsive again? What are we doing to say that they are more than the sum of their deeds, that even as prisoners they have value – a value that is hardly noticed and yet is inalienable, the value of human beings justified by God?

Isn't it appropriate to make a human gesture, to begin to build a bridge across to this strange other world? A gesture, a bridge that will reconcile our society with those who have done these things – who are not just criminals, but first and foremost human beings – and reconcile them with us? A gesture, a bridge that will make a way from that strange other world back into our society? Will we stretch out our hand to do that? Or would we prefer the judgement and punishment of the law to have the last word and the unjust stay unjust? We will have to draw the final political conclusion from God's pardon for sinners, that life imprisonment is a measure which contradicts the worth of the person. This is definitely an unreasonable demand. But that should not prevent us from emphasizing very clearly that those who have been condemned to life imprisonment are no longer in a position to see themselves as persons recognized by this society.

(b) But what we have just said has direct relevance even for the status we give those in our achievement-oriented society who can do little or nothing for themselves. Children and the elderly are the most natural representatives of the absolute primacy of persons over their works. They are essentially recipients and cannot yet or can no longer do anything for themselves. It is only when we perceive them as of benefit to us, only when we respect their worth instead of asking how their value can be increased or decreased, that our worship will beam the gospel into the everyday world so that our achievement-oriented society becomes worthy of being called a human society. The same goes for our attitude toward the sick, not only for our personal attitude, but also for the way we treat sick people socially in our law-making.

(c) Up to this point, we have been giving our attention to those who are on the fringe of society, those who are on the bottom. This is appropriate. Those who live by God's righteousness will allow their eyes to follow the inexorable downward gaze of the God who justifies us. However, it is important to turn this attention in the opposite direction as well. We love to make fun of those in charge! After centuries of Protestantism's being far too subject to authority, today we seem to see those who hold political power – who, after all, have been elected by us – as non-persons whose personhood disappears behind the political mask which they only too often wear for show. And when – as can happen – those who have the power are seduced into some scandalous misuse of power and this is exposed, then we are apt to see this as the rule, rather than the exception. We Protestants have a fundamentally unbalanced relationship to power and make those in power suffer by mercilessly putting them down as being nothing more than 'those in charge', the ones we would be happiest seeing fall as low as possible. It is true to say that God casts the powerful *down* from their thrones (Luke 1:52). But he does not cast them *out*, for they are sinners in need of grace, just as we are. Their worth as persons recognized by God is not up for grabs. Those who live by God's righteousness will develop political culture to such a degree that they find, even among those who have political and economic power, *persons* who are to be distinguished from their deeds and misdeeds, persons who have their inalienable worth, just as each of us has.

IV. Secular justice

Finally, let us turn our attention again to the concept of the righteousness of God himself and ask what God's justifying action means for our own struggle for secular justice. Any system of evangelical ethics worthy of the name starts from the given that divine action cannot be directly translated into secular action, that is, that our human acts can never be any sort of continuation of divine action. The only thing that is directly in keeping with *divine action* is *human being*, which was made by God himself. Our daily struggle for secular justice can only ever correspond in an indirect way to divine action. We owe our being to God alone. Conversely, we ourselves determine our actions, even when we are wanting to act in obedience to God's command. Our being is a gift of the gospel. But our actions are required of us. They are subject to the demand of the law. If we were to see our human action as a kind of extension of divine action, we would be turning the gospel into a new law. And that would be a denial of justification.

When we nevertheless ask what is the meaning of God's justifying action for our own striving for secular justice, it is because secular justice is, or should be, nothing other than true *human* righteousness. God's righteousness became actualized among us in the fact that God became *human*, suffered as a human being for us and died for us. It is the humanity of God that not only allows us but obliges us on the basis of God's righteousness to demand *human* justice and to set up criteria for human righteousness worthy of that name, so that the existing secular system of justice is made more just by being made more human. However, it will not become more human by denigrating the powers that be, but only by their betterment

– while totally avoiding the situation where people are uncertain of their legal position.

We can call to mind the crucial factor here by looking back at the point we made above. God is the triune God who exists in trinitarian fellowship so that Father, Son and Holy Spirit give each other their due. The crucial factor about divine righteousness is that it grants and puts in place rights where rights belong. This is so that all those who are part of the community of justice will seek not their own rights, but those of others. The point here is not 'I want my rights and I'll take them', but 'I'll concede that you are right and I'll seek your rights'. (This is what Aristotle meant when he claimed that justice was a virtue which above all was able to bring people into relationship with each other.) Justice, when seen in this light, not only safeguards the relational riches of those who live with others. It also organizes the fundamental relationships of life so that their interconnections exist for the greatest possible mutual benefit. This is what the Bible calls peace, *shalom*. Divine righteousness aims at *peace*. This means it has in view the *whole* of the community of justice and the *wholeness* of each person belonging to it. This is what the Bible understands to be peace: wholeness. This does not mean the totality of a whole that is only held together by some external force, without which it would fall apart. No, it means the peaceful wholeness of good order, where every single person seeks the rights of the other. Where this happens, 'righteousness and peace will kiss each other' (Ps. 85:10).[7]

---

[7] Recent, communist, social theories have highlighted similar points. They emphasize the common cultural and social shape of society through which primarily the inner satisfaction of society's members is achieved. This is in critical contrast to a liberal theory of society that develops a view of society as a union of persons conceived of atomistically whose communality is restricted to a mutual recognition of only a few elementary rights to freedom. Michael Walzer came up with the notion of 'complex equality' to develop a third way beside the totalitarian or individualistic social order. In Walzer's schema, the members of a society stand in a relationship of mutual benefit in various aspects of social dealing (see Walzer, *Spheres of Justice*, 3–30).

Have we got to that point yet? If only! It is clear we will never build the kingdom of God on earth. We remain justified sinners. But as such we are already living by the righteousness of God and we can and should in this life risk earthly similes to the kingdom of heaven. In the political realm as well.

As we do this we must emphasize especially that God's righteousness always extends beyond the original community of justice and includes the other, the stranger. God's existence in the trinitarian community of mutual otherness is such that he defines himself as a God who chooses. He allows Israel to participate in its own divine righteousness by establishing a covenant, that is, a community of justice between himself and the people of Israel. And as the God who justifies he includes the whole of humanity in this community of justice by taking the sin of the whole world on himself as the founder of the new covenant, so that he can give the world a part in his right- eousness. By the fact that it is such a communicable divine attribute, by proving to be a righteousness that grants others a part in itself and that makes them righteous, the righteousness of God stands in stark contrast to all self-righteousness. That is precisely why we can live by it while self-justifying life is perishing.

If our human justice must now be *consistent* with divine righteousness without being misconstrued as an *extension* of it, it will base itself on this criterion and thus it will also aim to seek the rights of others. In this way it will create a wholeness where the persons who are part of that whole and the basic conditions of life stand in a relationship of the greatest possible mutual benefit. It will prove itself to be righteousness by creating a peace that is no longer seen as just the opposite to war. As human justice that corresponds to divine righteousness it will not be extreme or disproportionate. It will not follow the motto *fiat iustitia et pereat mundus* [let justice prevail though the world may perish] or even *fiat iustitia et pereat homo*. Justice must come about in such a way that even those who in the worldly sense are unjust can live humanly or learn to live humanly again. Human justice worthy of the name will be mindful that the

God of justice is in the right by his *grace*. Only then will the height of justice not mean the height of roguery [*summum ius summa iniuria*, Cicero, *The Offices*, I, 10, 33 (Tr)]. Even human justice only earns its name when we are able to live by it.

Another part of this is to practise remembering that not only divine but also human justice is *communicable*. Human justice does not leave out in the cold those who exist outside our community of justice. It includes them and thus gives strangers a part in our own societal justice. Those who live by the righteousness of God which is foreign to us will never wish to reserve earthly justice for themselves. It is quite obvious what that means for the way we relate to foreigners.[8] Just as clear is the fact that we ourselves would not be righteous if we were to accept or even come to terms with blatant injustices in other communities, for example, the infringement of human rights.

As we have seen, true justice always goes beyond the personal righteousness of those who are righteous. That is why Aristotle could say it shines brighter than the evening or morning star.[9] There must also be a temporal outworking of the fact that true justice extends beyond each community of justice. Thus it is an integral part of the righteousness we are to cultivate at present that it should protect and strive for *the rights of future generations*.

---

[8] Regarding foreigners in a society, Michael Walzer defines as 'the principle of political justice': 'the processes of self-determination through which a democratic state shapes its internal life, must be open, and equally open, to all those men and women who live within its territory, work in the local economy, and are subject to local law ... Political justice is a bar to permanent alienage ... At least, this is true in a democracy' (Walzer, *Spheres of Justice*, 60–1). However, a distinction must be made between naturalization and emigration; the latter is strictly a matter for individual countries. It is not that the consequences for the naturalization of foreigners are obviously based on charity; they are a matter of justice: 'The theory of distributive justice begins, then, with an account of membership rights. It must vindicate at one and the same time the (limited) right of closure, without which there could be no communities at all, and the political inclusiveness of the existing communities. For it is only as members somewhere that men and women can hope to share in all the other social goods – security, wealth, honor, office, and power – that communal life makes possible' (ibid., 63).

[9] See above, p. 52.

As the Bible sees it, righteousness even includes the whole of creation by restoring the original creation peace for at least one day on the Sabbath and prohibiting all intrusions into the surrounding world on this day. So we shall need to discover whether we human beings are only obliged to be just towards other human beings. If righteousness and peace are to kiss, human justice will need to have an effective reach beyond the community of justice – at least as far as stopping the non-human creation from degenerating at our hands into mere resources.

It is the task of the church to preach the gospel of justification of the ungodly, and of course it must itself make no political laws. 'The gospel does not introduce any new laws about the civil estate.'[10] Thus the church will be able to do no more regarding secular justice than to *make demands of the law-givers* from a gospel perspective. At the same time it will remember that it is a sign of our presumed resemblance to God when we make laws and have to make them in order to rule, when we dispense justice and have to do so in order to avoid destruction. The church will also remember that human beings, having aspired to this divine office, must fulfil it according to God's will until the last judgement. But as they do this, Christians hope for that day when this office will again be exclusively God's, and we will be released from the necessity to rule and judge, because the righteousness of God will be all in all.

This hope extends to our human yearning for earthly justice a promise that makes bearable the burden of ruling and judging. That is why any yearning for earthly, even human justice that has a right understanding of itself will keep coming back to the worship that proclaims God's righteousness as being justification of sinners. In earthly matters those who live by this righteousness will never cease to pray: 'Forgive us our trespasses, as we forgive those who trespass against us' (Matt. 6:12 [AV]). For human activity that is consistent with divine action will always be dependent on this prayer being answered. Despite all disappointment and despondency, from the answer to this

---

[10] *ApolCA* XVI, *BC*, 222–3.

prayer, justified sinners will ever gain the freedom to start their human activity all over again. But the most important thing is that when we pray for forgiveness of our sins we trust in the righteousness of God that makes us righteous. It is indeed more wonderful than the evening or the morning star. Or, to stay with the metaphor: it is the Sun of Righteousness that outshines all other stars.

INDEX OF REFERENCES TO THE BIBLE
AND TO DEUTEROCANONICAL WORKS

INDEX OF GREEK TERMS

INDEX OF LATIN WORDS AND PHRASES

INDEX OF AUTHORS

GENERAL INDEX

Abel 10, 107
Achievement/Performance 181, 207, 268
Accountability 7
Accusation 39
Acquittal 173, 205
Actant(s) 164, 228
Action
  representative 234f.
  sacramental 235f.
Adam 55, 94, 121, 124, 127, 129, 132, 133, 135f., 178, 187, 218, 224, 265, 266
Addressing
  evil 94
  humans 201
  prisoners 270
Adjutrix 171
Adoptionism 21
Advocate 171
Affirmation
  mutual 105
  divine 237
Alienation 156, 249
Ambivalence 248
Amen 251
Amour social 87
Analytic judgement 173, 209, 210
Anathema 176, 186, 196, 207f., 215, 245, 249f.
Angel 20
Anonymity 95, 97
Anthropocentricity 263
Anthropology 38, 40, 115, 147, 190. 195, 238
Antitrinitarianism 119

Apostles' Creed 15
Apostolic succession 254
Appeasement 159
Arbitrariness 34, 37, 39, 42, 238
Ark 157
Arminians 119
Article by which the Church stands or falls 16
Ashamed of the Gospel 68
Assurance of faith 230, 242–6
Atonement 18, 20, 32, 82, 153, 155, 158ff.
Ausgleichende Gerechtigkeit 51
Authority 4, 6, 43, 66, 96, 335, 347, 253, 255f., 271
Auxiliatrix 171

Baptism 121f., 169, 232ff., 252
Battle 22
Being, undivided 155f., 160, 166
Belief 15, 32, 36f., 122, 131, 226, 239f., 266
Benefit, mutual 235f.
Bible 8f., 18, 20, 53, 55, 57, 61, 84, 86, 97, 117f., 123, 132f., 142, 200ff., 228, 262, 273, 276
Birth, new 88, 253, 356
Bishop 254
  Bishops' Conference 25, 224
  Bishops, Catholic 224, 255
Blame 141, 203, 262
Blood 10, 161, 167, 169, 186, 230, 233, 255
Boldness 108
Bondage 31, 47, 179